The Measurement of Unemployment

Methods and Sources in Great Britain
1850–1979

Warwick Studies in Industrial Relations

General Editors: G.S. Bain and H.A. Clegg

Also in this series

The Measurement of Unemployment

Methods and Sources in Great Britain
1850–1979

W. R. GARSIDE

BASIL BLACKWELL · OXFORD

© Social Science Research Council 1980

First published in 1980 by
Basil Blackwell Publisher
5 Alfred Street
Oxford OX1 4HB
England

British Library Cataloguing in Publication Data

Garside, William Redvers
    The measurement of unemployment. – (Warwick
    studies in industrial relations).
    1. Unemployment – Great Britain – History
    2. Economics, Mathematical – Great Britain
    I. Title   II. Series
    331.1′37941   HD5765.A6

    ISBN 0–631–12643–0

Typeset by Gatehouse Wood Ltd,
Sevenoaks, Kent.
Printed and bound in Great Britain
by Billing and Sons Limited,
Guildford, London, Oxford, Worcester.

To my wife Glen
and my children David and Amy

Contents

List of Tables

Editors' Foreword

The University of Warwick is the major centre in the United Kingdom for the study of industrial relations. Its first undergraduates were admitted in 1965. The teaching of industrial relations began a year later in the School of Industrial and Business Studies, and it now has one of the country's largest graduate programmes in this subject. Warwick became a national centre for research into industrial relations in 1970 when the Social Science Research Council, a government-funded body, located its Industrial Relations Research Unit at the University. The Unit has a full-time staff of about twenty and undertakes research into a wide range of topics in industrial relations.

The series of Warwick Studies in Industrial Relations was launched in 1972 as the main vehicle for the publication of the results of the Unit's projects. It is also intended to disseminate the research carried out by staff teaching industrial relations in the University. The first six titles in the series were published by Heinemann Educational Books of London, and subsequent titles have been published by Basil Blackwell of Oxford.

This volume stems from the Unit's desire to produce a set of definitive guides to labour statistics which will be of value to both the general inquirer and the specialist researcher. It examines in detail the complex issues associated with the measurement of unemployment. A thorough survey is made of a very wide range of primary and secondary sources to illustrate the nature of British unemployment statistics from the mid-nineteenth century to the present time. In addition the author has provided a critical appraisal of the data, illustrating problems of interpretation and methodology and how they have changed over time. One of the particular strengths of the book is its discussion of the extent to which the scope and content of the official unemployment series have reflected contemporary views of the working of the labour market. There is no comparable study available in this country.

This is in many ways a most timely publication. The current pre-occupation with rising and persistent unemployment can only benefit from an objective assessment of precisely how far we understand the nature of the problem to be tackled, Moreover, our increasing tendency to recall the conditions of the past will be instructive only if it based on a clear appreciation of the strengths and weaknesses of the available data.

George Bain
Hugh Clegg

Preface

My interest in the nature and sources of unemployment statistics
developed as part of a research project on interwar unemployment in
Britain, on which I am presently engaged. Critical guides to the complicated subject of the measurement of unemployment are comparatively
rare and when available rather chronologically patchy. It seemed particularly useful, therefore, to investigate the problem in a comprehensive way and to try to meet the needs of those interested in the
historical record as well as those currently involved in labour market
analysis. The essential purpose of this book, however, is not to provide
a statistical digest but to indicate the major sources of relevant material
and to discuss problems of methodology and interpretation.

An investigation of this sort involves a considerable amount of
painstaking research into official and semi-official documents. I am very
grateful to the staff of the Department of Employment, and in particular to Mr. B. Wainwright, Chief Statistician, for generous help at
various stages of my work. I also wish to record my gratitude to the
Social Science Research Council for financing the project.

Professor George Bain, University of Warwick, has been a constant
source of inspiration and assistance throughout the entire study. He
and Professor Hugh Clegg read and commented upon the complete
manuscript and together they saved me from many errors of omission
and expression. I benefited too from the comments and criticisms of
David Deaton and John Bowers on the treatment of the post-1945
period. The manuscript was typed with great patience and efficiency by
Celia Charlesworth, Yvonne Jacobs and Susan Kennedy.

This book is dedicated to my wife and children for making it all
worthwhile.

W.R. GARSIDE
University of Birmingham

Introduction

Prior to 1888 there were no continuous, reliable or comparable official statistics of unemployment in Great Britain, though scattered sources of data were available.[1] It is not surprising that the number out of work escaped systematic analysis for most of the nineteenth century, however, since the very existence of unemployment as a serious theoretical and practical question was almost wholly ignored. Most classical economists stressed the logical impossibility of a general imbalance between supply and demand. Unemployment, or to use the more conventional terminology 'want' or 'inconstancy' of employment, was regarded as a temporary and self-correcting phenomenon, the existence of which lay in the idleness and moral delinquency of workmen. The word 'unemployment' was not introduced into the language of political economists until 1888 and its first formal definition, in terms of involuntary idleness of the able-bodied, was advanced by J.A. Hobson in 1895.[2]

By the end of the last decade of the nineteenth century unemployment was being recognized as a major problem attracting specific analysis and empirical investigation. Charles Bradlaugh, impressed by the statistical work of various Labour Bureaux in America,[3] had moved a resolution in the House of Commons on 2 March 1886 that 'immediate

1. See below pp. 10–11
2. J. Harris, *Unemployment and Politics. A Study in English Social Policy 1886–1914,* Oxford 1972, p. 4. According to the *Oxford English Dictionary* the word 'unemployment' first came into common use in about 1895. T.W. Hutchison, *A Review of Economic Doctrines, 1870–1929,* Oxford 1953, p. 409.
3. E.H. Phelps–Brown and M.H. Browne, 'Carroll D. Wright and the Development of British Labour Statistics', *Economica,* 30, 1963.

1

steps should be taken to ensure in this country the full and accurate collection and publication of labour statistics'.[4]

The task of implementing this resolution was originally entrusted to the Board of Trade although at the time it had no direct concern with the problems of unemployment, employment or trade unions.[5] Various witnesses before the Royal Commission on Labour during the early 1890's had pressed for the establishment of a strong government statistical department which could assist in formulating decisions on labour matters.[6] By 1893 the Board had established a separate Labour Department charged, among other things, with the duty of obtaining a 'further record of . . . slackness of employment',[7]

An additional function of this new Department was to publish the *Labour Gazette* as a regular monthly journal 'for the use of workmen, and of all others interested in obtaining prompt and accurate information on matters specially affecting labour'.[8] The publication has continued in unbroken sequence ever since under the successive titles of *Labour Gazette* (May 1893-January 1905), the *Board of Trade Labour Gazette* (February 1905-June 1917), the *Labour Gazette* (July 1917-May 1922), the *Ministry of Labour Gazette* (June 1922-May 1968), the *Employment and Productivity Gazette* (June 1968-November 1970) and the *Department of Employment Gazette* (December 1970-continuing). It is referred to throughout the rest of this book simply as the *Gazette*.

Despite the passage of time it is still notoriously difficult to describe, analyse or measure unemployment adequately for want of a precise and universally accepted definition of its scope and meaning. Few words are

4. Hansard 1886, Ser. 3, CCCII, Col. 1769.
5. *Memorandum explaining arrangements made by the Board of Trade for collecting and publishing statistics of Labour,* LXXI, 205, 1886; *Memorandum explaining our progress made in carrying arrangements,* CVII, 121, 1888. The Board's responsibilities in this context were transferred in 1917 to the Ministry of Labour.
6. 'A Labour Department and Labour Statistics' in *Fifth and Final Report of the Royal Commission on Labour,* 11, C.7421, 1894.
7. For details see R. Davidson, 'Sir Hubert Llewellyn Smith and Labour Policy 1886-1916', unpublished Ph.D thesis, Cambridge 1971; D.F. Schloss, 'The reorganisation of the Labour Department', *Journal of the Royal Statistical Society,* LVI, 1893; *Memorandum on progress of work of Labour Department.* 1893-94, LXXXII, 363; *Report on Work of Department since its formation; with Supplement of Labour Statistics.* C.5765, 1894.
8. *Gazette,* May 1893.

surrounded by so much ambiguity. The measurement of unemployment has long been a matter of statistical convention but the actual meaning of the terms used are often so technical as to defy general use or so subjective as to encourage misleading assumptions. Unemployment can be used to describe a condition—being not at work, an activity—seeking work, an attitude—desiring a job under certain conditions, or a need—that of needing a job.[9] The term is often further confused when meaningful distinctions are sought between 'voluntary' and 'involuntary' unemployment, when it is used as a measure of the number of people in need or distress, or when it is treated as a purely economic phenomenon capable of indicating the degree of excess labour supply nationally and by region for purposes of economic management.

A survey of unemployment in history has led one author to observe that:

What actually has been done for the unemployed and about unemployment has depended upon the intervention of moral and religious attitudes, the sense of what is economically possible, the locus of political power in society, and the extent to which those who possess the power are aware of how unemployment affects both its victims and their own interests.[10]

There is little doubt, however, that the substance and direction of unemployment policy in the past have also been affected, often in a negative way, by the extent to which the problem of joblessness was understood in terms of its volume, rate, duration, seasonal and cyclical sensitivity, and its distribution by industry, sex, occupation, and region. Published works offering critical analyses of the methods and sources of British unemployment data since the nineteenth century are few in number compared with those dealing with the nature and impact of official unemployment policy.

There are some notable exceptions at both primary and secondary level but it is not intended to list the relevant titles here since the substance of their various criticisms of the unemployment figures has

9. 'Statistics of unemployment in the United Kingdom', *Gazette*, May 1974. J.A. Hobson described unemployment as 'perhaps the most illusive term. . . which confronts modern industrial society', 'The Meaning and Measure of "Unemployment"', *Contemporary Review*, 67, March 1895, p. 415.
10. J.A. Garraty, *Unemployment in History. Economic Thought and Public Policy*, New York 1978, p. 9.

been included in the appropriate parts of the text. Suffice to say that none of the available commentaries cover the chronological span of this present book nor survey within such a period the relevant secondary and non-government primary or near-primary sources in sufficient detail to meet the requirements of both the specialist researcher and the general reader.

The need for a critical analysis of what precisely the published unemployment figures mean, either currently or in the past, requires little justification. As governments doggedly pursued the search for full-employment in the post-1945 period, figures of registered unemployment were commonly regarded as perhaps the most important and reliable indicators on which to base public policies of demand management, regional growth, the control of inflation and welfare provision. Yet although unemployment figures were freely used in the most complex investigations of the workings of the economic system there was for many years a marked reluctance to investigate the nature and validity of the various components of the official series. This is partly explained by the low level of recorded unemployment during the period (the published rate for Great Britain only once rose above 2.2 per cent between 1948 and 1966). But the serious economic recession of recent years has altered the situation. The strategy and direction of government economic policy and the public understanding of the unemployment problem have proved extremely sensitive to movements in the gross unemployment figures, as was so clearly demonstrated in 1971 and 1972. A close investigation of the reliability and completeness of the data, therefore, can provide as illuminating an insight into the relevance of central government activity as might the most detailed survey of ministerial pronouncements.

In the interwar years attention was increasingly focused on the sheer magnitude of the level of aggregate unemployment and on its cyclical fluctuations. Scant attention was paid to the extent to which the published unemployment series adequately reflected the changing nature and composition of unemployment or to how far they were being influenced by administrative practices. But it is known that there were important deficiencies in the scope and coverage of the statistics even at national level. It is important therefore not to infer from them more than a close scrutiny of their internal methods of computation would justify, particularly so when the magnitude of the problem readily distracts attention from the comparative seriousness of its constituent parts. Problems of interpretation and reliability are perhaps more acute when the sources of data are scanty and generally unrepresentative of the situation as a whole. The particular characteristics of pre-1914 unemployment cannot be properly understood, for example, without a clear appreciation of the strengths and weaknesses of the limited sources of data. Indeed, comparisons of pre- and post-1914 conditions are hardly worth pursuing unless details of the origins, scope and meaning of the available statistics are firmly grasped.

The purpose of this book is therefore threefold. First, to indicate the sources and nature of unemployment data from the mid-nineteenth century onwards; second, to assess the reliability of each source, largely in terms of the confidence with which one can use the published results; and third, to identify changes in definition and coverage in order to assess the degree of comparability between different series and within a given series over time. The text is almost exclusively concerned with official government sources largely because, with the exception of the trade union data prior to 1926, there has been no regular or systematic effort among industrialists or private organizations to develop an 'unofficial' unemployment series, itself a telling indication of the importance generally attached to the government's figures. In judging the reliability of the various published series a conscious effort has been made to summarize the main issues and arguments developed by contemporary observers, including those of the very recent past, many of whom are less concerned with offering final verdicts than in helping to define the exact nature of the modern debate about unemployment.

Even the most casual reader will be aware of my debt to past and present authors in this field. If my summary of their often highly specialized work appears somewhat perfunctory my purpose has nevertheless been consistent—to present a thorough survey of the critical literature in order to encourage precision in the assessment of the magnitude and characteristics of the unemployment problem. This is an essential prerequisite to both sound historical judgement and to current labour market analysis.

Part I

Counting the Unemployed

1

Towards Unemployment Insurance

'Exact statistical measurement of "the unemployed", or even a close estimate of the total number of those "out of work" at any given time is ·impossible at present. The miserably defective character of our statistical machinery forms an adequate basis of ignorance upon which to base discreet official answers to awkward questions.'

– J.A. Hobson, 1895

Comprehensive statistics of unemployment only became available after the introduction in 1920 of an unemployment insurance scheme covering the bulk of the working population. Until then, and especially before 1913, the principal sources of information were obtained from returns made to the Board of Trade by trade unions, employers and local correspondents of the Board's Labour Department. The information obtained from these various sources was not compiled in any uniform way and is of somewhat limited value. It was assembled for publication purposes in two ways. First, in the form of district reports, which enabled the condition of employment in particular districts to be compared from month to month; and second, by trades, in the form of special reports on particular industries. A summary of all this information was published in the *Gazette* as a monthly memorandum on the state of the labour market. These early sources of data, or the sum of them all, could not, however, in any way purport to represent a true statistical measure of the extent of unemployment.

Statistics Obtained from Trade Unions

A large number of trade unions in the engineering, shipbuilding, metal, printing, woodworking, building and other trades made payments of one sort or another to their unemployed members. The records of the persons entitled to such benefit, including those who were still out of work after having exhausted their claim, provided the basis for the well-known 'trade union' unemployment series. Returns showing the percentage of the total union membership unemployed at the end of each month were made monthly to the Board of Trade by a number of trade unions from 1888. In 1893 the basis of the return was widened by the inclusion of additional trade unions. The industrial coverage of the trade union sample depended upon the development of out-of-work pay schemes in the various trades. These were first instituted in the engineering, shipbuilding, and metal industries which together accounted for about three-quarters of the total membership covered by the returns in 1860–70.[1] This proportion rose to nearly 60 per cent during 1881–90, falling to 46 per cent in 1894 and to 39.1 per cent in January 1908, then rising to 42.6 per cent in December 1921. There are variations, therefore, in the extent to which the figures for certain industries affect the results at different periods in time. The trade union sample also drew from manufacturing (printing, bookbinding and paper, textiles and, later, clothing and pottery), mining and building, but excluded workers in agriculture, transportation, communications, domestic service, government and commerce.

Although regular monthly returns of unemployment among selected trade unions date only from 1888, the Board of Trade carried the figures backwards (on an annual basis) to 1860 and, in the case of the engineering, shipbuilding, and metal trades, to 1851. Information on unemployment before 1851 is particularly scarce. When available it is usually descriptive or, if statistical, based on very specific data, often for a single industry during a critical phase of the trade cycle.[2]

---

1. W.H. Beveridge, *Full Employment in a Free Society*, London 1944, p. 41.
2. The economy of pre-industrial Britain suffered more from chronic rural under-employment than from unemployment (see D.C. Coleman, 'Labour in the English Economy of the Seventeenth Century', *Economic History Review*, VIII, 1956). There is little doubt that the multifarious changes in industrial development and technique from 1760 to 1850 produced frictional, structural, technological and cyclical unemployment but the intensity of such unemployment—and even of unemployment in general—cannot be

The Board of Trade series from 1888 was constructed from monthly reports of the total membership of particular unions and the number of members unemployed at the end of the month, excluding workers who were sick, superannuated, on strike or locked-out. The comparison of the two figures gave an 'unemployment percentage'. The combination of all the returns was commonly cited as the 'general unemployment percentage'. For earlier years this method was supplemented by data of the amount paid per head of total membership as unemployment benefit. This amount, divided by the weekly amount allowed, gave the average number of weeks of unemployment per head, or the average per head per year over the whole membership, from which the percentage was deduced.[3]

---

adequately measured. Some general indication of the nature and seriousness of unemployment during the first half of the nineteenth century can be obtained from A.D. Gayer, W.W. Rostow, and A.J. Schwartz, *The Growth and Fluctuation of the British Economy, 1790-1850*, 2 vols. Oxford 1953, and A.D. Gayer, 'Unemployment in British Industries 1815-1850', D. Phil thesis. Oxford 1930. More detailed information exists of unemployment in particular towns and industries during the recession of 1841-2. See R.C.O. Matthews, *A Study in Trade Cycle History, 1833-1842*, Cambridge 1954; E.J. Hobsbawm, 'The Tramping Artisan', *Economic History Review*, III, 1951; E.J. Hobsbawm, 'The British Standard of Living, 1790-1850', *Economic History Review*, X, 1957; *Hand-Loom Weavers. Report of the Commissioners*, 1841, (296), X. For the situation in the 1850s see J.R.T. Hughes, *Fluctuations in Trade, Industry and Finance: A Study of British Economic Development, 1850-1860*, Oxford 1960; N. Gash, 'Rural Unemployment', *Economic History Review*, VI, 1935.

The most detailed statistical returns of pre-1850 unemployment refer to a single occupational group—ironfounders—whose trade was especially subject to cyclical fluctuations. See Gayer, Rostow, and Schwartz, op. cit., vol 2; W. Woytinsky, *Three Sources of Unemployment*, Geneva 1935, p. 19. Unemployment records from 1854 of members of the Friendly Society of Ironfounders are in Marie Dessauer, 'Monthly Unemployment Records, 1845-1892', *Economica*, 17, August 1940.

The reports of the Poor Law Boards from 1848-59 indicate for England and Wales and selected counties therein the number of able-bodied outdoor paupers in receipt of relief on account of being out of work. But the figures are seriously defective in a number of important respects. See Marie Dessauer, 'Unemployment Records, 1848-59', *Economic History Review*, X, 1940.

3. Details of the data prior to 1888 can be found in Board of Trade, *British and Foreign Trade and Industrial Conditions (Second Series)*, Cd. 2337, 1905, pp. 79ff. A general unemployment percentage for all unions in engineering, shipbuilding, and metal, together with percentages for the principal unions—

To what extent do the trade union unemployment rates adequately reflect the level of unemployment in the trades covered and how valuable are they as an indicator of the general state of unemployment over a period of years? The statistics of the earlier years are extremely selective and narrowly based. The total trade union membership covered by the returns did not reach 100,000 until 1872. The basis of the general unemployment percentage grew gradually stronger from 1888 as the number and variety of reporting unions increased and as the proportion of the total working population represented in the returns expanded. Details of various groups of unions reporting to the Labour Department of the Board of Trade and subsequently to the Ministry of

----

Amalgamated Engineers, Iron Founders and Iron Moulders – are provided for the period 1851 to 1903. Details for the Boiler Makers and Iron and Steel Shipbuilders are available from 1872 to 1903. There are, in addition, unemployment percentage figures relating to: Amalgamated Carpenters and Joiners (1860–1903); all Unions in Woodworking and Furnishings (1867–1903); Principal Unions therein, namely United Coachmakers (1867–1903; Furnishing Trades Association (1868–1903); Amalgamated Millsawyers– known later as Woodcutting Machinists (1873–1903); All Unions in Printing and Bookbinding Trades (1856–1903); Principal Unions therein, namely London Compositors (1860–1903); Typographical Association (1863–1903) and London Bookbinders (1856–1903); All other trades (1867–1903).

The regular Board of Trade returns were published in the *Gazette* providing monthly trade union percentages from 1888 to 1926 (with separate percentages for the following trade groups: engineering, shipbuilding, and metal; carpenters and joiners; other woodworking and furnishing, and printing and bookbinding) and on a yearly mean basis for 1881 to 1887.

In addition the *Gazette* provided a detailed breakdown of trade union percentages in its reports on employment in the principal industries between 1904 to 1912, providing for certain industries, and sometimes occupational groups, regional details of the monthly percentage of members returned as unemployed. Before 1904 regional data on industrial unemployment did not appear frequently enough or on a sufficiently comparable basis to permit close investigation, though details are available elsewhere of the monthly trade union returns for London during the period January 1895 to October 1906. See *Royal Commission on the Poor Laws,* Appendix XIX, Cmd. 4795, 1909, pp. 158ff.

Tables of the trade union unemployment percentage were also given in each issue of the *Abstract of Labour Statistics.* The *Eighteenth Abstract* (1926) contains detailed tables, giving separate figures for a number of groups of trade unions: carpenters, joiners, and plumbers, engineering, ironfounding, boilermaking etc.; miscellaneous metal trades; paper manufacture, printing and bookbinding; boot and shoe operatives; and the furnishing trades.

TABLE 1 TRADE UNION UNEMPLOYMENT RETURNS

	1908 Unionists included	Percentage by each trade	1913 Unionists included	Percentage by each trade	1926 Unionists included	Percentage by each trade
Building	61,057	9.4	73,708	8.3	–	–
Woodworking	35,200	5.4	45,248	5.1	36,793	3.8
Furnishing					30,010	3.1
Coalmining	126,725	19.5	163,614	18.5	143,869	14.7
Engineering	164,088	25.2	284,918	32.2	342,706	35.1
Shipbuilding	58,424	9.0				
Other metal trades	31,751	4.9	63,010	7.1	48,738	5.0
Printing and Bookbinding	56,376	8.7	62,850	7.1	105,618	10.8
Textiles	93,900	14.5	124,237	14.1	125,725	12.9

Labour in January of selected years are reproduced above in Table 1. By comparison the proportion of the number of unionists included in the returns for 1894, contributed by building, woodworking, and furnishing was 21 per cent, by coalmining 19 per cent and by engineering, shipbuilding, and other metal trades 46 per cent.

By 1914 the membership of the reporting unions had increased to 993,000. From 1900 to the outbreak of World War I it represented about one-quarter of the total membership of trade unions and other employees' associations in the United Kingdom. After the war, the proportion fluctuated from about one-sixth to about one-fifth, the reported numbers reaching a peak of 1,603,000 in 1920 contracting to 833,000 in 1926 when the trade union series was discontinued.[4]

4. J. Hilton, 'Statistics of Unemployment Derived from the Working of the Unemployment Insurance Acts', *Journal of the Royal Statistical Society*, LXXXVI, March 1923.

   The returns, however, were not consistent in every case. Struck by the high percentage reported as unemployed in the Card and Blowing Room branch of the cotton industry 1905, despite general improvements within the trade, the Labour Department discovered on further investigation that women who ceased work on marriage but who continued to pay 1d. per week for funeral benefit were being counted as unemployed. It was estimated that by excluding such groups the number normally returned as out-of-work could be reduced by 75 per cent. PRO, Lab.2/1478, 1905.

During the first World War men in the armed forces were excluded from the base in calculating the trade union percentages. The figures from 1921 exclude pottery trade operatives and from July 1924, building trade operatives.

Contemporary observers were reasonably confident that the unemployment rates given for specific unions did not substantially falsify the employment position in the trades covered. The Labour Department of the Board of Trade commented in 1893 that 'though these absolute percentages only apply strictly to the organized workers in certain groups of trades, their monthly changes probably afford an index of changes in the total volume of employment in the skilled trades of the country.'[5] The statistics should nevertheless be treated with caution. They would be more valuable if the relation between the number of workers covered by voluntary insurance and the total number of workers generally employed in corresponding industries and occupations was known precisely and if it could be ascertained how far changes in the figures reflected variations in the trade distribution of the members of the unions included and in the rules under which out-of-work benefits were paid. Comparisons over time of the industrial classification of the unemployed derived from trade union data should take account, moreover, of the conditions of administration of the insurance schemes themselves and of the extent to which trade unions altered the industrial classification of their members.

The available evidence indicates that with the exception of employees in public authorities, whose unemployment was due normally to more exceptional circumstances, the only principal trade group in which the majority of the organized workmen were in unions which paid no unemployment benefit was mining and quarrying where slackness of work was met systematically by short-time, and not by deductions in employment (see Table 2).

It is difficult to compare the absolute amount of unemployment in one union, or in the same union over long periods of time, unless a proper correction is made for changes in the scale and conditions of benefit payments. Moreover, unemployment benefit was often continued only for a stipulated period so that during long periods of depression the statistics tended to under-estimate the degree of suffering involved as men out of work for protracted periods ceased to be recorded. Nevertheless statistics of trade union expenditure on unemployment benefit provide some indication of prevailing conditions.

5. *Gazette,* June 1893.

TABLE 2 UNIONS AND UNEMPLOYMENT BENEFIT, 1906

	Unions paying one or more forms of Unemployment Benefit		Unions paying no Unemployment Benefit	
	No.	Membership	No.	Membership
Building	53	175,434	43	20,902
Mining & Quarrying	40	251,858	29	319,262
Metal, Engineering & Shipbuilding	164	314,396	58	46,570
Textile	204	280,586	55	20,299
Clothing	20	55,095	17	4,419
Transport	9	115,391	49	73,570
Printing, etc.	36	63,472	5	979
Woodworking & Furnishing	90	41,849	8	480
Miscellaneous	123	89,045	70	34,501
General Labour	6	68,991	12	42,843
Employees of Public Authorities	2	860	68	85,481
Total	747	1,456,977	414	649,306

SOURCE
Royal Commission on the Poor Laws and Relief of Distress, Appendix XXI (C), p. 614.

Allowances must be made, however, for fluctuations in the rate and conditions of benefit and of the extent to which workmen were encouraged to accept out-of-work pay rather than work for less than standard wages.[6]

6. For figures of unemployment expenditure see the financial summary of 100 principal trade unions in the *Annual Reports on Trade Unions from 1892.* The unions covered constantly represented *c.* 60% of the total membership of all unions but their expenditure on unemployment benefits represented 80% of the total expenditure of all unions for this purpose in 1906 and 1908–the only years before 1914 for which full particulars regarding unemployment benefits are available for all unions.

   Details of the changing rates of benefit and conditions of eligibility are in Royal Commission on Unemployment Insurance, *Minutes of Evidence,* 17 April 1931, Memorandum of Evidence by the Ministry of Labour–Payment of Unemployment Benefit by Trade Unions. See also G. Wood, 'Trade Union Expenditure on Unemployment Benefit since 1860', *Journal of the Royal Statistical Society,* LXIII, 1900; E.L. Hartley, 'Trade Union

It has long been recognized that the trade union returns cannot be regarded as an adequate indicator of the condition of employment either of the total working population, or of industrial manual workers, or even of all trade unionists. As the Controller General of the Statistical Department of the Board of Trade explained in 1908:[7]

If we could read into these figures something more than is there, namely, that they give a basis for calculating the total unemployment in the country, we should all be very glad; but I do not think we can do that, and I do not think it would be safe to try to do that. After all, we only get the figures for some 600,000 Trade Unionists, and I am somewhat sceptical about applying them to the 2,000,000 trade unionists. One reason is . . . that I think we have got figures from some trades which are particularly susceptible to changes in bad times, such as the shipbuilding, the building, and the engineering. Then another reason is that among the trade unions we leave out there are large bodies of men who are seldom out of employment at all. . . . Therefore, I do not think it would be safe to apply our unemployed figures to the trade unions as a whole; and a fortiori, I do not think it is safe to apply them to the 11,000,000 of working people, and I do not think that anybody would suggest that one could apply the definite information which we have got as to the 600,000 to the 11,000,000. Each trade has got to be considered by itself, and each trade has a history of its own. Even when you take the 11,000,000 people, you will find there are a large number who are not unemployed as a rule. There are the railway servants, the rest of the coal miners not included in our figures, and there are the textile workers. None of those people are unemployed much. On the other hand, there are a large number of people in certain trades who are at times very considerably unemployed. I should like to mention this as regards our own figures: We can only get the figures for the carpenters and plumbers in the building trade; although they show

---

Expenditure on Unemployment Benefit', *Journal of the Royal Statistical Society,* LXVII, 1904. See also 'The Growth of Trade Unions with Particular Reference to the Payment of Unemployment Benefit', *Royal Commission on the Poor Laws and Relief of Distress,* Appendix XXI (C).

7. *Royal Commission on the Poor Laws and Relief of Distress, Minutes of Evidence,* Q.98850, 6 April 1908. Cf. Bowley's statement made in 1906: 'When it was asked in the House of Commons a month ago as to how many persons there were unemployed, the Board of Trade returned the numbers already published in the *Labour Gazette,* which we know all about. Nobody knows what is the factor by which you multiply them.' A.L. Bowley, 'The Problem of the Unemployed', *Sociological Papers,* III, 1907, p. 337.

considerable unemployment at the present time, I should say that there are probably more unemployed among the bricklayers, the labourers and the masons, because theirs is outside work. Therefore, in that particular trade, our figures, which illustrate the position of the carpenters and plumbers, may not, I think, fairly represent the amount of unemployment in the building trade, in fact, I think they probably underestimate it. Our figures may exaggerate in some particulars, and underestimate in others, the amount of employment even in the case of the trade unions.

The general unemployment percentage was clearly not a complete record of unemployment. Its adequacy within its own restricted field depended upon the degree of registration within unions of all their unemployed members. Even when such returns were regarded as reasonably trustworthy they did not indicate the total loss of employment at any time since by concentrating on the wholly unemployed they ignored short-time working. The trade union percentage failed to cover all trades and occupations excluding, for example, shopworkers and clerks but more especially those in trades which enjoyed considerable stability of employment such as agriculture, railways, and domestic service. Nor were the occupations included in the series fairly represented; some were over-represented, some were under-represented. In the building trade, for example, the returns referred to the condition of carpenters and joiners and plumbers; no reference was made to bricklayers, plasterers, masons or painters.[8] Only a fraction of all textile operatives was included in the count of the unemployed while the whole mass of casual and generally low-skilled labour was almost completely ignored.

Nor is it possible to determine precisely whether the trade union returns are a satisfactory index of unemployment among non-unionists.[9] Using information derived from the operation of the first unemployment insurance scheme in 1913-14, Beveridge compared the benefits paid directly to workmen in certain insured industries with those paid

8. For details of the relevant trade union returns for London during 1896–1906 see N.B. Dearle, *Problems of Unemployment in London Building Trades,* London 1908.

9. Local correspondents of the Board of Trade carried out a special investigation of the extent to which non-unionists were out of work in 1908. See PRO, Cab.37/95, 'Report of Unemployment in the United Kingdom in September 1908', 10 October 1908.

by trade unions and concluded that the trade union unemployment rate was slightly greater than it would have been if full account was taken of unorganized workers.[10]

A more fundamental problem arises from the fact that the trade union data refer only to those unions paying unemployment benefit, cover a limited number of industries, and even within those industries apply only to trade unionists, themselves predominantly skilled men whose conditions of employment were far from representative.[11] Moreover, because the series was weighted on the basis of trade union membership and not in proportion to the actual number of workers in the different industries it tended to exaggerate fluctuations in employment by over-representing workmen in the shipbuilding, engineering, and metal trades, particularly sensitive to cyclical depression, and under-representing those in building, vulnerable to seasonal unemployment, and those in mining and textile industries which normally reacted to downturns in activity by working short-time.[12]

The proportion of the total membership of the recorded returns accounted for by the engineering, shipbuilding, and metal groups in 1860–70 was about three-quarters, in 1870–80 about three-fifths, in

10. Beveridge, *Full Employment*, op.cit., pp. 328–30.
11. For contemporary criticism on the same lines see Schloss, loc.cit., p. 53; J.A. Hobson, *The Problem of the Unemployed*, London 1896; A. Mercer, 'Unemployment', *Economic Review*, XVII, 1907; *Select Committee on Distress from Want of Employment, Minutes of Evidence*, H.C. 365, 1895, Evidence of H. Llewellyn-Smith.

Bowley had drawn attention as early as 1896 to the inadequacy of using trade union returns without relating the numbers involved to the wider trade union population. See A.L. Bowley, 'The abstract of labour statistics 1894–5', *Economic Journal*, September 1896. Beveridge claimed that in 1904 less than one-fifth of all occupied males recorded at the 1901 Census in industrial occupations were in trade unions and less than one-fifteenth of these were in unions giving unemployment pay. *Royal Commission on the Poor Laws and Relief of Distress, Minutes of Evidence*, Vol. VIII, Cd.5066, 1910, Q.77832. See also L. Chiozza-Money, 'The Extent of British Unemployment', *The International*, 2, 1908.

12. There were other sources of data on the regularity of employment in these trades supplied by employers. See below pp. 24–27. In places such as Lancashire, for example, it proved extremely difficult to provide an adequate measure of the extent of unemployment because of the lack of systematic data from trade unions on short-time working and female unemployment. See S.J. Chapman and H.M. Hallsworth, *Unemployment: The Results of an Investigation made in Lancashire*, Manchester University Press, 1909.

**TABLE 3   UNEMPLOYMENT RATES IN DEPRESSION YEARS,
SELECTED TRADE UNIONS**

	General Unemployment, all Unions included in returns	Engineering, Shipbuilding & Metal Trade Unions	All Unions except Engineering, Shipbuilding & Metal Trade Unions
	%	%	%
1858	11.9	12.2	2.5
1868	7.9	10.0	3.5
1879	11.4	15.3	6.1
1886	10.2	13.5	5.6
1893	7.5	11.4	4.0

1880-90 rather under three-fifths, while from 1890 to the early 1900s it remained at about two-fifths. The effect of the change in the relative importance of this group was to exaggerate the fluctuations of general unemployment in the earlier years of the series. The years of deepest depression during the last quarter of the nineteenth century affected this group of trades in particular, reinforcing the important part which their unemployment figures played in the general average, as Table 3 indicates.

While there were exaggerated fluctuations in the earlier percentages, the gradual reduction in the overriding influence of particular groups of trades over others had the effect in later years of altering the basis on which the general unemployment percentage was calculated. The crude average rate tended in effect to understate unemployment as compared with previous years. If we compare 1894 and 1909, the group of trades which normally resorted to dismissals during periods of recession—Building, Woodworking, Engineering, Shipbuilding, Other Metal, Printing and Bookbinding—covered 77 per cent of the total members returned in 1894 and 60.6 per cent in 1909. A second group which often resorted to short-time working—the coalmining, textile, paper, leather, and miscellaneous trades—covered 23 per cent of the returns in 1894 and 39.4 per cent in 1909. The general unemployment percentage in 1909 (7.7) was composed of 11.36 per cent unemployed in the first group and 2.06 in the second group. If, however, the various trades had been represented as in 1894 when the general percentage was 6.9 the 1909 figure would have been 9.2, an increase of 2.3 per cent in 1909 over 1894 in contrast to only 0.8 per cent in the recorded data.[13]

The Board of Trade, aware of the excessive weight of this particular group within the trade union series, prepared a 'corrected' unemployment percentage based on the unweighted mean of the percentages for

TABLE 4   AVERAGE PERCENTAGE OF MEMBERS OF TRADE UNIONS RETURNED AS OUT OF WORK

	Uncorrected	Corrected		Uncorrected	Corrected
1860	1.9	1.8	1882	2.3	2.3
1861	5.2	3.7	1883	2.6	2.6
1862	8.4	6.0	1884	8.1	7.1
1863	6.0	4.7	1885	9.3	8.5
1864	2.7	1.9	1886	10.2	9.5
1865	2.1	1.8	1887	7.6	7.1
1866	3.3	2.6	1888	4.9[a]	4.1
1867	7.4	6.3	1889	2.1	2.0
1868	7.9	6.7	1890	2.1	2.1
1869	6.7	5.9	1891	3.5	3.4
1870	3.9	3.7	1892	6.3	6.2
1871	1.6	1.6	1893	7.5	7.7
1872	0.9	0.9	1894	6.9	7.7
1873	1.2	1.1	1895	5.8	6.0
1874	1.7	1.6	1896	3.4	3.5
1875	2.4	2.2	1897	3.5	3.6
1876	3.7	3.4	1898	3.0	3.1
1877	4.7	4.4	1899	2.4	2.4
1878	6.8	6.2	1900	2.9	2.8
1879	11.4	10.7	1901	3.8	3.8
1880	5.5	5.2	1902	4.4	4.6
1881	3.5	3.5	1903	5.1	5.3

SOURCE
Cd. 2337, op. cit., pp. 83, 90. For details of the 'corrected' percentages for the years 1904-26 see W.H. Beveridge, *Unemployment. A Problem of Industry*, London 1930, pp. 39, 432.

NOTE
a. Percentages from 1888 onwards were derived from returns of the number of unemployed at the end of each month. Those prior to that date were partly computed from expenditure on unemployment benefit. See above p. 11.

13.   N.B. Dearle, 'English Statistics of Unemployment', *International Conference on Unemployment, Paris, September 1910*, Paris 1911, Report No. 25, pp. 1-3.

the two groups 'engineering, shipbuilding, and metal trades' and 'all other trades'. This was equivalent to giving the former group a constant weight equal to half of the total throughout the entire period, in place of a changing weight fluctuating from three-quarters to two-fifths. The effect was to reduce the level of unemployment in years of depression, though from 1881 the correction appears to make little difference. Indeed there is no reason to suppose that the arbitrary system of averaging which the Board of Trade adopted necessarily represents a more correct estimate of unemployment than the unadjusted figures.[14] The details of the two series are listed in Table 4.

A further revised series is available for the period 1912–22 in which the percentages for each of the reporting unions are combined with weights corresponding roughly with the estimated numbers in the industries. The details, from Hilton, are shown in Table 5.

To what extent can the trade union percentages be considered a valid index of general unemployment over the period covered by the series? Contemporary government statisticians, acutely aware of the deficiencies of the trade union figures, especially as a reflection of the total *volume* of unemployment, did not reject them entirely as a barometer of the state of the labour market. The cyclical fluctuations in the trades covered, while exaggerating the general fluctuations of industry in the whole country, tended also to propagate waves of prosperity and depression. Llewellyn Smith wrote in 1895:

It is precisely the trades included . . . which are the most violent in their oscillations. For this reason, and partly because they exaggerate the fluctuations, the variations in the percentage of their unemployed members afford a very sensitive test of change in the labour market. It is believed therefore that the percentage of unemployed among Trade Unions making returns is a good index of the state of employment, but it is quite misleading to suppose that the percentage itself can be directly applied to all the working population, or to the whole body of Trade Unionists.[15]

14. Beveridge, op. cit., p. 41; W. Galenson and A. Zellner, 'International Comparison of Unemployment Rates', in Universities–National Bureau Committee for Economic Research, *The Measurement and Behavior of Unemployment,* Princeton 1957, p. 561.

15. PRO, Cab. 37/38. *Memorandum on a Recent Estimate of the Number of the Unemployed,* 8 January 1895. The same point was reiterated by Churchill in 1909: PRO, Cab. 37/97, *Estimate of the Number of the Unemployed in the United Kingdom and Notes Upon the Difficulties of Making Satisfactory Calculations,* 2 January 1909.

TABLE 5   COMPARISON OF ORIGINAL AND ADJUSTED TRADE UNION PERCENTAGE

	Original	Adjusted
1912	3.2	3.3
1913	2.1	2.1
1914	3.3	3.3
1915	1.1	1.1
1916	0.4	0.4
1917	0.7	0.6
1918	0.8	0.8
1919	2.4	2.1
1920	2.4	2.0
1921	14.8	13.5
1922	15.2	12.8

SOURCE
C.H. Feinstein, *National Income, Expenditure and Output of the United Kingdom 1855-1965*, London 1972, table 11.9, p. 225. For a commentary on this adjusted series see Hilton, *Journal of the Royal Statistical Society*, March 1923, loc. cit. Feinstein has applied these adjusted percentages for 1912-18 and for 1920, the original trade union percentages for 1881-1911 and the Board of Trade 'corrected' percentages for 1855-80 to data of the civilian working population to provide estimates of the total number wholly unemployed in these periods. The details are in Feinstein, op. cit. table 57. Feinstein's somewhat different revision of the rate of unemployment during the period 1921 to 1938 is discussed below, pp. 58-60.

NOTE
The trade union series was known to be incomplete for 1919 and an alternative estimate of the national number unemployed was made on the basis of the records of the out-of-work donation scheme.

In 1903 the Labour Department was to confess again that in its search for reasonably accurate employment indicators it was 'continually . . . thrown back on the old Trade Union statistics as the most trustworthy guide'.[16]

Bowley's ingenious effort in 1912 to improve upon existing measures of employment[17] lent support to the view that the trade union figures

16.   PRO, Cab. 2/1478, 1903.
17.   See below pp. 00-00.

were still a valid index of the general state of unemployment, as were the figures provided by the introduction of unemployment insurance. Reviewing the trade union series in 1922 Hilton, former Director of Statistics at the Ministry of Labour, concluded that

the experience which has been gained since the records of the proportions unemployed among insured workpeople became available, suggests that in times of good employment the Trade Union percentage has approximated very closely to the general percentage unemployed, but that in times of serious depression the over-representation of the engineering and shipbuilding trades in the figures has (as was believed to be the case) tended to raise the general percentage for all unions included to a level appreciably too high to represent accurately the average proportion of workpeople unemployed in the country as a whole.[18]

If Hilton's conclusions are accepted then only in 1908 and 1909, the two years of severe depression in the decade before 1914, could the trade union percentages not be regarded as close approximations to the general level of unemployment. And there is reason to suppose that even in these two exceptional years the distortion arising from the potential over-representation of the engineering, shipbuilding, and metal groups has itself been exaggerated. Galenson and Zellner have suggested that the overstatement in 1908-9 was not as great as that during the more serious downturn in 1921 when the three trade groups constituted a higher proportion of the union sample and had greater unemployment percentages relative to those of other groups in the earlier period.[19] Other comparisons of the trade union returns with the unemployment insurance statistics have tended to confirm the validity of the former as fairly representative of conditions generally over a period of years and not only in the trades directly represented.[20] At most, however, the trade union returns remain an index of the variations of employment generally, i.e. 'whether employment is going

---

18. Hilton, loc. cit., p. 182.
19. Galenson and Zellner, op. cit., p. 565.
20. Beveridge, *Full Employment*, op. cit. pp. 328–35. W.A. Berridge, 'Employment and the Business Cycle', *The Review of Economic Statistics*, January 1922; Committee on Industry and Trade, *Survey of Industrial Relations*, London 1926. pp. 33, 244ff; *Final Report of the Royal Commission on Unemployment Insurance*, London 1932, pp. 85–6.

up or down, whether it is better or whether it is worse'[21] and cannot
be relied upon as an absolute measure of the total amount of unemployment in all industries at any particular date. It is virtually impossible, as
Feinstein has pointed out, 'to arrive at a precise statistical assessment of
the possible under- or over-statement involved in the use of the trade
union series as a measure of the general unemployment rate. In relation
to such stable industries as the railways, domestic service and certain
branches of agriculture, it will undoubtedly be too high, in relation to
unskilled and casual workers it would be too low; and the net effect—
which would probably vary over different phases of the trade cycle—is
uncertain'.[22]

Returns from Employers and Local Correspondents

In addition to the data supplied by trade unions the Board of Trade
obtained certain employment statistics from employers and from trade
correspondents who were secretaries of employers' associations. This
information was of a rather different character to that supplied by the
unions and related to certain groups of industries in which the percentage of workpeople unemployed was either not obtainable or did not
afford a satisfactory indication of the fluctuations in employment.
In certain industries such as coalmining, changes in the level of
economic activity tended to give rise to a greater or smaller number of
days worked per week rather than to increases or decreases in the total
number employed; similarly the total number of shifts worked in iron
and steel or the number of blast furnaces at work at the end of each
month were regarded as 'furnishing a more or less direct measure of
quantity of employment'.[23]

21. *Royal Commission on the Poor Laws and Relief of Distress, Minutes of
    Evidence,* Q.98,893, 6 April 1908.
22. C. Feinstein, *National Income, Expenditure and Output of the United
    Kingdom, 1855–1965,* Cambridge 1972, p. 225.
23. *Royal Commission on the Poor Laws and Relief of Distress, Minutes of
    Evidence,* Appendix XXI (B), p. 604. The Board of Trade undertook
    separate studies of the irregularity of employment in selected industries
    including coal (*Gazette,* April 1894–December 1899); iron (ibid., November
    1894), the textile and hat trades (ibid., January–March, July–August 1895,
    July 1897–December 1899) and clothing (ibid., March 1906). Information
    for agriculture was obtained, not from local correspondents, but from a
    special agricultural correspondent appointed by the Board of Trade.

The information furnished by employers referred in the main to the larger, more fully established firms and took no account of the loss of employment due to failures and to the dissolution of businesses. Descriptions of the principal returns are shown in Table 6.

TABLE 6 EMPLOYERS' EMPLOYMENT RETURNS
DATA SUPPLIED

(a) The number of days worked per week in the coalmining industry. The number given as 'days worked' was the number of days (allowance being made in all the calculations for short days) on which coal was hewn and wound at the collieries included in the returns received. It was not necessarily implied that all the persons employed at these collieries worked the whole number of days. No allowance was made, therefore, for actual unemployment.

(b) The number of days worked per week in iron mines.

(c) Number of tinplate mills working at the end of each month.

(d) Number of furnaces in blast in the pig-iron industry.

(e) Number of persons employed and average number of shifts worked per week in iron and steel works.

(f) Number of workpeople employed, and their total earnings in one week in each month, in the cotton, woollen and worsted, carpet, bleaching, printing, dyeing and finishing, linen, jute, lace, silk, hosiery, shirt and collar, boot and shoe, brick, porcelain, china and earthenware, and glass trades. This information was taken by contemporaries to indicate the variations in employment during any one month. The figures did not distinguish between the unemployed and those who might be underemployed due to a shortening of hours. Although the figures of total wages paid took account of short-time they were affected by changes in wage rates and by fluctuations in employment, so that they are unsuitable for comparisons over a long time.

(g) Number employed in a few particular trades, of which the most important was dock and riverside labour in London.

Apart from reporting numbers unemployed many branch unions commented generally upon employment prospects. In the earliest days it was the custom of the Labour Department to group the number of branches in particular industries into three distinct categories, according to their descriptions of the state of trade: 'fair to very good', 'moderate or quiet', and 'dull to very bad'. This information was supplemented, and later superseded, by reports on the state of employment in various trades and districts[24] supplied by local correspondents of the Board of Trade. It was precisely because the trade union returns ignored the unskilled, the skilled workers who did not belong to a trade union, and those organized skilled workmen whose unions did not pay unemployment benefit, that a demand grew for specially appointed local agents to supply more complete information of the regularity of employment and of the occupational distribution of those out of work.[25]

The district reports provided little or no statistical information, except in regions where benefit-paying trade unions predominated. They consisted largely of subjective assessments of prevailing conditions with descriptive comments ranging from employment being 'healthy' or 'bad' to there being a 'slight falling off in the number unemployed' or 'a perceptible improvement' in the numbers at work. Nevertheless this information provided the basis of the Labour Department's own largely verbal summary of employment conditions customarily printed in the forefront of the *Gazette*.

The reports from local correspondents on the state of employment in the important industries in their area were published individually in the *Gazette* until 1903. Thereafter they were pooled with information from other sources, including employers' and trade union returns, to provide a series of articles on the state of employment in various industries. This method continued until 1939, though not on a strictly comparable basis.[26]

24. Including Tyne and Wear, Oldham, Bolton, Burnley, Accrington, Manchester, Liverpool, Middlesbrough, Stockton, Leeds, Bradford, Huddersfield, Barnsley and the Yorkshire mining districts, Sheffield, Hull, Wolverhampton, Birmingham, Nottingham, Leicester, the Eastern Counties, Bristol and the South West, Cardiff, South Wales and the Forest of Dean mining districts, Edinburgh, Glasgow, Dundee, the West of Scotland, Dublin, Belfast and London, for which comparatively more information was usually available.
25. Schloss, loc. cit., pp. 52–5. Schloss himself suggested that the local correspondents should arrange to have their reports displayed in every local post office.
26. While the trade union index figure of unemployment referred in 1911 to some 800,000 workpeople the total number included in all the series of numerical returns of one kind or another made to the Board of Trade amounted to *c.* 6 million. Balfour Committee on Industry and Trade, op. cit., p. 245.
    The industries and trades included in the series before 1922 included coalmining; iron, shale and other mining and quarrying; pig iron; tinplate and steel sheet trades; iron and steelworks; shipbuilding trades; engineering

The numerical and verbal reports and returns from local correspondents, offering a mass of not very promising material, were used by
Bowley in 1912 as the basis of an experiment in the measurement of
the level of employment. His central aim was to ascertain whether such
disparate data could be made to yield a curve similar in general character to the curve derived from the trade union returns. The results, based
in part on the quantification of verbal descriptions, were not strictly a
measure of unemployment but he succeeded in constructing for the
period 1894 to 1911 a quantitative index of the rise and fall in the
volume of employment and by inference an index of the movement of
total unemployment and short-time.[27]

Unemployment Insurance and Labour Exchanges

The introduction of the first scheme of compulsory unemployment
insurance in 1911 provided a new series of statistics. Initially only a
limited number of industries were covered: building, construction of
works, shipbuilding, mechanical engineering, construction of vehicles,
and sawmilling carried on in connection with any other insured trade.
The scheme was extended in 1916 and again in 1920.[28] From September 1912 it was possible to calculate an unemployment percentage rate
nationally and by districts by expressing the number of insured persons
unemployed at monthly dates as a percentage of the total number of
insured persons. The unit for counting for this purpose was the 'lodged'
unemployment book, the card to which contribution stamps were
fixed. When an insured person became unemployed he had to obtain
his unemployment book from his employer and 'lodge' it at an Employment Exchange for the entire period of his unemployment. The book
was handed to a new employer when work re-commenced.

----

trades; miscellaneous metal trades; cotton trade; silk trade; lace trade;
carpet trade; bleaching, printing, dyeing and finishing; felt hat trade;
tailoring trades; shirt and collar trade; other clothing trades; leather trade;
boot and shoe trades; brick and cement trades; building and construction
of works; paper, printing and bookbinding trades; pottery trades; glass
trades; food preparation trades; agriculture, fishing industry, dock and
riverside labour and eamen. For details of changes from 1922 see below
p. 219.

27. A.L. Bowley, 'The Measurement of Employment: an Experiment', *Journal
of the Royal Statistical Society*, LXXV, 1912.
28. See below, pp. 30–32.

Detailed statistics derived from the operation of the National Insurance Act, 1911 are given in the *First Report on the Proceedings of the Board of Trade under Part II of the National Insurance Act, 1911, with Appendices* (Cd. 6965, 1913) and in the unpublished *Report on the Proceedings of the Board of Trade under the Labour Exchanges Act, 1909, and under Part II of the National Insurance Act, 1911 to July 1914.* Statistics of the number insured under the 1911 Act and under the insurance scheme as extended in 1916 are given in the *Nineteenth Abstract of Labour Statistics* (Cmd. 3140, 1928).

The information furnished by the work of the Exchanges does not, of course, represent an exact measure of unemployment. Applications by workmen and vacancies notified by employers may not necessarily reflect the state of the labour market. Many workers ignored the Exchanges altogether. In periods of recession others may not have registered because of a general feeling of hopelessness in obtaining work while employers may, under similar conditions, have felt it preferable to seek labour other than through the Exchanges. The Exchange data in the early years over-represented some trades compared with the general occupied population, especially those particularly liable to unemployment. In addition, persons could register who were employed but seeking other work; others could register at different Exchanges and therefore be counted more than once.

Although the introduction of limited national insurance and the establishment of a national system of Labour Exchanges widened public awareness of the condition of labour and of the sexual composition of those seeking work, they did not alter the fact that down to 1914 statisticians could do little more than indicate general trends in unemployment and in distress from unemployment. The absolute level of unemployment nationally and locally and its variations within industry and occupation escaped precise definition in both trade union and State records.

2
From War to Welfare State, 1913–1948

It has been determined so far that until 1912 almost the only statistics of unemployment readily available were those relating to unemployment among members of certain trade unions paying unemployment benefit. Other information was fragmentary. The sums paid in outdoor relief and the number of persons relieved had been regularly issued over a number of years; and from 1905 there were records of committees operating under the Unemployed Workmen Act but these were more an indication of the distress caused by unemployment than a precise measure of the total out of work. From 1910 information was available of the number of applications for work at the newly-established Labour Exchanges, but these figures reflected the development of Exchange activities more than changes in the state of employment. Reports from employers of the state of employment in various trades and districts had been published regularly in the *Gazette* since 1883, and, to a limited extent, they threw some light on the trend of unemployment in pre-war years. But only the trade union figures gave a rate of unemployment which itself had to be interpreted very cautiously.[1]

The trade union unemployment percentage was published regularly until the end of 1926. With the widespread extension of unemployment insurance in 1920 statistics of a much more representative character than the trade union series became available. Nevertheless the trade union returns had provided the main source of unemployment data for the First World War period[2] and were not without some value thereafter.

---

1. See Chapter 1, pp 10–24 and below pp. 58–60.
2. In addition special investigations were made of the impact of the war upon employment. The Board of Trade addressed an enquiry 'to nearly all the

The Extension of Unemployment Insurance

The extension of unemployment insurance after 1916 marked the beginning of a more comprehensive and detailed statistical treatment of unemployment. In July 1916 approximately 1.5 million workers engaged in machine woodwork, the repair of metal goods, the manufacture of munitions, chemicals, rubber, leather, bricks, wooden cases, artificial stone and other artificial building materials were added to the 2.1 million or so persons over 16 already insured under the 1911 National Insurance Act.

During the period 1919 to 1920 considerable numbers of demobilized ex-servicemen and civilian workers, including juveniles over 15 and under 18, whose war work had come to an end were temporarily unemployed. Few had any rights to benefit under the insurance scheme so temporary arrangements were made for non-contributory benefits, known as Out-of-Work Donations, to be paid to them for limited periods. Holders of OWD policies were obliged to lodge them at an Employment Exchange and to sign them daily when unemployed. Though details were available of the number of policies issued it was not possible to compute percentage rates of unemployment during the period of the operation of the scheme (November 1918–November 1919)[3] as the total number of persons who would have been entitled to out-of-work donations when unemployed was not known. The OWD figures themselves do not provide an exact measure of the volume of

---

principal manufacturers' and estimated 'the total contraction in the volume of employment due to war, and of its distribution by trades and localities', PRO, Cab. 37/120, Unemployment Due to War, 28 August 1914. Details of unemployment among women in various districts appeared in the *Gazette* in November 1914 and February, March 1915. From early 1915 statements also appeared of the number of trade unions in particular industries to which emergency grants had been made in aid of exceptional expenditure on unemployment benefit arising out of the war. In addition see *Memorandum on the steps taken for the Prevention and Relief of Distress due to War*, Cd. 7603, 1914.

3. Though the civilian scheme ended in November 1919 ex-servicemen and women and certain classes of merchant seamen continued to benefit from the arrangements until March 1921. Details of the number claiming donation under the extended scheme in insured and uninsured trades and by Ministry of Labour Divisions are in the *Gazette*, January, February, May, September 1920. For further details see *Report of Committee on Re-Employment of Ex-Servicemen*, Cmd. 951, 1920.

unemployment among those to whom they related because the data were affected by changes in administration and, in the later months especially, by the exhaustion for many individuals of the right to benefit under the scheme.

From January 1919 the *Gazette* provided details of the number of OWD policies issued to civilians (men, women, boys and girls) and demobilized members of H.M. Forces (sailors, soldiers, airmen, and women's corps) for each Ministry of Labour Division in the United Kingdom. Statistics were also available of the number of policies remaining lodged each month at Employment Exchanges which had been signed during the preceding six days by those in insured and uninsured trades. The data for uninsured trades must be used cautiously. During 1919 workers recently employed in the insurable munitions industries were reclassified in large numbers under their normal peacetime occupations which, in the case of women, were largely in uninsured trades. Increases in the figures of policies lodged for uninsurable occupations were not wholly attributable to lack of employment in these occupations but were due partly to the return of workers from munitions industries.[4]

The largest expansion of the unemployment insurance scheme came in 1920 when it was applied to all persons of 16 years and over who were employed under a contract-of-service or apprenticeship and, if non-manual workers, receiving remuneration not exceeding £250 a year. The principal persons excluded from the scheme were those occupied in agriculture[5], forestry, horticulture, and private domestic service whose risk of unemployment was not thought to be serious.

4. The percentage of civilian and demobilized persons reabsorbed into industry in relation to the total number of those to whom policies had been issued was published in the *Gazette,* March, April 1919. Full details of the operation of the OWD scheme can be found in *Report on National Unemployment Insurance to July 1923.*

5. The total number of employees (regular and casual) in agriculture fell during the years 1914 to 1920 but the variations in the number employed were distorted by the employment of soldiers, German prisoners and relatives. In addition there was a regular seasonal ebb and flow between the employment figures for July and January each year suggesting that there were workers engaged in the industry for the summer period who sought other jobs in the winter. The Committee on Agriculture and Insurance tried to obtain information on agricultural unemployment during December 1920 from the National Farmers' Union, the National Union of Agricultural Workers, the District Agricultural Wage Committees, and the Employment Exchanges. The reports from the first and second sources were very partial and incomplete. The

Other excluded groups included persons in military service, teachers, the police, certain excepted classes employed by local authorities, railways and certain other public utility undertakings, nurses, and established civil servants.[6] To this extent the insurance scheme and the statistics derived from it related to groups of workers who were more likely to be unemployed than was the workforce as a whole. The insurance statistics did not, of course, cover the total of those 'gainfully occupied'. At the 1931 Census nearly 19½ million persons within the insurance age limits were counted as gainfully occupied, of whom only 12½ million were insured against unemployment.[7] The basic problem is to define precisely those who ought to be counted among the unemployed. Official definitions ranged from those persons 'capable of and available for work', unable to obtain suitable employment', 'genuinely seeking work' to those 'normally employed in insurable employment'. The count of the unemployed became therefore a count of those individuals who, having regard to the law and administrative practice of the time, had sufficient motive to record themselves at the Employment Exchanges as out of work.

Committee was prepared to accept that there was little unemployment in the industry in the accepted sense given the absence of any substantial protest against the exclusion of agriculture from the 1920 Unemployment Insurance Act. *Report of the Committee on Unemployment Insurance in Agriculture,* Cmd. 1344, 1921.

Some of the difficulties in determining the extent of agricultural unemployment are discussed in PRO, Lab. 2/1184, National Council of Social Service, Conference on Rural Unemployment, n.d. An apparent increase in unemployment among agricultural workers was noted in the *Report of the Proceedings under the Agricultural Wages (Regulation) Act, 1924,* July 1931.

6. The following changes were made in the scope of the scheme thereafter: in 1928 persons aged 65 and over ceased to be insurable on becoming entitled to pensions under the Widows', Orphans' and Old Age Contributory Pensions Act, 1925; women aged 60 and under 65 ceased to be insured against unemployment on 1 July 1940. The following became insurable in the years given: boys and girls aged 14 and 15 in 1934; persons employed in agriculture and horticulture in 1936; private gardeners in 1937; domestic servants in clubs, institutions, hospitals, etc., and chauffeurs in private service in 1938, from 2 September 1940 non-manual workers earning between £250 and £420 per annum. The scheme was revised entirely in 1948. For further details see below pp. 49–53.

7. Some of the problems encountered in trying to estimate the degree of unemployment amongst certain excepted classes are discussed in W.M. Kotsching, *Unemployment in the Learned Professions,* Oxford 1937.

Insurance Statistics and the Count of the Unemployed

The basis of all insurance statistics is the total number of insured persons. Upon becoming unemployed insured persons in the inter-war period were required to lodge their unemployment books at an Employment Exchange in order to claim unemployment benefit and to seek fresh employment. To arrive at a percentage rate of unemployment it is necessary to know the total number of insured workpeople to which the unemployment figures relate. This number was estimated in July of each year from the annual issue of new unemployment books in exchange for those of the previous year's currency, classified by industry, sex, and locality. The number of insured persons was never precisely known, however, because of unrecorded deaths, migrations, and shifts between insurable and non-insurable occupations. Allowance had to be made for those whose books only became available for exchange later in the year and for those books written out in respect of persons who turned out subsequently not to have been in insurance at the date of the exchange.[8]

It would seem relatively simple to compute and analyse the number of insured workpeople who at any particular time were unemployed. The total of 'lodged' unemployment books in the files of the Employment Exchanges represented an approximate measure of the gross total of insured persons who were not at work in an insured trade. 'Books Lodged' was in fact adopted as the basis of the official computation of the number of insured workpeople unemployed[9] but its method of calculation was by no means straightforward. The total of 'Books Lodged' always included some persons who ought not to have been counted as unemployed and omitted some who were unemployed.

The total of unemployed insured persons was not confined to those in receipt of benefit. It was obtained by counting those lodged books represented by current claims to benefit, applications for work on the

---

8. It has been suggested that as a result of evasion of national insurance by both employers and employees the insured workforce was consistently understated between the wars by at least 250,000. S. Glynn and J. Oxborrow, *Interwar Britain: A Social and Economic History*, London 1976, p. 147.

9. This series of statistics was originally described as 'Number of unemployment books remaining lodged' but in later years it was altered to 'Number of insured persons recorded as unemployed'. On the omission of the 'Two Months file' the definition became 'Number of Insured Persons Registered as Unemployed'. See below pp. 40–44.

part of insured non-claimants, and the books passing through what was known as the 'Two Months file'. In the case of a person not in receipt of benefit who ceased to attend an Employment Exchange to maintain his registration his book was placed in a special file and included in the statistics of unemployment for a period of two months from the date on which the person was last in touch with an Employment Exchange. Thereafter the book was transferred to a 'Dead file'[10] if the economic condition of its owner was still unknown, whereupon it was no longer included in the statistics of unemployment.

The period of two months selected for the retention in the statistics of persons whose condition was unknown was arbitrary but was believed to furnish a total in which those persons actually unemployed but no longer being counted were roughly counterbalanced by the inclusion of persons who, without knowledge of the Exchange, had ceased to be candidates for employment in insured industries. The number of books in the Two Months file was published separately in the *Gazette* from February 1926.[11]

Whether on balance the Two Months file represented an under- or over-allowance for genuinely unemployed persons who would otherwise have been omitted remains a matter for conjecture. Investigations by the Ministry of Labour into the rate at which books were 'lifted' from the Two Months file either because the person had got insured work or because he desired to renew his claim to benefit indicated that there was no reason to believe that a longer or shorter period would have given a more appropriate measure.[12] The Economic Advisory

---

10. Statistics of the 'Dead file' were not regularly published though certain figures derived from them were given in *Memorandum on the Influence of Legislative and Administrative Changes on the Official Unemployment Statistics*, Cmd. 2601, 1926. The Ministry of Labour concluded that the measure of unemployment would not be seriously affected by disregarding the Dead file but including the Two Months file, *Memorandum on Certain Points Concerning the Statistics of Unemployment and of Poor Law Relief*, Cmd. 2984, 1927, pp. 3–4.
11. Similar estimates were not generally available before that date but the total number in the Two Months file for each month during 1924 and 1925 were published in Cmd. 2601, op. cit., p. 5.
12. Royal Commission on Unemployment Insurance, *Minutes of Evidence*, 3 July 1931, p. 1161. Cf. the comment of W. Beveridge: 'It seems likely . . . that the Two Months file is an excessive allowance for persons unemployed and available for work but not caring to register. This file automatically carries for two months every married woman disallowed as being not really in the industrial

Council claimed in 1930 that 38,000–40,000 of the books in the Two Months file at any date related to persons who had definitely passed out of unemployment insurance.[13] It was generally conceded, however, that such cases were offset by the unemployment represented by books in the Dead file which were not included.

In arriving at the net figure of insured unemployed the books of those persons who were known to be working in an uninsured trade, or who were sick or deceased or known to have emigrated or who had retired from employment, were excluded. Insured persons who were disqualified from receiving unemployment benefit under the trade dispute disqualification were also excluded. Thus, by discriminate counting, the files of current claims, applications for work, and books in the Two Months file yielded a total of insured persons regarded for statistical purposes as unemployed.[14]

The fact that an unemployment book was lodged on a particular day at an Employment Exchange indicated that the person was not working on that day in an insured occupation. The only insured persons who might have refrained from lodging their books would be those who believed that they had no current prospects or future hope of obtaining either unemployment benefit or employment or who did not wish to make application for it. The potential number of such persons was reduced, however, by two factors. First, many poor law authorities required as one of the conditions on which outdoor relief was given that an able-bodied applicant should maintain registration at an Employment Exchange. Second, by registering at an Exchange when unemployed persons who after 1928 were insured under the Health Insurance Scheme had their health card franked and thus avoided an accumulation of arrears of health insurance contributions.

However the increase in registrations following administrative changes in 1928 and 1929 and legislative changes in 1928, 1930, and

---

field who does not think it worthwhile to register for work', 'An Analysis of Unemployment', *Economica*. 1936, p. 368. Some books were retained in the Two Months file even after the period of two months had expired if it was definitely known that a person was out of work and desiring employment. Such definite knowledge was rare.

13. PRO, Cab. 58/146, Economic Advisory Council, Committee on Unemployment Statistics, 22 March 1930.
14. For details of the possible omissions and retentions of insured persons in the count of Books Lodged see Hilton, loc. cit.

1934, which favoured claimants, and the decrease following the restrictive changes introduced in 1928 and 1931 are evidence that not all the unemployed had in fact registered.[15] On balance it does not appear likely, in view of the various provisions attached on the receipt of unemployment benefit, that much long-term unemployment among the insured population went unrecorded. Although there is no way of explicitly determining the extent to which non-registration of the insured unemployed affected the statistics some indication of its influence can be gained from a comparison of unemployment insurance and Census returns.[16]

The net total of Books Lodged did not claim to represent anything other than the number of insured persons who, as far as was known, were not at work on the day of the count for reasons other than those given above. Whether the figures of Books Lodged can be regarded as an adequate measure of unemployment depends to a large extent on whether 'not at work' necessarily meant 'unemployed' within the meaning and provisions of the Unemployment Insurance Acts. In pre-war days the dock labourer who had done four days work and 'played' the fifth day would not have been referred to as 'unemployed'. Textile operatives during a spell of short-time working would not have described themselves as out of work. By the early 1930s such groups, if they maintained a claim to benefit, lodged their unemployment books and maintained registration when not actually working, were counted among the unemployed. In the gross total of 'insured persons unemployed' they did not loom very large; but they were certainly an inflation of the numbers 'unemployed' according to the pre-war conception of what constituted unemployment. The term 'unemployment' in the insurance statistics did not therefore necessarily mean that the person was definitely without a job. Persons who were not at work because they were suspended, 'stood off', or on short-time and whose unemployment books were lodged at the Employment Exchange were counted in the statistics of unemployment.[17] The Assistant Secretary to the Ministry of Labour, not unduly concerned about the matter, told the Royal Commission on Unemployment Insurance in 1931:

I cannot estimate the measure of the inflation that is due to this counting everyone as "unemployed" who is not at work on the day of the

15. See below pp. 46–53.
16. See below pp. 133–5.
17. *Royal Commission on Unemployment Insurance. Minutes of Evidence,*
   J. Hilton, 3 July 1931, pp. 1160–61.

count. In some classes of people—and one such class is undoubtedly married women—the overstatement must be very considerable . . . but in the gross total of insured persons unemployed I cannot think that the all-over inflation is such as seriously to enlarge the unemployment figure.[18]

From the early days of unemployment insurance statistics efforts were made to distinguish those persons without a job who were on short-time. The early returns were more narrowly based and less useful than those of the later 1920s which in turn were never themselves entirely comprehensive. From December 1920 the statistics of the insured population included those persons employed in establishments where, owing to trade depression, the number of working days had been reduced on a systematic basis in such a manner as to entitle claimants to unemployment benefit.[19] Such data cannot be taken as

18. ibid., p. 1183. For further discussion see below pp. 48–61.
19. The number of insured persons who took advantage of the systematization of short-time was only a small proportion of the total number on short-time. An attempt to measure the total extent of short-time in 19 industries using scattered *Gazette* material on average earnings, loss of hours of work, and the number of manshifts worked in particular industries can be found in J. Astor, *The Third Winter of Unemployment,* London 1923, p. 25 *passim.* Lost time, other than total unemployment, was expressed as the percentage that the aggregate hours lost bore to the aggregate hours that would have been worked if all connected with the industry were working in September 1922. Some approximations of the percentage addition to recorded unemployment necessary to account for that degree of short-time working between 1923 and 1928 excluded from official returns can be found for particular industries in C.G. Clark, 'A Graphical Analysis of the Unemployment Position 1920–1928', *Journal of the Royal Statistical Society,* XCII, 1929. Details of short-time working in the engineering industry in 1928 and 1933 are in *Unemployment. Its Realities and Problems.* Engineering and Allied Employers, National Federation, July 1933. By their nature the official statistics also excluded the intermittent and spasmodic unemployment of the type experienced in the cotton industry. For tentative estimates of unrecorded unemployment in the Lancashire cotton industry in the late 1920s and 1930s see Board of Trade, *An Industrial Survey of the Lancashire Area (excluding Merseyside),* London 1932, pp. 104–9; E.M. Gray, 'Under-Employment in Cotton Weaving: A Recent Wage Census', *Manchester School,* X, 1939. See also E.W. Daniels and J. Jewkes, 'The Post-War Depression in the Lancashire Cotton Industry', *Journal of the Royal Statistical Society,* XCI, 1928; International Labour Office, *Unemployment: Some International Aspects, 1920–28,* Geneva 1929, p. 211 (percentage of workers on short-time in the British cotton industry since 1924); the *Gazette* April, July, October 1929 and January 1930.

indicative of the total amount of short-time worked in industry generally. The number of persons included in the returns depended more upon the employers' ability to organize the working week so as to enable workpeople to claim systematic short-time benefit than upon the extent to which short-time was actually being worked. Persons working one day short-time per week or reduced hours on particular days were excluded.

Until October 1922 the estimated numbers of workers on organized short-time were published separately. From November 1922 to October 1923 half the insured contributors who were claiming benefit in respect of systematic short-time were counted with the unemployed. From November 1923 to December 1925 persons who were suspended, 'stood off', or on systematic short-time were included as unemployed.

From 1926 a distinction was made in all monthly figures of insured unemployment between the number 'wholly unemployed' (in the sense that they were definitely without a job), those 'temporarily stopped' i.e. working short-time[20] or otherwise temporarily stood off on the understanding that they were shortly to return to their former employment,[21] and those unemployed casual workers. The separation of the groups did not in any way affect the total figures of insured unemployment which were strictly comparable with the corresponding figures published since 1921.[22]

20. These figures must not be confused with the earlier returns relating to persons working 'systematic short-time'.
21. In cases where there was no definite prospect of a return to former employment within six weeks the individuals were included in the statistics as 'wholly unemployed'. An exception to this rule arose in the small number of cases where, although the expectation of resumption within the six weeks' period was not realized, a definite date for resumption of work had nevertheless been fixed. In such cases the individuals were included under 'temporary stoppages'.

    The Report of the Industrial Transference Board noted in 1928 that the extent of short-time working in the coal industry was much greater than the Ministry's figures of persons temporarily stopped. In its view the more preferable statistics were the Mines Department figures of the number of persons who had worked less than the full normal number of weekly shifts.
22. Special analyses of the extent of short-time working were included in the *Gazette*, December 1929 and January 1933. The latter report gave the proportion of the workpeople employed by firms in the 55 industries making returns who were reported to be working less than full-time in the week ending 24 October 1931.

It must be emphasized too that the statistics derived from insurance records related only to insured persons. The statutory exclusions were overwhelmingly of persons who, it was possible to surmise, suffered rates of unemployment below the average, e.g. agricultural workers, civil servants and juveniles. To this extent the insurance statistics exaggerated the volume of unemployment among wage and salary earners as a whole. A regular opportunity to readjust the classification of individual insurance books arose at the time of the annual exchange. Questions of locality, sex, and juvenility presented no serious difficulty in principle as the returns on which such statistics were based were sent to the Ministry of Labour headquarters by each local Employment Exchange.

The data on unemployment by age, however, were particularly poor. The unemployment book carried age information only in the case of juveniles so there was no readily available means of ascertaining the age distribution of insured persons with 'books lodged'. The age at last birthday of every insured person having a 'live claim' to unemployment benefit was recorded but not systematically analysed.[23] Most of the available information regarding age and unemployment between the wars was derived from the various samples of insured persons and claimants to benefit conducted by the Ministry of Labour. Such data generally showed the age distribution of the unemployed, the unemployment percentage in each age group, and variations in duration of unemployment with differences in age.[24] But as the incidence of disqualification for benefit varied in this period and proved very uneven among different age-groups, figures relating to the age distribution of claims to benefit cannot be readily used for drawing conclusions as to the incidence of unemployment among different age groups in the insured population.

23. Early in February 1922 a classification of adult claimants to unemployment benefit by age, sex, and marital state was made at all local Employment Exchanges in Great Britain and Southern Ireland and the results published by F. Morley, 'The Incidence of Unemployment by Age and Sex', *Economic Journal*, XXXII, 1922.
24. See below pp. 139–44. For comments on the significance of the data on age and unemployment contained in some of the Ministry's sample surveys see W.H. Beveridge, 'An Analysis of Unemployment III',*Economica*, IV, 1937, and Mary Gibson, *Unemployment Insurance in Great Britain*, New York 1931, p. 185 *passim*. For an interesting study of unemployment during 1937–39 among youths aged 18–25 see C. Cameron, A. Lush and G. Meara, *Disinherited Youth*, Edinburgh 1943.

One of the most noticeable deficiencies in the scope of published material on unemployment by age related to the juvenile population under the age of 18, and especially to those under the age of 16. There was no readily available index of the rate of juvenile unemployment, even among 16 to 18-year-olds alone, or published statistics of the duration or regional and industrial distribution of unemployment among the under 18s as a whole during the interwar period.[25] A careful search of the statistical evidence available in selected secondary or near-primary works and of a variety of unpublished Cabinet and Department of Employment papers can provide relevant data not normally found in the more common abstracts of labour statistics. But the most thorough examination of the scattered sources will never provide totally satisfactory results since the existence of unrecorded unemployment was particularly prevalent among the juvenile population.[26]

The Live Register

Although the unemployment insurance scheme was the foundation of the overwhelming proportion of all inter-war unemployment statistics the work-finding function of the Employment Exchanges provided another basis on which a count of the unemployed could be built, namely the number of persons 'registered for employment', otherwise known as the Live Register. It related to those who, by signing the register at the Employment Exchanges at the appointed times, indicated that they were seeking employment and were capable of and

25. Even less was known of the problem before 1914. See A. Greenwood and J.E. Kettlewell, 'Some Statistics of Juvenile Employment and Unemployment', *Journal of the Royal Statistical Society,* LXXV, 1911–12.
26. For further details and for estimates of unemployment among the insured juvenile population and of the size of the juvenile Live Register between the wars, nationally and by Ministry of Labour Division see W.R. Garside, 'Juvenile Unemployment and Public Policy Between the Wars', *Economic History Review,* XXX, May 1977 and W.R. Garside, 'Juvenile Unemployment Statistics Between the Wars: A Commentary and Guide to Sources', *Bulletin of the Society for the Study of Labour History,* XXXIII, 1976. See also D.K. Benjamin and L.A. Kochin, 'What Went Right with Juvenile Unemployment Policy Between the Wars: A Comment', and W.R. Garside, '. . . A Rejoinder', *Economic History Review,* XXXII, 4, November 1979. Juvenile unemployment did occasionally figure among the Ministry of Labour's sample surveys. See below pp. 139–44.

available for work. The Live Register figures distinguished between men, women, boys, and girls and were published weekly in the Press in respect of Great Britain and monthly in the *Gazette* from December 1922 distinguishing Great Britain, the United Kingdom and each Administrative Division.

The weekly statistics of 'persons on the Registers' indicated the number of all those who were registered at Employment Exchanges on the day of the count as applicants for employment. By its nature this total excluded two classes of persons who were included in the insurance figures, namely unemployed persons belonging to the industries which had special schemes (banking and insurance), except in so far as they registered at Exchanges as applicants for work, and those persons included in the 'Two Months file'. On the other hand the Live Register totals included two groups who were not represented in 'Books Lodged', unemployed persons, such as agricultural workers, domestic servants, and boys and girls under 16 as long as they remained outside the scope of the insurance scheme, and persons, whether insured or uninsured, who were actually in employment but wished to change jobs. The anomaly of employed persons being included in a count of the unemployed arose from the dual purpose of the Live Register return, i.e. as a measure of the work of the Employment Exchanges and as a measure of the extent of unemployment. The total number thus involved was too insignificant to cause any undue concern.[27]

The extent of the differences in the coverage of 'Books Lodged' and the 'Live Register' was regularly indicated in the *Gazette* after February 1926 in a table entitled 'Composition of Statistics'. It included for men, boys, women, and girls details of (1) claims to unemployment benefit admitted or under consideration, (2) claimants disqualified from benefit but maintaining registration, (3) insured nonclaimants, (4) uninsured persons on the register, (5) persons on the Two Months file, (6) persons insured in special schemes within the few industries which had contracted out of the main insurance scheme.

27. Nevertheless Ministry of Labour officials regretted the fact that although the Live Register figures represented the number of persons registered at the Exchanges the public nevertheless invariably took them to indicate that all persons included in the figures were unemployed. See PRO, Cab. 2/2175, T.S. Chegwidden to A. Reeder, 3 October 1931. Difficulties did arise, however, in the case of dock workers and the procedure for counting the unemployed was changed accordingly. See below pp. 43–4, 50.

Adding together (1), (2), (3), and (4) gave the total number of persons on the Live Register. The total of (1), (2), (3), (5), and (6) gave the total number of Books Lodged, i.e. the number of insured persons recorded as unemployed. Clearly, therefore, the insured persons included in the Live Register were not all actually in receipt of unemployment benefit.

Until December 1931 the Live Register count was taken on the Monday of every week but from January 1932 it was made on one Monday only in the latter part of each month. Unemployed persons were counted as on the register on a Monday if they signed the register on that day or if they had signed on the last preceding signing day (usually Friday) and were not known to have found work in the meantime. Although this was a convenient method of counting it did mean that the figures tended to overstate the volume of unemployment by a small but significant amount by including a number of persons who had in fact started work on the Monday without informing the Employment Exchange. In order to eliminate this unreal element from the figures the method of counting was altered in September 1937 to ensure that persons on the Live Register, but not actually unemployed on the day of the count, were not included in the total. The new method consisted of identifying specifically the cases of uncertainty and ascertaining, in the week following the day of the count, whether the day of the count was in fact a day of unemployment. The cases in which it was not a day of unemployment were then excluded from the figures.[28]

The Live Register statistics included all unemployed persons on the Employment Exchange registers, irrespective of whether or not they were in the unemployment insurance scheme. In addition to the numbers of those who were actually without jobs, separate figures were obtained of those who, though they were not unemployed, were reg-

28. Details of the figures compiled under the old and new procedures within each Ministry of Labour Division at 13 September 1937 were published in the *Gazette,* December 1937. The net effect of the adjustment on this date was to reduce the total number of insured unemployed by 43,687 and the rate of unemployment among insured persons from 10.1 to 9.7. In addition the new method reduced the applicants for unemployment benefits under the general scheme by 6.2 per cent and under the agricultural scheme by 5.3 per cent. Applicants for unemployment assistance allowances were reduced by one per cent.

istered at Employment Exchanges owing to short-time working[29] or other temporary stoppages. From January 1932 the number recorded under short-time working and temporarily stopped comprised only those who happened to be out-of-work on the day of the count. A count was also made of the number of unemployed persons on the registers who normally obtained their livelihood by means of casual employment. For a greater part of this period this category consisted largely of dock labourers. In the case of these workers a special difficulty in the counting procedure arose at certain ports where there were registration schemes. At such ports dock workers did not prove unemployment by attendance at an Employment Exchange. They were merely required to attend twice a day at various call stands within the docks, and at the end of each call when the requisite labour had been engaged, all those remaining had to obtain a special card as proof of their non-engagement. These cards were current for each week ending on Wednesday and at the end of a week the used cards were sent to the Employment Exchanges which held the men's claim for benefit. Local offices therefore had no information on any given Monday as to whether such men were at work or not on that day as their latest records related to the previous week. It was decided for administrative convenience that each claim for benefit should be regarded as current if a worker had proved unemployment on either the Monday, Tuesday or Wednesday of the week in question. Since the number on the Live Register was obtained in the main by counting the number of current claims it followed that the count of dock workers included not only those who were unemployed on the Monday but also those on the Tuesday or the Wednesday in the week preceding the date to which the figures related. The effect of this procedure was to inflate the figures relating to dock workers.[30] During any week or fortnight, however, there would be

29. Before 1924 the figures excluded workers on systematic short-time but included people suspended or stood off from work. In October 1924 those workers who, though employed on a basis of systematic short-time, were actually employed on the dates of the counts were included in the figures for the first time. Statistics of th total number on the registers, including persons working systematic short-time at weekly dates during the period 1921–31, are given in the *Eighteenth, Nineteenth and Twentieth Abstracts of Labour Statistics.*

30. *Royal Commission on Unemployment Insurance, Minutes of Evidence,* J. Hilton, 3 July 1931, p. 1166. The change in the procedure for counting unemployment among dockers caused the unemployment register to be

many other workers temporarily unemployed than were ever recorded in the official figures.

The two principal series of unemployment statistics developed from 1921–the Live Register, which included all unemployed persons on the registers of Employment Exchanges irrespective of whether or not they were insured under the Unemployment Insurance Acts, and the count of unemployed insured persons, were continued with slight modifications throughout the war years and until 1948.[31] With the introduction of the national insurance scheme in 1948 only one series was maintained. But even before 1948, when all employed persons became insurable, the emphasis in official statistics had changed to insured workers only, especially from October 1945. This was due mainly to the fact that the uninsured consisted largely of boys and girls who had just left school and had not entered industry.

From 1939 the count of the number of insured persons unemployed excluded the books in the Two Months file, the number of which had become artificially inflated. The effect of their exclusion on the comparability of the figures was very slight. The file formed a relatively small proportion of the pre-war insured unemployed (little more than 5 per cent on the average) and represented about half of one per cent of the total insured population.[32] Account was taken thereafter only of those persons who were actually registered for employment and the series formerly described as 'Number of insured persons recorded as unemployed' became known as 'Number of insured persons registered as unemployed'.

The scope of the unemployment insurance scheme had been extended in 1928, 1934, 1936, 1937, and 1938 and a number of wartime and

---

reduced by about 11,000 persons. See above pp. 43 and below pp. 50, 208. For details of the regularity of work among Liverpool dockers and their claims to unemployment benefit between 1924 and 1929 see F.G. Hanham, *Report of Enquiry into Casual Labour in the Merseyside Area,* Liverpool 1930. An analysis of insured unemployment within Dock, Harbour, River and Canal Services, indicating for the first time its extent within the Port Transport Industry during July 1931–November 1939, is in PRO, Cab. 2/2177, Stats. 297/1935.

31. See below pp. 52–3, 62–3.
32. See above pp. 33–5. The number of persons who ceased to maintain registration in the two months preceding the date of the count but who were not known to have found work and who were excluded in January 1939, was 93,000.

post-war amendments altered it further. Women aged 60 and under 65 ceased to be insured against unemployment on 1 July 1940. The unemployment figures on which the percentage rates were based up to and including June 1940 related to males and females aged 14 and under 65, but for July 1940 and subsequent dates, to males aged 14 and under 65 and females aged 14 and under 60. From 2 September 1940, non-manual workers earning between £250 and £420 per annum first became insurable. The age groups included from mid-1948 following the raising of the school-leaving age, were 15-64 for males and 15-59 for females.[33] The Live Register data were also affected by minor alterations in the classes of persons who, for various reasons, entered or left the unemployment register.[34]

33. For further details see below pp. 52-3, 62-3. Monthly and annual rates of unemployment amongst the insured population in the U.K. from September 1912 to June 1948 can be found in Department of Employment, *British Labour Statistics: Historical Abstract, 1886-1968,* HMSO 1971, tables 160, 161 (with the exception of the months of February, March, May, June, August, September, November, December in 1943 and 1944, and of February, March, and May in 1945). The publication (referred to hereafter as *Historical Abstract)* is kept up to date in an annual *Yearbook of Labour Statistics* (hereafter *Year Book).* Both sources contain brief comments on the reliability of various unemployment series and in effect replace the previous source of general reference, *Guide to Official Sources, No. 1 – Labour Statistics,* Interdepartmental Committee on Social and Economic Research, HMSO 1958.

  Detailed information of insured unemployment in the period 1911 to 1914 is contained in *First Report on the Proceedings of the Board of Trade under Part 11 of the National Insurance Act, with Appendices,* Cd. 6965 1913, and in an unpublished report entitled *Report on the Proceedings of the Board of Trade under the Labour Exchanges Act, 1909 and under Part II of the National Insurance Act, 1911 to July, 1914.* For a discussion on unemployment among insured workers in 1939 see R.G.D. Allen, 'The Unemployment Situation at the Outbreak of War', *Journal of the Royal Statistical Society,* CIII, 1940. For later years see Beatrice Reubens, 'Unemployment in War-Time Britain', *Quarterly Journal of Economics,* LIX, 1945.

34. See below pp. 48-57. During the period January 1943 to October 1945 the Live Register count was made at quarterly and not monthly intervals. Thereafter the monthly computation was resumed but details of the regional breakdown of the uninsured unemployed were discontinued. Data of the total number of persons (insured and uninsured) registered as unemployed monthly and by region, Great Britain and the U.K. during December 1922 to June 1948 are in Department of Employment, *Historical Abstract,* table 162.

  Because of the tendency of the public to concentrate on the total and not the consituent items of the published unemployment series there was pressure

Measuring Inter War Unemployment

It is still uncertain precisely how far the volume and rate of inter-war unemployment are adequately reflected in the available statistics. The issue is complicated for the early years of the period by the existence of two separate returns on unemployment: those derived from the trade unions and those from the workings of the unemployment insurance scheme. The former were never regarded as a trustworthy measure of the general amount of unemployment. During the years 1913 to 1926 when the two series overlapped there were times when the trade union percentage was higher and lower than the insurance percentage (see Table 7). In the period 1913 to 1914 the trade union percentage was uniformly lower but this was a time when the unemployment insurance scheme was confined to trades particularly subject to fluctuations in employment. During a time of heavy unemployment at the end of 1920 the two series rose together, yet the trade union percentages were higher than the insurance ones during the eighteen months ending 1922 but lower during the subsequent four years.

The differences between the two series are noticeable only during the 1920s. Exhaustions of benefit on the part of considerable numbers of workers in mid-1921 led to their failure to continue registration at the Exchanges and consequently to inaccuracies in the count of 'Books Lodged' as a measure of unemployment. At the time the percentage rate of unemployment fell below the recorded trade union percentage but immediately rose thereafter. The subsequent divergence may be connected with the exclusion of those persons whose trade union membership had lapsed but who may well have been unemployed. If, however, the discrepancies are ignored and it is assumed that the co-existence of unemployment insurance did not, in practice, affect the benefit-procedure of trade unions, then the two series can be regarded as registering much the same reading for the severe state of industrial affairs. And if, moreover, the trade union percentages for various groups of allied trades are considered in proportions roughly corresponding to the approximate number of workpeople employed in these trades, instead of in the proportion of the actual number of members in the

within government during 1941 to discontinue the monthly Live Register series, because it was thought to encourage our Allies to believe that the country was not exerting its full effort in the war. PRO, Lab. 17/138, 'Publication of Unemployment Figures', May 1941.

TABLE 7
UNEMPLOYMENT PERCENTAGES DERIVED FROM TRADE UNION AND UNEMPLOYMENT INSURANCE STATISTICS

	Trade Union[a]	Unemployment Insurance
1913	2.1	3.6
1914	3.3	4.2
1915	1.1	1.2
1916	0.4	0.6
1917	0.7	0.7
1918	0.8	0.8
1919	2.4	n.a.[b]
1920	2.4	3.9
1921	14.8	16.9
1922	15.2	14.3
1923	11.3	11.7
1924	8.1	10.3
1925	10.5	11.3
1926	12.2	12.5

NOTES
a. Original series.
b. No figures are available between December 1918 and October 1919 when the Out-of-Work Donation Scheme was in force.

unions represented by the returns, the effect is to reduce the disparity between the two series even further.[35]

The comparison must not, however, be pressed because of the particular characteristics of each series. The mean unemployment rate recorded by the trade unions before 1914 may be biased upwards on account of the exclusion of unorganized workers; on the other hand the same returns may have failed to record some unemployment. In important industries such as coalmining and textiles the returns included only the wholly unemployed and not those working short-time; in other industries the terms under which trade union benefit was available may have discouraged workmen suffering short spells of unemployment from registering as such and those men who remained

35. J. Hilton, 'Statistics of Unemployment derived from the Working of the Unemployment Insurance Acts', *Journal of the Royal Statistical Society,* LXXXVI, 1923. *Survey of Industrial Relations* (Balfour Committee on Industry and Trade), 1926, p. 245. See above, pp. 21–2.

unemployed for some time might have failed to be recorded by virtue of having lost their trade union membership. In contrast the recording of unemployment after 1921 was more complete, and likely to have included persons as unemployed who before 1914 would not have been so recorded. The growing familiarity with the unemployment insurance scheme encouraged most claimants to lodge their books immediately on ceasing work and in some cases to maintain signature after benefit had been disallowed. It is difficult, however, to be precise as to the degree of possible overstatement that this involved.

The official unemployment statistics for the inter-war years must themselves be interpreted cautiously. The count of the unemployed was not a compulsory census but merely a count of those individuals who, according to the law and administrative practice of the time, felt it worthwhile to record themselves as out of work at an Employment Exchange. The record therefore is affected by changes in law or administration. The definition of unemployment was not a concept of universal application or acceptability but rather that definition arising from the provisions of the Unemployment Insurance Acts. If the law aimed to compensate only a certain portion of those who were out of work then to that degree the number receiving benefit would be less than the total number unemployed. The most important influences therefore on the comparability of the figures of the extent of unemployment have been the changes influencing the conditions for the receipt of benefit which have had a direct bearing on the incentive to register at an Exchange. Details of the specific alterations in law and administration which affected the unemployment estimates are given in Table 8.

In considering the effect of new legislative and administrative provisions on the statistics of unemployment it is necessary to bear a number of points in mind. The various estimates indicated below were made on the basis of such information as was available at the time and they are valid only for periods shortly after the changes took effect. When a period of some months had elapsed it became impossible to distinguish the effects on the statistics of a change in legislative or administrative conditions from those of other influences, and it is impossible to say to what extent the increases or decreases shown in Table 8 continued to affect the totals for subsequent dates. Furthermore, the additions to the Live Register figures represent the process by which the figures became a more complete statement of the amount of unemployment in the country; they did not necessarily represent real increases in unemployment. Persons whose claim to unemployment benefit had been disallowed were entitled to maintain registration as applicants for employment, and as long as they did so they were counted on the unemployment registers. Some would maintain registration in order to secure evidence of unemployment in the event of an appeal against disallowance being successful; from July 1928 there was, as indicated, the further inducement that by continuing registration one could help avoid falling into arrears with health insurance contributions.

TABLE 8

EFFECT OF LEGISLATIVE AND ADMINISTRATIVE CHANGES ON THE STATISTICS RELATING TO THE NUMBERS OF PERSONS REGISTERED AS UNEMPLOYED

Date and Nature of Change	*Estimated approximate increase (+) or decrease (−) caused in number registered as unemployed*
February 1924 Removal of certain special restrictions on the grant of uncovenanted benefit to persons with other means of support, and abolition of the three weeks' gap in uncovenanted benefit.	+ 13,500[a]
August 1924 Relaxation of certain conditions for the receipt of both standard and extended benefit.	+ 70,000[a]
August 1925 Restoration of the special conditions for extended benefit which were removed in February 1924.	− 10,000[a]
January 1928 Persons aged 65 and over ceased to be insured under the Unemployment Insurance Acts.	− 25,000
The number removed from the unemployment register by this change represented little more than 7 per cent of the number of insured persons of 65 and upwards. As this was lower than the average unemployment rate, the change had the effect of raising slightly the recorded rate of unemployment.	
April 1928 Relaxation of the conditions for the receipt of benefit	+ 40,000

Table 8 – *continued*

May 1928
Institution of the system of franking the Health
Insurance Cards of persons registered at Exchanges.   + 25,000

June 1929
Reference of certain classes of applications for benefit
to local Board of Assessors (effect by 16th December)   +   5,000

March 1930
The unemployment insurance returns sometimes
included people who were not really in the labour
market either because they were incapable of
ordinary work or, more importantly, because their
attachment was extremely tenuous. Early in 1930 the
condition was dropped that those claiming benefit
had to show that they were 'genuinely seeking work'.
This caused a number of people, mostly married
women, to register as unemployed to receive benefits
even though they were not purposely seeking
employment. The effect during 1930–31 was to
increase substantially the rate of female unemployment as expressed as a percentage of the corresponding
rate among males relative to previous years. The extent
of abuse by those not looking for work at the time of
their claim was exaggerated by contemporaries, even
with regard to married women. Nevertheless the figure
of 60,000 considerably understates the addition to the
registers that eventually took place as a result of this
change in the law. It was found impracticable,
however, to make a satisfactory estimate of the total
number when the effects of the changes had become
fully operative. One complication was the fact that the
abolition of the test coincided with recession in those
trades traditionally employing large numbers of
married women.   + 60,000

October 1931 to May 1932
Restrictions in the condition for receipt of
unemployment benefit and transitional payments
(principally the Anomalies Regulations and the
Transitional Payments Scheme) and alterations in
method of reckoning the number of unemployed.
The effects began to be felt in October 1931.

In January 1932 a change in the procedure for
counting unemployment among dockers caused
the unemployment register to be reduced by 11,000
and about 3,000 persons registered for a change of

Table 8 – *continued*

situation although still in employment were excluded
from the figures for the first time. No estimates for   – 180,000 to
later dates have been made.   190,000

It has been estimated that the recorded rate of
unemployment for males and females together in
1930 and 1931 overstated the amount of unemployment by a maximum of 1.5 percentage points.
(Galenson, op. cit., p. 578). The rate of female
unemployment subsequently fell after the 1931
Anomalies Regulations Act imposed certain conditions on married women and seasonal workers which
excluded from benefit a larger proportion of women
than men. (See *Report on the Operation of the
Anomalies Regulations,* Cmd. 4346, 1933). The effect
of the tightening of the conditions for the receipt of
benefit in late 1931 was to reduce the unemployment
rate by an estimated one per cent. (*Gazette,* April
1932). An American survey of British unemployment
statistics in the early 'thirties noted more generally
that:

'At a time when unemployed insured persons and other
insured persons were probably most respondent to
changes in the conditions governing the payment of
benefit, the unemployment percentages were influenced
to the extent of only 1.0 to 1.5 percentage points. It
does not seem unwarranted to conclude that these
1.0 to 1.5 percentage points represent the maximum
effect which changes in the regulations governing
conditions of the right to benefit have had on the
insurance unemployment rates.' (Galenson, op. cit.,
p. 578).

Even so, although we have a general idea of how many
persons left the register during this period there is no
means of estimating the number of people who became
unemployed afterwards and who did not trouble to
register—either because they expected to be refused
payment of benefit or because they were unwilling to
present themselves before a Public Assistance Committee.

January and February 1935
Introduction of Unemployment Assistance Scheme.   + 10,000 to
                                                                                        20,000

Table 8 – *continued*

May 1936 and February 1937
The extension of unemployment insurance to
agriculture, horticulture etc., in May 1936 and to
private gardeners in February 1937 resulted in the
registration of agricultural and horticultural workers
and private gardeners who might not otherwise have
registered as unemployed. The numbers varied according
to the seasons of the year, and precise estimates of the
numbers added to the register could not be made.

April 1937
Changes in Unemployment Assistance regulations
admitted to assistance unemployed persons irrespective
of their insurance contribution record.   + 20,000

The change affected the comparability of the statistics
of duration of unemployment since the additional
numbers included a large proportion of persons subject
to long-term unemployment. See below pp. 184–5.

September 1937
Change in method of counting unemployed.   – 50,000

April 1938
The extension of the Unemployment Insurance Scheme
to institutional and outdoor domestic workers in April
1938 caused a small increase in the number of persons
registered as unemployed but insufficient information
is available for a precise estimate of the increase to be
made.

Statistics of unemployment among the newly insured
classes were published monthly from July 1938. In
the General Scheme of insurance the inclusion of the
new classes reduced the percentage rate of male
unemployment in Great Britain on 18 July 1938 by
0.1 and by 0.3 for females. The combined percentage
rate fell by 0.1 in the case of both the General and
the Agricultural Schemes. The addition of the new
classes had a much greater effect on the percentage
rates of unemployment for individual industries,
particularly in the case of males.

The effect of the change was to bring an extra
240,000 persons aged 14–64 into insurance in Great
Britain as a whole.

September 1939
Registration of women for war work.   + 50,000
                                                             (uninsured)
July 1940
Women aged 60–64 excluded from insurance.   – 2,000
Men at Government Training Centres excluded from
unemployment statistics.   – 8,000

March 1942
Persons classified as unavailable for ordinary
employment excluded from unemployment statistics.   – 25,000

---

a. Details of the effect of these changes on the monthly totals of the Live
   Register and Books Lodged series can be found in *Memorandum on the
   Influence of Legislative and Administrative Changes on the Official
   Unemployment Statistics*, Cmd. 2601, 1926. This includes a particularly
   detailed study of the extraneous deflation of the Live Register between 24
   August 1925 and January 1926 due to the greater restrictions on the receipt
   of benefit imposed during July–August 1925.
b. The persons still excluded from the unemployment scheme immediately
   before it was replaced by national insurance in 1948 were:
   (i)   boys and girls aged 14 who were no longer insurable after the change in
           the minimum school-leaving age in 1947
   (ii)   employees over insurable age (men 65+; women 60+)
   (iii)   employees of local authorities, railways and public utility concerns
   (iv)   civil servants
   (v)   teachers
   (vi)   police
   (vii)   farmers' sons and daughters employed in agriculture
   (viii) female professional nurses
   (ix)   private indoor domestic servants
   (x)   non-manual employees earning in excess of £420 p.a.
   (xi)   men and women working less than 30 hours a week
   (xii)   employees and self-employed

In cases where persons who were no longer entitled to insurance
benefit or transitional payments remained unemployed, their unemployment books remained lodged whether or not they continued to register
as applicants for work. If they maintained registration they were
included in the number on the register and their books remained on
the Live files. If they discontinued registration without obtaining
unemployment they ceased to be included in the number on the
register. Where their personal or economic situation was unknown they
were classified in the Two Months file and included in the statistics, and
later, if necessary, in the Dead file and thereby excluded from the
statistics. An abnormal change in the number of books in the Two
Months file thus furnished an indication of the extent to which persons

disallowed benefit under new conditions had discontinued registration
while remaining unemployed.[36]

Since the size of the population from which registered persons on
the Live Register were drawn was indeterminate it was not possible to
derive from such statistics a true percentage rate of unemployment.
For most of the inter-war period it was not known how many employed
and unemployed agricultural workers, domestic servants, and uninsured
juveniles there were to which to relate the figures of registrations of
uninsured persons at the Exchanges; there was no means of ascertaining
what proportion of the real total of unemployment among such groups
was represented by the registrations at the Exchanges nor how many
insured workpeople would, had they all been unemployed, have had
'live claims' to benefit.

The Live Register, apart from leaving out of account the uninsured
who failed to register for work, was also less comprehensive in regard to
insured persons than the Books Lodged series because it excluded the
Two Months file and the unemployed persons covered by special
schemes for banking and insurance. The Ministry of Labour indicated
in 1925 that the exclusion of the file would tend unduly to understate
unemployment, especially after the introduction of administrative and
legislative changes concerning the right to unemployment benefit.
Changes which tended to make benefits easier to obtain resulted in the
registration of unemployed insured persons who had not hitherto
registered while restrictive changes led to the withdrawal of some
registrations or to failure to register. When unemployed insured persons
ceased to register the effect was immediately reflected in the more
sensitive Live Register where they ceased to be counted, although they
continued to be counted for a period of two months among Books
Lodged. The Live Register thus responded more rapidly to legislative
and administrative changes but tended also to understate the actual
volume of unemployment.

36. Cf. J. Hilton's statement to the Royal Commission on Unemployment Insurance: 'There would appear to be a critical point above which unemployment
insurance admits dubious accretions to the statistics of unemployment, and
below which it begins to operate in the contrary direction of reducing
unemployment to a minimum and of discouraging the registration of any
persons other than those really desiring work. It is not possible to deduce
from known facts the exact point at which this reversal of tendency will
occur, but it is probably in the region of between 6 and 8 per cent of
unemployment', *Minutes of Evidence*, 3 July 1931, p. 1168.

The influence of administrative and legislative changes on the unemployment statistics discussed above did not, therefore, affect both the Live Register figures and the Books Lodged figures to the same degree. When changes in legislation or administration added a greater number of unemployed insured persons to the Live Register, the addition was mainly at the expense of the number of books in the Two Months file. The principal reason for an unemployment book passing from the live file to the Two Months file was that the insured person had had a claim for unemployment benefit disallowed and did not thereafter consider it worthwhile to continue registration at an Exchange. In such a case the person would no longer appear as on the Live Register but his unemployment would be transferred from the Books Lodged file to the Two Months file; he would continue to appear in the Books Lodged statistics for two months. Although, therefore, the Live Register total might fall by reason of an increase in the number of disallowances of benefit, there would not for two months be any fall in the number of Books Lodged. Because the first effects would be to increase the size of the Two Months file, it was variations in the content of that file that gave a clue to the influence of conditions of benefit on movements in the official statistics.

As soon as the conditions for the receipt of unemployment benefit were relaxed or a change in administration made it easier to succeed in an application for benefit, persons who remained unemployed but whose claims had been disallowed renewed their claims and their books were transferred to the live file from the Two Months file. This action also resulted in a transfer of books from the Dead file to the live file. Since the Two Months file was included in the Books Lodged statistics but not in the Live Register figures, transfers of books from that file to the live file were merely the transfers of individuals included in the Books Lodged figures from one section to another, but represented a real addition to the Live Register figures. When a book was transferred from the Dead file to the live file, it resulted in an addition both to the Live Register and to the Books Lodged figures, since the Dead file was not included in either.

Though all signatures on the Live Register were statistically equivalent in the total they did not represent problems of the same urgency. To this extent a certain amount of unemployment was recorded merely because of the conditions attached to the claim for monetary relief and would probably not have come within the measurements adopted by the trade unions before the war. Moreover the aggregate Register figures could do little to distinguish sufficiently between the different types of unemployment, its concentration in particular areas and industries, or the degree of constant change month by month in the personnel of the unemployed, each of whom suffered unemployment of varying durations.[37] These deficiencies did not escape the attention of the Cabinet which was informed in 1928 that:

Substantially the unemployment figures published weekly (the Live Register) represent the aggregate number of signatures of unemployed persons at Employment Exchanges on Monday in each week. For purposes of the aggregate total all signatures must be valued alike. But the slightest familiarity with the working of the employment market and a short reflection on the irregularity of employment inseparable from a highly complex industrial structure, make it clear that as a "problem of unemployment" there is a wide difference between the docker signing as unemployed on Monday, employed Tuesday, Wednesday and Thursday, idle Friday and at work Saturday, and the miner in the Rhondda Valley who presents himself at the Exchange regularly every day for a long period.

While, therefore, movements in the aggregate live register reflect well enough movements in the employment market, the Register by itself is an insufficient index of the problem of unemployment with which the Government may feel compelled to deal by special means. It is, again, the composition that matters.[38]

Since, therefore, the Live Register reflected on one day the registrations of workpeople with varying motives, incentives, and claims to benefit and who in total bore an unknown relation to the entire workforce in need of employment it proved impossible to draw from it any conclusions about the unemployment situation as a whole. The register total did not, of course, represent a standing army of unemployed entirely unable to find work and surplus to the needs of industry. It consisted of persons with widely differing expectations of reabsorption into industry. Even though every claimant to unemployment benefit had to be 'available for work' all were not available for *any*

37. Some aspects of the adequacy of the Live Register as a measure of unemployment can be found in J.A. Dale, 'The Interpretation of the Statistics of Unemployment', *Journal of the Royal Statistical Society*, XCVII, 1934.
38. PRO, Cab.27/378, Interdepartmental Committee on Unemployment. Memorandum by the Ministry of Labour on the Live Register and the Unemployment Problem, 29 October 1928. Governments were particularly concerned about the undue emphasis placed upon the aggregate Live Register figures by the general public and by overseas commentators.

work wherever it was and however different from their ordinary occupations. Furthermore it is unlikely that all uninsured persons registered
at Employment Exchanges when unemployed and, as noted already,
legislative and administrative changes had the effect to some extent of
increasing or reducing the number who thought it worthwhile to
register. In addition those persons who were working for part, though
not the whole, of a week but who were claimants to unemployment
benefit and counted on the register had not formerly been part of the
recorded figures of the unemployed before 1920.

All unemployment figures prior to 1937 tended to overstate by
a small margin the volume of unemployment because of the procedure used for counting the unemployed. The change in the counting
method adopted in September 1937 lowered the general unemployment rate by 0.3 per cent on average. Persons included in the Live
Register as unemployed on the day of the count included those
employed on short-time and until 1932 the Register included a small
number of persons in employment who were registering for other work.
On the other hand the official statistics ignored unemployed persons
who did not register at Employment Exchanges, especially juveniles
under the age of 16, failed to reflect the extent of concealed or disguised unemployment, especially among women, and, except for the
building industry, gave virtually no indication of the occupational
incidence of unemployment within British industry. Nor did they take
full account of the extent of short-time working or provide any
meaningful indication of the actual time lost through unemployment.
In the absence of adequate data of the extent to which the actual
working week of the employed fell short of the hours of the standard
working week it was difficult to gauge the full extent of under-
employment. Without comprehensive records of overtime or short-time
the total volume of unemployment cannot be measured with accuracy.[39]

39. Cf. Harold Wilson's assessment of the statistics of the interwar period:
    'The twenties, the thirties, all saw the development of departmental statistics.
    No Government, no Parliament could have had fuller information about
    unemployment. The only reason that nothing was done was that the economists
    were wrong, providing almost unanimous support to the deflationary Estab-
    lishment philosophy known as the Treasury view.' Statistics and Decision-
    making in Government—Bradshaw Revisited: Address of the President, The
    Rt. Hon. J. Harold Wilson, delivered to the Royal Statistical Society on
    Wednesday, November 15th, 1972', *Journal of the Royal Statistical Society*,
    A, 136, 1973, p. 10.

Beveridge, acutely aware of the deficiencies in the trade union series compared with the unemployment insurance returns, suggested that the pre-war trade union unemployment rate which had averaged 4.8 per cent during the years 1883–1913 should be reduced by 0.8 per cent to cover unorganized as well as organized workers, then increased by a quarter to account for the extent to which the post-war series included short intervals of unemployment in the data on 'temporarily stopped' and increased by as much again for the generally more complete coverage of the insurance statistics in respect of prolonged unemployment and in other ways. The combined effect was to raise the mean trade union unemployment rate during the years 1883–1913 from 4.8 to 6.0 per cent. The implication was that on the evidence of national insurance returns the trade union figures understated the true volume of unemployment before 1914.[40] On this calculation the average unemployment rate for Great Britain and Northern Ireland of 14.2 per cent between 1921 and 1938 appeared to be nearly 2½ times the true rate of unemployment before the first World War.

A recent revision of the estimates of unemployment among the labour force as a whole, on the other hand, has gone so far as to suggest that 'national average rates of unemployment during most of the inter-war period were probably not significantly higher than the rate which prevailed before 1914'.[41] This claim is based largely on the results of Feinstein's correction of the insured unemployment rate for the inter-war period. His comparison of the 1931 Census returns with the insurance figures revealed a higher unemployment rate among the insured population than among the labour force as a whole.[42] His estimates of the rate of unemployment of the total workforce for the period 1921 to 1938, using Chapman's data of man years of employment as the basis of the numbers employed,[43] take account of groups of persons normally excluded at one time or another from the official returns. They are based, too, on the assumption that the unemployed persons omitted from the insurance statistics during the years 1921–30 accounted for the same proportion of the total as was found for 1931

40. Beveridge, *Full Employment,* op. cit., pp. 72–3; 328–37.
41. A.E. Booth and S. Glynn, 'Unemployment in the Interwar Period: A Multiple Problem', *Journal of Contemporary History,* October 1975, p. 617.
42. Though his new rate is dependent in part on data of the temporarily stopped and is not therefore a 'true' rate in the strictest sense.
43. A.L. Chapman and R. Knight, *Wages and Salaries in the United Kingdom, 1920–1938,* Cambridge 1952.

(16.8%) and a constant 13.8 per cent from 1932 to 1938.[44] The results suggest that the insurance figures tended to overstate the unemployment rate by approximately 20 per cent.[45]

The validity of Feinstein's estimate of the degree of over-statement in the insured unemployment data is difficult to judge precisely. The extrapolation was from a year of severe cyclical unemployment and was based for most of the period on an assumption, incapable of verification for the majority of years, that the relative difference between unemployment rates for certain groups excluded from the insurance scheme remained stable. There is no reason to believe that the Census recorded unemployment among non-insured persons more accurately than among insured persons. It is probable that Feinstein's figures tend to underestimate the average level of insured unemployment. The two important revisions in the unemployment insurance scheme in 1930 and 1931 to which we have already referred produced severe fluctuations in the recorded unemployment percentage.[46] The Census data on which Feinstein relies were collected when the unemployment percentages were abnormally swollen.

Booth and Glynn, on the other hand, argued that Feinstein's data are, if anything, an over-estimate because of his extrapolation from a year in which unemployment among the uninsured was unusually high,[47] though they offer no evidence in support of this claim. Nor do they appear to be sufficiently aware of the extent to which the particular nature of the pre-1914 data on unemployment makes direct comparisons with inter-war estimates extremely hazardous. Unless and until we can determine more precisely the extent to which insurance data are an adequate measure of unemployment among the workforce

---

44. The difference in percentages was due to the additional insurance data that were available after 1932. For more details see above pp. 50–52.
45. Feinstein, op. cit., p. 215 *passim* and tables 57 and 58. An earlier estimate by C. Clark suggested that the unemployment insurance returns in 1931 indicated a percentage rate of unemployment about one-third higher than that for the total workforce. *National Income and Outlay*, London 1937, pp. 31–32. A less ambitious estimate of the total number of persons unemployed in each quarter between March 1921–March 1939 calculated by adding to the Live Register the total number in the Two Months file and in the special schemes for banking and insurance can be found in E.M. Burns, *British Unemployment Programs, 1920–1938*, Washington 1941, p. 343. This total still, of course, ignored the unemployed persons who did not register at the Exchanges.
46. See above pp. 50–51.
47. Booth and Glynn, loc. cit., pp. 613–14.

in general between the wars and can compare them with a pre-1914 series devoid of most of the deficiencies of the conventional trade union returns, especially in terms of industrial coverage, then it will remain a matter of conjecture how far the available unemployment data are a reasonably accurate guide to conditions over the entire period from the 1860s to 1939.

Another potential source of inaccuracy in the official series is voluntary, benefit-induced unemployment among the 'work-shy', the existence of which would tend to inflate the figures as a measure of genuine unemployment. The level, duration, and real value of unemployment benefits rose appreciably during the 1920s in particular and the possibility of serious abuse became a prime issue of political concern. Two American economists have suggested that the persistently high rate of unemployment in inter-war Britain was largely due, not to deficient aggregate demand, but to high unemployment insurance benefits relative to wages[48] so much so that:

the army of the unemployed standing watch in Britain at the publication of the *General Theory* was largely a volunteer army.[49]

They estimate that had the ratio of benefits to wages remained at its 1913 level the recorded unemployment rate would have averaged more than one-third lower; and, more specifically, that over the period 1920 to 1938 the insurance system raised average unemployment by *c.* 5–8 percentage points.[50]

The effect of the introduction of the Anomalies Regulations in October 1931 on female unemployment rates in particular suggest a relationship between the level and availability of unemployment compensation and the recorded rate of unemployment. The direct effect on female unemployment is by no means statistically proven even for the 1930s. But the attention devoted internationally in more recent years to the unemployment-inducing effects of insurance[51] must make it worth applying the accepted theoretical and econometric techniques to

48. Strictly defined as: $$\frac{\text{weekly benefit of adult male with one adult dependant and two dependant children}}{\text{average weekly earnings of full-time employees}}$$
49. D.K. Benjamin and L.A. Kochin, 'Searching for an Explanation of Unemployment in Interwar Britain', *Journal of Political Economy,* 87, 1979.
50. ibid.
51. See H.G. Grubel and M.A. Walker, *Unemployment Insurance. Global Evidence of its Effects on Unemployment,* The Fraser Institute, 1978.

earlier time periods. Unfortunately such attention has focused to date on plotting the most direct statistical evidence of benefit-induced unemployment with only the slightest regard to the criticisms levelled against similar analyses of the British situation in the 1960s, especially in terms of specification and aggregation.[52] Thus Benjamin and Kochin neglect the extent to which wide variations in the family composition, sex, age, duration of unemployment, and levels of previous income of those out of work acted independently or in combination with each other to affect the incentive to work between the wars. Moreover, although the legal conditions attached to eligibility for unemployment benefit were systematically relaxed during the 1920s, the strict manner in which the rules were administered often denied benefit to many individuals who failed to convince local officials that they were not malingering. Deacon has shown quite convincingly that the operation of the 'genuinely-seeking work' clause in the decade before 1931 was dominated by Ministerial pressure to check abuse, and by a degree of local discretion which, especially after 1927, laid great emphasis upon the assessment of an individual's attitude to work as grounds for with-holding benefit, whatever the state of the labour market. Between March 1921 and March 1930 nearly 3 million claims for benefit were refused because the claimants were unable to satisfy the condition that they were making all possible efforts to find work. Even after the abolition of the 'genuinely-seeking work' clause in March 1930 it appears that the number of claimants who were not genuinely unemployed was certainly less than popularly believed.[53]

The econometricians presently engaged in explaining inter-war unemployment in Britain as principally, though not exclusively, the result of many thousands of people choosing, because of relative financial gain, to remain out of work may in time shed some interesting light on the operation of the unemployment insurance scheme. Precisely how the highly specified models of benefit/income ratios are to be evaluated in light of contemporary evidence of the power of the work-ethic, of the existence of substantial under-employment among those who would rather have remained in rather than out of work, and of the largely immeasurable but very real psychological and social effects of being out of work has yet to be determined.

52. See below pp. 102–9.
53. A. Deacon, *In Search of the Scrounger. The Administration of Unemployment Insurance in Britain 1920–1931*, Occasional Papers in Social Administration, Number 60, 1976.

3
The Post-War Period, 1948–1979

The Nature of Unemployment Statistics since 1948

The introduction in 1948 of both the national insurance scheme and a new Standard Industrial Classification had an immediate effect on the nature and scope of official unemployment statistics. The new insurance scheme related to all persons who worked for pay or profit and to all persons in unpaid work under a contract of service. It included classes of employment, such as private domestic service, which had previously been outside the scope of the unemployment insurance scheme. The main exceptions related to self-employed men aged 70 and over and women aged 65 and over, and self-employed married women who opted not to be insured under the scheme. Since 1948 the only significant alteration to the scheme has resulted from the raising of the school-leaving age to 16 in 1973. The total number of employees under the new scheme in Great Britain at mid-1948 was 20,500,000 compared with 15,760,000 under the old unemployment insurance scheme. For administrative reasons it was not found practicable after 1948 to continue the former practice of counting the total number of insured persons each July on the renewal of the unemployment insurance books. Instead, insurance cards of different colours (marked A, B, C, and D) were issued at random and all cards of the same colour were exchanged at quarterly dates; the count now being based on random 25 per cent samples at the end of each quarter. The samples proved sufficiently reliable to give aggregate figures of the number of insured persons, but not detailed analyses of the numbers of employees by industries and localities. From June 1949, therefore, employers of five or more persons were required to state the total number of cards held by them.[1]

Before 1939 the published unemployment series referred separately to the insured unemployed and to the total unemployed registered at the Exchanges. The monthly unemployment data published from July 1948 included all the registered unemployed whether they were insured or not. The rate of unemployment before 1948 had been obtained by expressing the insured registered unemployed as a percentage of the estimated total number insured under the Unemployment Insurance Acts, and was not therefore representative of the labour force as a whole. Thereafter it was calculated by expressing the total number of unemployed persons on the register as a percentage of the estimated total industrial population (i.e. the estimated total in civil employment plus the total registered unemployed) at the appropriate mid-year. Whereas in July 1948 there were 15.8 million persons insurable under the Unemployment Insurance Acts in Great Britain the number in civil employment and the registered unemployed amounted to 19.4 million.

The incidence of unemployment among the labour force excluded by the pre-1948 insurance scheme was much less than among those included. The extension of the insurance scheme to previously excluded categories makes it difficult to compare pre-1939 and post-1948 unemployment rates. For example, the published rates for December 1953 related to all the registered unemployed and all employees while that for September 1939 related only to the insured population, which then excluded people whose incidence of unemployment was very small. A comparable figure for September 1939, covering the entire employee labour force would give a much lower unemployment percentage for that date.[2]

The denominator for calculating the unemployment percentage was based on counts of national insurance cards until 1971 and on census of employment data thereafter. Annual estimates of the number of employees in employment analysed by industry and area were obtained

1. R.B. Ainsworth, 'The Sources and Nature of Statistical Information in Special Fields of Statistics. United Kingdom Labour Statistics', *Journal of the Royal Statistical Society,* CXIII, 1950, p. 39. For further details see N. Buxton and D. MacKay, *British Employment Statistics,* Oxford 1977, pp. 58–64.
2. E. Devons, *An Introduction to British Economic Statistics,* Cambridge 1961, pp. 71–3.

from 1971 by means of a postal enquiry of employers. Full censuses are conducted only every three years, as in 1973 and 1976. Between these years, forms were not sent to very small pay-points with less than three employees. The returns exclude working proprietors; partners; the self-employed; directors not under a contract of service; wives working for husbands; husbands working for wives; persons working in their own homes; private domestic staff working in private households, and civil servants working outside the U.K.

Despite the fact that age distributions of the unemployed, by duration category and later in aggregate, were regularly published twice a year in the post-war period, age-specific unemployment rates were not generally available. This deficiency has been emphasized particularly in recent years by the growing incidence of unemployment among younger workers. To produce reliable unemployment rates by age it is necessary to have estimates of the age distribution of employees in employment. By combining Census of Employment data of employees in employment with EEC Labour Force Survey estimates of percentage distributions by age since 1975, the Department of Employment has calculated age distributions of numbers of employees in employment from which unemployment rates by age have been obtained every six months from July 1975 to July 1978 and quarterly thereafter.[3] A considerable degree of estimation is involved, however, with regard to the younger age groups (under 18), the data for whom should be used cautiously. The rates for the youngest age group inevitably reflect the inclusion of school leavers at the end of the school year. The statistical evidence of unemployment by age covers only those who are registered as unemployed. The propensity of young people of both sexes to register is thought likely to vary between periods of low and high unemployment; the registration behaviour of school leavers, on the other hand, has been positively influenced both by changes in the school-leaving age in relation to the minimum age at which they can claim supplementary benefit and by the relaxation of rules governing the time of the year in which school leavers can enter the labour force (which itself varies between England and Wales and Scotland).

The completeness of the unemployment data depends on the extent to which persons seeking employment register at the Exchanges. The current series show for Great Britain and the UK and for each administrative region the number and rate of unemployment of wholly

3. *Gazette,* July 1977, November 1978, January 1979. The quarterly returns were made possible by the introduction of a new quarterly age analysis of the unemployed in 1978.

unemployed persons, i.e. those males and females who were unemployed and capable of and available for work on the day of the
monthly count. Persons are so classified in accordance with standard
rules based on a type of 'case law' built up over the years.[4]

Disqualification from benefit for reasons other than unavailability
for work does not prevent someone registering as a non-claimant and
therefore remaining in the unemployment count. Thus the official
series may include those who fail to fulfil the various contribution
conditions for benefit and those who are disqualified for having left
their employment voluntarily without just cause or because they
were dismissed for misconduct. Men aged more than 65 but less than
70 and women aged more than 60 but less than 65 who choose not to
retire may receive benefit while unemployed and therefore have an
incentive to register. Over those respective ages they lose their entitlement to benefit, but are still entitled to register as unemployed. Those
excluded from the series are those sick for more than three days, some
pesons who are severely disabled and unlikely to obtain work other
than under special conditions (who are covered by a separate monthly
count), women receiving a National Insurance maternity allowance, and
a small number of persons who are not claiming any benefits and who
are registered only for part-time work. Figures of temporarily stopped
workers who are registered in order to claim benefit are published
separately.

From July 1971 a new series was introduced of the wholly unemployed (excluding school leavers and adult students) and estimates
were provided of equivalent data for the period 1967-71. The origin of
the new series lay in the fact that the underlying movement in the
various seasonally adjusted data of wholly unemployed (excluding
school leavers only) was being obscured by the growth since the
summer of 1967 in the number of adult students registering for temporary employment during vacations. Separate monthly count figures
of temporarily registered adult students were subsequently published
in the monthly national and regional analyses in the *Gazette* from
August 1972 to March 1976. Thereafter, because the flow of over
100,000 persons on to and off the register was felt to distort the

4. Since 1930 claimants have been required to accept suitable employment or
   be disqualified from receiving benefit for a specified period. 'Suitable
   employment' refers to a person's usual employment at generally recognized
   wages and conditions. It excludes jobs which become vacant as a result of a
   trade dispute.

reality of the unemployment problem, the government decided to separate entirely from the statistics adult students who registered for vacation employment. Their numbers continued to be published in the unemployment press notice but separately from the unemployment figures. The adult student group had already from October 1975 been excluded from detailed analysis of the unemployed by age, duration, and other characteristics.

Under the Employment and Training Act 1973 responsibility for the employment services was redistributed between the Employment Service Agency (operating from a local network of employment offices) and the careers service of education authorities. The effect on the unemployment statistics from mid-1973 was that they no longer distinguished separately those under 18 and those aged 18 and over (except in the regular six-monthly analyses by age). Special provision was made however for the separate publication of statistics of the number of unemployed school leavers under 18. The official definition of the unemployed school leaver is a person aged under 18 who has had no full-time employment since completing full-time schooling and who has voluntarily registered with a local employment office or careers office. As such the definition excludes those who do not choose to register, those who have reached the age of 18, and those who have taken up full-time jobs and become unemployed almost immediately.[5]

A number of changes were made to the system of counting registered unemployed persons in 1972. Although the unemployment count traditionally related to a Monday, the official figures were not finalized until the total of those who had in fact left the register before the count day were excluded and those who were subsequently found to have been unemployed on that day were included.[6] Until May 1972 these net adjustments were applied both to the total unemployment figures and to all separate analyses except those by occupation. Thereafter the adjustments were applied only to the total figures (including the totals for the wholly unemployed and temporarily stopped and totals for males, men and boys, and females, women and girls). Separate analyses by age and duration, for example, remained unadjusted in this

5. For further details see A.J.H. Dean, 'Unemployment Among School Leavers: An Analysis of the Problem', *National Institute Economic Review,* 78, November 1976.

6. This did not always clarify the situation. In an industry such as cotton where a system of stopping two days in a week was not unknown the count would be particularly inflated because of the general practice of stopping on Mondays.

respect. The adjustment to the total figures, which had normally reduced the total number unemployed by a few thousand, was itself discontinued from October 1975 when the day of the count was changed from Monday to Thursday. The level of unemployment counted on a Thursday was found to differ very little from the average of the preceding and succeeding Monday. The change, therefore, had a negligible effect on the published figures. Nevertheless the national total of wholly unemployed (excluding school leavers) can, strictly speaking, only be compared before and after October 1975 if account is taken of the exclusion since then of this particular statistical adjustment and, later, of that relating to adult students.

Casual workers were separately distinguished in the unemployment statistics until April 1972 but excluded from analyses by occupation, age, and duration of unemployment. They are now included in all statistics of the unemployed. Until November 1972 those persons who were temporarily suspended from their jobs could be identified statistically in the total register of the unemployed. The Government's interdepartmental working party on unemployment statistics[7] regarded such persons as being in a different category from the 'wholly unemployed' and recommended that they should be shown separately.[8] Consequently the published unemployment rates before and after this date are not strictly comparable and the full extent of short-term fluctuations in unemployment are less readily observable.[9]

7. Appointed in 1972 at a time when the sharp rise in the jobless total had led to criticisms of the adequacy of official data in reflecting the 'true' unemployment position. See *Unemployment Statistics. Report of an Inter-Departmental Working Party,* Cmnd 5157, November 1972. The Working Party adopted as its terms of reference: 'To consider whether the statistics which are at present collected relating to the registered unemployed, and others in the population of working age who are neither in employment nor registered as unemployed, need to be further sub-divided, supplemented or presented differently in order to provide a more accurate indication of the real level of unused labour resources in the economy', ibid., p. 1.
8. See below pp. 73–5.
9. Statistical details of the count of the unemployed since 1948 are available as follows:
   Number of persons registered as unemployed and unemployment rates, monthly 1948–1968 distinguishing total numbers, males, females, wholly unemployed, temporarily stopped, Great Britain, United Kingdom; number and rates of wholly unemployed excluding school-leavers, seasonally adjusted, total numbers, males, females, Great Britain, Department of Employment, *Historical Abstract,* table 165.
   Total registered unemployed and unemployment rates: annual averages, by

Do the Unemployment Figures Measure What They Ought to Measure?

The Department of Employment readily acknowledges that its regular series of unemployment statistics, dependent as they are upon a strict definition of unemployment and limited by and large only to the detailed analysis of those who genuinely seek and are capable of and available for work, are imperfect indicators either of the pressure of the demand for labour or of social distress. This is true not only of the series in general but also of the data of the wholly unemployed excluding school leavers and adult students (seasonally adjusted) which are generally regarded as the best indicators of the *trend* of unemployment. Yet without doubt unemployment statistics have a crucial impact on the formulation of economic policy not least because of the post-war emphasis on achieving a high and stable level of employment.

With the significant increase in the level of total unemployment since 1966 and especially since 1971, considerable concern and alarm has developed about the validity of the official unemployment data. The volume of criticism has increased sharply during recent years, though in contradictory directions. The official series have been condemned as fundamentally misleading and potentially harmful in their influence on economic policy. Some observers have argued that the published figures exaggerate the situation because they include people who are not genuinely seeking work or who are 'unemployable'; others claim that the figures underestimate the number of those who are looking for jobs without registering as unemployed, while others again

---

region 1949–68, males, females and unemployment rates by region, monthly 1948–68, U.K. and Great Britain, Department of Employment, *Historical Abstract*, tables 168, 169 and appropriate *Year Books*.

Number of persons wholly unemployed (distinguishing the number of whom were school leavers and adult students) and unemployment rates since 1969 total, males, females, Great Britain, Department of Employment, *Historical Abstract*, tables 165–7, appropriate *Year Books* and monthly *Gazette*.

Number and rate of wholly unemployed excluding school leavers and adult students, seasonally adjusted, total, Great Britain, United Kingdom; males, females (numbers only) since 1969, Department of Employment, *Historical Abstract*, tables 165–7, appropriate *Year Books* and monthly *Gazette*.

Twice a year, in January and July, the registered unemployed are analysed by age and sex (percentage of total registered in each age group). Analyses of duration of current spell of unemployment by age are conducted quarterly (nationally and by region).

have sought to identify a whole range of omissions and miscalculations in the data, trying at the same time to suggest more adequate ways of measuring unemployment.[10]

A more fundamental criticism frequently levelled against the statistical treatment of the unemployed is the extent to which the percentage figures overstate the level of 'real' unemployment by their exclusion of the self-employed, employers, and the armed forces, i.e. causing the divisor (unemployment) to be too large and the denominator (employees) too small. Wood maintains that the published unemployment percentage remained higher for longer periods between 1958 and 1968 than it would have done had the numbers wholly unemployed been expressed as a percentage of the working population.[11] The Government's committee on unemployment statistics examined the same problem for later years (see Table 9).[12]

The committee declared that 'information about the numbers in the total working population is not available for local areas' and considered that 'it would only cause confusion to use different definitions for the national and local rates', preferring to retain the existing method of calculation.[13] It is a moot point, however, whether the loss in being

10. See for example, B. Hunter, 'Who are the unemployed?', *New Society,* 23 July 1970; P. Jay, 'Where have all the workers gone?', *The Times,* 9 October 1971; G. Standing, 'A million unemployed already', *New Society,* 14 October 1971; J.B. Wood, *How Much Unemployment?,* Institute of Economic Affairs, 1971; M. Peston, 'Unemployment: Why We Need a New Measurement', *Lloyds Bank Review,* 104, April 1972; D. Metcalf and R. Richardson, 'The Nature and Measurement of Unemployment in the U.K.', *Three Banks Review,* 93, March 1972; *Unemployment Statistics, Report of an Inter-Departmental Working Party,* Cmnd. 5157, November 1972; N. Bosanquet and G. Standing, 'Government and Unemployment 1966–1970: A Study of Policy and Evidence', *British Journal of Industrial Relations,* X, 1972; S. Brittan, 'Some ways to improve the unemployment figures', *Financial Times,* 22 November 1972; J. Bourlet and A. Bell, *Unemployment and Inflation. The Need for a Trustworthy Unemployment Indicator,* Economic Research Council, October 1973; J.B. Wood, *How Little Unemployment?,* IEA, October 1975; J. Hughes, 'How Should We Measure Unemployment?' *Industrial Relations Journal,* 7, *Relations,* 13, November 1975; J. Hughes, 'The Measurement of Unemployment: An exercise in political economy?' *Industrial Relations Journal,* 7, 1976/7; R. Cutler and K.J. Rowles, 'The Unemployment Statistics and Government Policy', *Journal of Industrial Affairs,* 4, 1977.
11. Wood (1972), op. cit., pp. 14–15.
12. Cmnd. 5157, op. cit., para. 2.10.
13. ibid.

TABLE 9
UNEMPLOYMENT PERCENTAGE RATES (TOTAL REGISTER)
GREAT BRITAIN: MONTHLY AVERAGES, 1969–71

	Published figures (using employees as denominator)	Figures using working population as denominator
1969	2.42	2.22
1970	2.63	2.41
1971	3.55	3.25

unable to produce for regions an unemployment rate based on the economically active population is not outweighed by the need to reflect more precisely the extent to which the country's potential labour force is out of work.

This raises the very issue which has been and still is at the heart of informed criticism of the published unemployment data—the extent to which arbitrary definitions of who should and should not be included in the statistical count of the jobless bear any close resemblance to the realities of the labour market.

Much of the argument among the commentators rests on whether a meaningful distinction can be made between voluntary and involuntary unemployment and to which of the conventional categories groups of the so-called unemployed belong. The familiar classification of unemployment distinguishes four principal types: frictional, short-run unemployment arising from the movement of workers between jobs and for whom jobs are available; structural, arising from a fundamental mis-match between the demand for and supply of labour, due for example to changing skills and structural change within industry; seasonal, that is unemployment due to seasonal changes in economic activity, and finally unemployment arising from an inadequacy of aggregate demand—demand-deficient unemployment. The latter, often referred to as Keynesian unemployment, has since the time of the *General Theory* encouraged a distinction to be made between frictional (including seasonal) and voluntary unemployment on the one hand and involuntary (demand-deficient and structural) unemployment on the other.

It is doubtful whether such distinctions are useful or meaningful from the point of view of the accurate recording of the unemployed.

Leaving aside for the moment the critical point of whether the categories can be separately identified in any statistical sense, there are serious problems in attempting to classify the unemployed thus. As Hughes has pointed out:

It might be convenient to regard frictional and structural unemployment as the short- and long-term components respectively of non demand-deficient unemployment. But since long-term spells of unemployment are also likely to be associated with demand-deficient unemployment then it becomes impossible to separate out the structural and the demand-deficient varieties from the long-term unemployed. Therefore, in order to test for an increase in structural unemployment, the effect of aggregate unemployment (which includes demand-deficient unemployment) upon long-term unemployment will have to be taken into account. If an increase in the long-term component cannot be explained by changes in aggregate unemployment then the increase is indicative of an increase in structural unemployment. However, if demand is deficient over a number of years then obviously the average duration of long-term unemployment will increase and a group of very long-term unemployed will emerge. Although not strictly structurally unemployed, given that aggregate demand is deficient, members of this group might suffer a considerable erosion of their skills so that when demand picks up again they experience difficulty in becoming re-employed. To the extent that this is likely to happen then the very long-term unemployed might be regarded as structurally unemployed—irrespective of the level of aggregate labour demand.[14]

And again

Although Keynes excluded frictional from involuntary unemployment (and also from voluntary unemployment) it is possible for someone to become unemployed involuntarily—for example, as a result of a redundancy situation—even though the subsequent spell of unemployment might be of short duration. Because it is of short duration the individual is regarded as being frictionally unemployed, but his unemployment is in no sense voluntary. . . . There is a difference between voluntary leaving and voluntary unemployment. For example an individual might voluntarily quit one job in the expectation that he will be able to obtain another within a certain time period—say four weeks. During his four weeks of job search he might best be described as voluntarily unemployed. But what if he takes twelve weeks to find a

14. Hughes, *British Journal of Industrial Relations,* 1975, loc. cit., pp. 318–9.

new job rather than the expected four? Is he voluntarily or involuntarily unemployed from the beginning of the fifth week to the end of the twelfth week?[15]

There is obviously a difference between a person who, having lost or left his old job, refuses alternative offers involving accustomed skills and rates of pay, and a willing searcher who can find work only at a subsistence wage by moving to a sheep farm in the Hebrides. Involuntariness is a matter of degree. The more a person is prepared to accept a dimimuition in any aspect of the work bargain—pay, conditions, distance from home, etc.—the more involuntary is his unemployment.[16] But the willingness of one individual to gain employment by lowering his reservation wage need not result in others following suit.

The marked increase in the absolute amount of unemployment suffered in Britain since the 1970s has brought such issues into sharper focus. Observers have been anxious to discern exactly who is unemployed and what statistical measurement of unemployment best reflects the unsatisfied demand for labour. Before turning to a critical assessment of these themes, it would be instructive to examine the nature and adequacy of the existing count of the unemployed.

Does the Count Include Persons Who Ought to be Excluded?
The official unemployment statistics are derived from a count of the unemployed in individual employment exchange areas on a particular day each month. In so far as the figures are merely a by-product of an administrative process (namely the registration of persons in search of a job and the payment of unemployment or supplementary benefit, or both) they refer in the main to the need for work by the involuntarily unemployed rather than to the potential supply of labour in terms of a schedule of wages. In practice some of those who register are non-claimants of benefits of any kind either because they are ineligible to claim, or have no wish to do so.

In the search for a measure of unemployment which excludes those persons who are not part of the reserve of labour but who might nevertheless be currently regarded as genuinely out of work the following groups have been identified as worthy of consideration:

(a) the temporarily stopped the the short-term unemployed,

15. ibid., p. 320.
16. S. Brittan, *Second Thoughts on Full Employment Policy*, London 1975, p. 36.

(b) school leavers and students seeking temporary employment during vacations,
(c) the 'unemployables',
(d) the disabled,
(e) fraudulent claimants to unemployment and/or supplementary benefits,
(f) the voluntarily unemployed and those not 'genuinely' seeking work.

(a) *The temporarily stopped and the short-term unemployed*   As a result of the recommendations of the Government's working party on unemployment statistics, the temporarily stopped were excluded from the official count of the total registered unemployed from November 1972 onwards, largely because they were not regarded as synonymous with the 'jobless' wholly unemployed. The figures of the temporarily stopped were viewed officially as 'a by-product of the unemployment benefit rules and not an accurate index of a particular form of under-employment'. They covered a wide range of circumstances and degrees of unemployment which were liable to erratic fluctuations between one count and another. Data continue to be published separately but refer only to those persons who satisfy the special conditions for benefit entitlement for short-time working.[17] The 'temporarily stopped' are defined as registered persons who, on the day of the count, are capable of and available for work, who are suspended from work by their employer but are expected to resume work with the same employer, and who are regarded as still having a job. They may or may not be entitled to unemployment benefit.

The existence of frictional unemployment arising from the natural turnover of labour raises the separate question of whether those who are not so much unemployed as between jobs ought to be included in the official data. The suggestion has been made that those whose unemployment lasts no more than eight weeks should be thus excluded.[18] The Centre for Policy Studies (CPS)—founded by Sir Keith Joseph and Mrs. Margaret Thatcher in 1974—has similarly campaigned for the exclusion of the job-changers, whom it defines as those unemployed for less than four weeks.[19]

17. Persons must not, for example, be in receipt of payments under the Employment Protection Act, 1975. Such data should not be confused with the monthly returns from employers of the numbers working short time in manufacturing industry which include the temporarily stopped.
18. Bourlet and Bell, op. cit.; Wood (1972) and (1975).
19. Centre for Policy Studies, 'What the July unemployment figures really show', press release 25 July 1976.

The problem here is that the available data on the duration of unemployment are unreliable as indicators of frictional unemployment. It is especially difficult to isolate the short-term unemployed. The development of flow statistics since 1966 has provided some indication of the extent to which people join and leave the register, thereby generating the monthly changes in the published levels of registered unemployed adults.[20] But the duration figures themselves are an inadequate guide to completed spells of unemployment. There is a close association between long-term and short-term unemployment. It is clear from analyses of duration of unemployment that, even if the exit rate from the register remained constant, a fraction of those actually on the register on the day of the count will be at the beginning of long spells of unemployment. All short-term unemployment is not frictional or voluntary or due solely to 'labour turnover' or 'redeployment'.[21] Neither the number of persons who, at the time of the count, have been on the register for four weeks or less nor the flow statistics adequately quantify the short-term unemployed; nor do they identify those who suffer recurrent spells of short-term unemployment. This is because such data include many who *will be* on the register for more than one month, thereby overstating what is sometimes described as frictional unemployment. The Department of Employment estimated in 1975 that according to actuarial calculations based on the experience of 1961-5 the number on the register who had been there for less than four weeks was about equal to the number on the register who would have been on it for up to 11 or 12 weeks by the time they obtained a job. Similarly, the number who had been on the register for eight weeks was approximately equal to the number who would have been on it for up to 20 weeks by the time they left.[22] On this basis, therefore, it could be argued that the exclusion of those persons who had been unemployed for up to eight weeks would underestimate 'real' unemployment.[23]

The principal difficulty in determining the most appropriate measure of frictional or short-term unemployment is that there is no way of distinguishing *ex ante* which individuals will be unemployed for a given

20. See below pp. 191–6.
21. See below pp. 124–5.
22. *Gazette,* March 1975, p. 180.
23. Hughes, *British Journal of Industrial Relations* (1975) loc. cit., p. 324.

period of time. The most that can be done is to gauge the varying probabilities that individuals have of leaving the register quickly.[24] But that is not the same as knowing precisely which individuals ought to be excluded from the count because their unemployment will be of a fixed and short duration. Revising the aggregate unemployment figures according to a strict and formal definition of frictional unemployment could be seriously misleading.

(b) *School leavers and students*   The fact that adult students were not generally regarded as part of the active labour force, did not depend entirely upon employment for financial support, and sought jobs of a temporary or seasonal nature only, led to demands in the early 1970s that they be excluded altogether from the published unemployment figures. The number of such students joining the unemployment register during their vacations was separately identified in the official unemployment series from July 1971 because its inclusion was obscuring the underlying movement in the total of wholly unemployed. They were not excluded entirely from the regularly published series until April 1976 because of the fact that some students gained work and thus constituted a net addition to the labour supply.[25]

The claim that school leavers represent a 'special case' and should be excluded altogether from the official unemployment statistics, partly because they have not previously been in the labour force, has little to commend it. Those school leavers who are successful in obtaining jobs without registering as unemployed will be automatically counted in the monthly statistics of employment. As Hughes has pointed out their exclusion would imply that:

School-leavers should be counted as part of the labour force if they find work, but excluded if they try and fail.... If their willingness to register at an unemployment exchange is taken to imply that they are engaged in job search ... then they should be regarded as part of the official unemployed since their non-employment is involuntary.... There seems to be no justification whatsoever in ignoring them, especially since demand conditions generally will influence the rate

24. See below pp. 196–205.
25. The fact that adult students do not figure in the principal aggregate series of unemployment data does not mean that they are ignored altogether. Separate data of the numbers registered for vacation employment are included in each issue of the *Gazette*.

at which new entrants in the labour market are absorbed into employment.[26]

This argument has been reinforced by the marked deterioration in juvenile unemployment since 1975, the result of both cyclical and structural changes in the labour market.

(c) *The unemployables*   In order to distinguish between those who are fit for normal and regular work and those who are not, it has been suggested that those individuals who can be classified as 'unemployable'– the elderly, the mentally and physically handicapped, and the work-shy–ought to be excluded from the count of the unemployed.[27] The critical problem in this respect is how such persons could be identified. At best unemployability is a relative concept. Judging whether or not an individual is 'unemployable' may in reality amount to no more than assessing his or her employability in a particular state in a particular labour market. As the working party on unemployment statistics pointed out:

It is this confusion which leads to the apparent contradiction that whilst some virtually "unemployable" individuals can be identified, the characteristics of these individuals cannot be used as a basis for the definition of a wider "unemployable" group.[28]

The so-called 'unemployables' constitute what is often described as the hard core of unemployment, the irreducible minimum. This group, however, has no fixed or absolute size: indeed, its number appears to be cyclically sensitive. The official surveys of the characteristics of the

26. Hughes, *British Journal of Industrial Relations,* 1975, loc. cit., p. 322. For a recent survey of unemployment among 14–24 year olds (with a separate analysis of those aged 14–19 inclusive) based on EEC Labour Force Survey data for 1973 and 1975 see M. Casson, *Youth Unemployment,* London 1979.
27. See for example F.W. Paish, *Policy for Incomes,* Hobart Paper 29, Institute of Economic Affairs, 1968 (4th ed); Wood (1972) Chapter 4, and (1975); and Centre for Policy Studies press releases, e.g. *The Times,* 25 August 1975. Both Wood and Paish agree that such persons should be transferred to a separate register.
28. Cmnd. 5157, op. cit., para. 4.32. Except that is for the severely disabled. These are excluded from the unemployment count on the grounds that they are not likely to obtain employment even under special circumstances. This exclusion does not apply to other registered disabled persons. See below pp. 77–8.

unemployed undertaken in 1964, 1973, and 1976 suggest that the number of persons classified as having poor prospects of securing long-term unemployment was dependent upon the overall level of unemployment, the number of personally deficient among the unemployed rising with unemployment. This is not surprising since the Department of Employment surveys were based on the subjective assessment of local office staff to an individual's employability. These assessments appear to have been influenced by the age of the unemployed and their duration of unemployment—each of which is likely to vary directly with the level of unemployment.

Such is the complex nature of the economic, social, and psychological factors affecting unemployment that it would be foolish to attempt to distinguish an 'unemployable' group within the unemployment register if only because so many of them, though out of work at particular times, may well be employed as the pressure of aggregate demand increases. One-third of those described as having 'poor prospects' in the June 1973 survey of the unemployed found employment within seven months.[29] Although they were obviously less employable in some respects than were other people they were not entirely 'unemployable'. The 'hard core' of the unemployed is noticeably soft at the edges.

(d) *The disabled*   The official unemployment statistics exclude registered disabled persons who are unlikely to obtain employment except under special conditions. Their numbers are published separately. Those disabled persons who choose to register and who are classified as suitable for ordinary employment are, however, included in the published count. Both groups are included in the Department of Employment's register of disabled persons as prescribed under the Disabled Persons (Employment) Acts 1944 and 1958.

The working party on unemployment statistics rejected the notion of separately identifying unemployed registered disabled persons who were not severely handicapped, arguing that:

Most registered disabled persons are readily employable on their own merits given the right rehabilitation and vocational training and given help to find the right job; and it would be wrong to suggest anything to

29. Details of the so-called 'unemployable groups' can also be found in subsequent surveys of the characteristics of the unemployed conducted during periods of greater industrial recession.

the contrary. It is true that some registered disabled persons at present classified as suitable for ordinary employment may be particularly hard to employ. These tend not only to be physically or mentally handicapped but also to suffer from other employment handicaps. . . . But it is not possible to identify such people separately.[30]

Even if the registered disabled were to be separately identified such data would be an inadequate reflection of employment among the disabled. Many of the unemployed who are eligible to register as disabled do not register as such,[31] moreover there are as many unregistered but registrable disabled persons in employment as there are registered disabled persons in employment.[32]

(e) *Fraudulent claimants*   The current level of unemployment and other social security benefits are thought sometimes to tempt individuals in areas of temporary or casual employment to make false claims to be 'unemployed'. To the extent that such people register as unemployed while possessing undisclosed and substantial earnings over and above those to which they would be legally entitled as claimants to benefit, the official statistics may disguise fraudulent unemployment. It is very difficult to quantify such cases with any degree of precision but the evidence available suggests that the incidence of fraudulent claims is nothing like as great as has been suggested.[33] The Fisher Committee[34] claimed that the majority of the long-term unemployed on supplementary benefit were unemployed because they could not get work. In 1973 the Department of Employment investigated the evidence of fraudulent claims among those in receipt of benefit on the basis of a sample of 14,000 workers, concentrating particularly on those occupations where the opportunities for abuse were greatest. Four hundred cases of fraud were established, about 2.9 per cent of the total sample.[35]

30. Cmnd. 5157, op. cit., para. 4.36.
31. See Inquiry by the Office of Population Censuses and Surveys, Social Survey Division, *Work and Housing of Impaired Persons in Great Britain,* by Judith R. Buckle. HMSO, 1971.
32. Cmnd. 5157, op. cit., para 4.36.
33. Cf. Sir Keith Joseph's allegation that probably 'one in ten of those registered unemployed fraudently draw benefit at normal times', *The Times,* 6 September 1974.
34. *Report of the Committee on Abuse of the Social Security Benefits,* Cmnd. 5228, HMSO, London 1973.
35. *Gazette,* August 1973, p. 768.

Subsequent investigation by the Department of Health and Social Security has demonstrated that the amounts of benefit fraudulently received (by all claimants and not just the unemployed) are small in relation to total benefit expenditure.[36] It is doubtful, in any case, whether the receipt of payments to which an individual is entitled is a sufficient basis on which to judge his or her right to be included in the unemployment figures. A fraudulent claimant may still be actively seeking work.

(f) *Not 'genuinely' seeking work* There is another group of persons to consider however—those who, while registered, may not genuinely be interested in work. It includes those people under 65 in receipt of an occupational pension who register as unemployed, not for work, but to have their national insurance contributions credited to them in order to qualify for a full state pension at the age of 65.[37] There appears to be no satisfactory way of distinguishing those in this category who genuinely seek work from those who do not and, despite Parliamentary efforts in the early 1970s to have the conditions of entitlement to unemployment benefit altered to recognize this anomaly, nothing has yet been achieved. For this reason the official data are subject to slight over-estimation. It is questionable, however, whether this group of occupational pensioners ought to be totally excluded from the official count. The 1973 survey of the characteristics of the unemployed showed that 17 per cent of such persons claimed to have registered to accumulate national insurance credits. There was no evidence to show, however, that they were not interested in finding work. In any event, because it is a fundamental principle of national insurance that benefits should be paid as of right then, clearly, the remaining 83 per cent of persons on the register should not be regarded as being unavailable for work until supporting evidence to that effect is available.[38]

There is a further difficulty in using job-search activity to determine who may or may not be voluntarily unemployed. The people who show

36. *Ninth Report of the Committee of Public Accounts,* HC 532, 1976–7, HMSO 1977. Cf. F. Field, 'Control measures against abuse', in F. Field (ed.), *The Conscript Army,* London 1977; F. Field *et al, To Him Who Hath,* Penguin Books 1977.
37. The question of how many people may be induced by social security payment to remain unemployed longer than necessary is discussed below, pp. 102–9.
38. Hughes, *Industrial Relations Journal,* 7, (1976/7), loc. cit., p. 10.

little or no interest in finding a job may, on account of their age, sickness, disability, or past unemployment record, be indistinguishable from those 'unemployables' who have a very low expectation of ever finding a job.[39]

Does the Count Exclude Persons Who Ought to be Included?

In so far as individuals who are available and looking for work do not register themselves as unemployed, the official statistics will understate the true extent of the total out of work. It is important therefore to try to identify the various sources of such hidden unemployment.

It is useful in this context to draw a distinction between 'primary' and 'secondary' workers in the labour force. The former are distinguished as normally being in the labour force at any given time (employed or seeking employment) and the latter as typically engaged in non-labour force activity but prepared to move into and out of employment depending on circumstances.[40] Fluctuations in the participation rate[41] of secondary or discouraged workers have given rise to doubts about the reliability of registered unemployment as a measure of unused labour resources.

The extent to which secondary workers leave the labour force or refrain from entering it depends in part upon the state of the economy, though it is not always clear in which direction the influence will work. As unemployment rises some workers may drop out of the labour force entirely rather than register as unemployed in view of the scarcity of suitable alternative job opportunities and/or the cost involved in obtaining work. Furthermore as labour market conditions worsen, secondary workers registered as unemployed may decide to stop registering; new entrants into the registered labour force may be similarly discouraged, as might those who were thinking of returning to the registered labour force in the near future.

39. Hughes, *British Journal of Industrial Relations* (1975), loc. cit., p. 331; Boulet and Bell, op. cit., have suggested that those on the register for between 8 and 26 weeks should be excluded as being voluntarily unemployed. No satisfactory reason was advanced as to why 26 weeks should represent the correct cut-off point.
40. See R.C. Wilcock, 'The Secondary Labor Force and the Measurement of Unemployment', in *The Measurement and Behavior of Unemployment,* op. cit., pp. 167–210.
41. i.e. the ratio of the economically active population falling in any age and/or sex category to the total population in that category.

On the other hand, rising unemployment, rather than having a 'discouraged worker' effect, might encourage fringe workers to enter the labour force in order to supplement the loss to family income arising from the unemployment of the 'bread winner'. Thus wives could take jobs, children might leave school earlier, or older persons might opt to work longer. Rising labour demand might also attract other fringe workers who are encouraged by employment prospects— the 'additional worker' effect.

Only empirical investigation can determine the final outcome of these two opposing forces. Inasmuch as participation rates change over the trade cycle unemployment statistics will fail to reflect accurately the manpower potential in the labour market. Hunter found that in Great Britain during the years 1951-60 expansion of demand was met by a relative increase in the participation rate of the civil labour force,[42] and in recessions there was a net reduction in participation. Rising unemployment on balance tended to discourage work seekers, and hence to moderate the growth of unemployment. Falling unemployment tended to attract extra workers and to ease the problems of excess demand for labour.[43] Subsequent studies of British experience during the 1950s and 1960s have pointed tentatively to a net 'discouraged registered worker effect' as unemployment rose.[44]

Turner found that during the recession in the cotton industry in 1952 there was a wide discrepancy between the estimated total number of cotton workers either out of work or losing paid work from short time and the total of registered unemployment among cotton workers. The latter proved a very defective index of involuntary idleness not least because the recession hit married women severely. They were immobile, had comparatively few opportunities for other jobs, and

42. The civil labour force was defined as consisting of the total in civil employment plus the total of wholly unemployed persons. The civil labour force participation rate expressed the number of persons in the civil labour force (or any section of it) as a percentage of the number of persons of working age in the total population (or any section of it).

43. L.C. Hunter, 'Cyclical Variations in the Labour Supply: British Experience 1951–60', *Oxford Economic Papers*, 15, 1963.

44. B.A. Corry and J.A. Roberts, 'Activity Rates and Unemployment: The Experience of the United Kingdom 1951–66', *Applied Economics*, 2, 1970; Corry and Roberts, 'Activity Rates and Unemployment. The U.K. Experience: Some Further Results', *Applied Economics*, 6, 1974; Bowers (1975) loc. cit., provides a good survey of British and American work in this field.

little incentive to register as unemployed. A large part of the unemployment in cotton remained concealed as marginal workers were driven off the labour market. The national unemployment index recorded only about one-third the increase of workers unemployed or on short-time up to May 1952.[45] Turner's later research indicated further that, judging by payroll trends in November 1958, there were perhaps half a million people (mainly married women or the elderly) who, because of industrial recession, were neither in employment nor registered as unemployed. On the assumption that no more than 100,000 people were out of work and unregistered for other reasons, he suggested that to have included the total of 'hidden' unemployment would have probably more than doubled the official percentage rate of unemployment for December 1958.[46]

Recent data from the General Household Surveys of 1973-6 of those persons reporting themselves as looking for work but who were not registered as unemployed strongly suggest that their numbers are inversely related to the general level of unemployment. Over the period 1971-5 the correlation coefficient of the two variables was -0.94 (significant at the 5 per cent level). It is possible that since most of the unregistered unemployed had no claim to benefit few of them actively sought work during periods of high unemployment because of a general belief that no suitable work was available—the 'discouraged worker effect'.

On the other hand, other investigations of the pattern of changes in the proportion of males and females (married and unmarried) registered as unemployed during the period 1971-6 indicate positive cyclical sensitivity. The significant rise in the propensity to register of unemployed females in the 1970s is thought to have arisen particularly from high levels of unemployment, enhancing the 'encouraged' registered worker effect.[47] Moreover there is reason to believe that to some extent variations in regional (registered) unemployment rates reflect, not real differences in the numbers unemployed, but differences

45. H.A. Turner, 'Measuring Unemployment', *Journal of the Royal Statistical Society*, 118, 1955.
46. H.A. Turner, 'Employment Fluctuations, Labour Supply and Bargaining Power', *Manchester School*, XXVII, 1959. Estimates of unregistered unemployment in December 1958 are in D. Bailey, 'Note on British Unemployment Statistics', *Applied Statistics*, 1, 1960.
47. Department of Employment, 'Survey Information on the Propensity to Register as Unemployed', Research Paper MC2330.

in the proportions registering, the numbers being generally higher in the less prosperous regions.[48] Clearly the balance between the substitution (discouraged worker) effect and the income (added worker) effect varies over different phases of the trade cycle. This may be particularly noticeable in the case of the young unemployed. As the Department of Employment notes:

Young people form a high proportion of those who are unemployed for short periods, and it may be that during a boom many young people are unemployed for such short periods that they do not register as unemployed. A small increase in the average duration of unemployment during a recession may induce this group to register as unemployed with a consequent disproportionate increase in the figure of registered unemployment for young people.[49]

The importance of all this so far as unemployment statistics are concerned is that there are certain groups of people who by reason of their temporary or tenuous attachment to the labour force create

48. See below pp. 241–2. It must not be assumed that the impact of demand is the sole or always the principal influence on activity rates. Real wage rates, the number and age of dependants, race, the industrial and occupational structure of the labour market, age, marital status, social attitudes, and opportunities for full-time education can all, in theory, have an influence. It is not the purpose here to evaluate their relative importance. But see J. Bowers, *The Anatomy of Regional Activity Rates,* Cambridge 1970; P. Galambos, 'The Activity Rates of the Population of Great Britain, 1951–64', *Scottish Journal of Political Economy,* February 1967; G. Davis, 'Regional Unemployment, Labour Availability and Re-deployment', *Oxford Economic Papers,* 19, 1967; S. Wabe, 'Labour Force Participation in the London Metropolitan Region', *Journal of the Royal Statistical Society,* 132, 1969; A.J. Brown, *A Framework of Regional Economics,* Cambridge 1972; I.E. Gordon, 'Activity Rates: Regional and Sub-Regional Differentials', *Regional Studies,* 4, 1970; Bowers (1975) loc. cit.; R. McNabb, 'The Labour Force Participation of Married Women', *Manchester School,* 3, 1977; Christine Greenhalgh, 'A Labour Supply Function for Married Women in Great Britain', *Economica,* 44, 1977; S.V. Berg and T.R. Dalton, 'United Kingdom labour force activity rates: unemployment and real wages', *Applied Economics,* 9, 1977; G. Standing, *Labour Force Participation and Development,* Geneva 1978; Christine Greenhalgh, 'Male Labour Force Participation in Great Britain', *Scottish Journal of Political Economy,* 26, November 1979; R. Layard, *et al.,* 'Married Women's Participation and Hours', *Economica,* 47, February 1980.
49. *Gazette,* August 1978.

problems of measurement by not registering as unemployed when out of work. They include seven identifiable categories:

(a) Married women who are not eligible for unemployment benefit because they choose not to pay full national insurance contributions. Since it is well known that Employment Exchanges play only a minor, though significant, part in placing workers, it is clear that the main incentive for registering at an Exchange is the need of or desire for social security benefits. Changes in rules governing the payment of unemployment and/or supplementary benefit, therefore, have an effect on the extent to which registered unemployment corresponds to the numbers seeking work.[50] Until May 1977 married women could choose to pay insurance contributions at a reduced rate and thereby forego their right to unemployment benefit or contributions credits while unemployed. Since May 1977, however, married women have not been able to choose reduced liability unless they have previously established that right. It does not seem possible to estimate the number of married women who are willing to work.

(b) Occupational pensioners who do not claim or who have exhausted their entitlement to unemployment benefit.

(c) Persons above normal retirement age who, though in receipt of state pensions, seek work to supplement their income.

(d) Those who are disqualified for one reason or another from claiming unemployment benefit (but who are nevertheless still unemployed) and who choose not to register as non-claimants. An important source of benefit disqualification arises from leaving employment voluntarily. Persons thus disqualified for a specific period (usually six weeks from the date of registration) have an increased tendency to seek alternative work without recourse to the Employment Exchange. Exhaustion of benefit entitlement can also lead to exclusion from the statistics, assuming that those affected do not register as non-claimants. Such potential exclusions could apply to those subject to short but repeated spells of unemployment. Under existing rules, where one spell is followed by another within 13 weeks they are linked so that many of those out of work exhaust their entitlement to one year's benefit before their current spell has reached 12 months.

(e) Widows, young entrants to the labour force, and the self-employed.

50. See below pp. 102–9.

(f) Those among the currently employed who are working short-time or who are temporarily employed at tasks that do not use their skills fully. In so far as fluctuations in employment express themselves in such ways the index of registered unemployment becomes increasingly inappropriate as a measure of the economic situation, of the social problem of unemployment, and of the extent of unused labour.

(g) Those people, mainly married women, who would enter the labour market if appropriate employment opportunities were available or who seek work only under special circumstances— the 'hidden female labour reserves'. This kind of unemployment is somewhat different from the 'discouraged worker' type referred to previously. It tends to occur in areas of few employment opportunities where married women especially do not bother looking for work because their entry into the labour market is not seriously considered as a real possibility.[51]

There are, of course, other sources of non-registration. Professional and skilled white-collar workers may not register as unemployed because of a feeling that it is beneath their dignity or pointless in terms of finding a job. In an effort to overcome such prejudices the Department of Employment has switched the emphasis of job-finding from the Exchanges to Jobcentres and has made a conscious effort to improve the services of the Professional and Executive Recruitment Register. The results of the 1966 Census indicate that there were strong occupational patterns of non-registration biased upwards for both men and women towards the higher socio-economic groups. In the case of males a strong upward trend was noticeable in the extent of registration with increasing age.

51. Taylor's study of hidden female labour reserves in the sub-regions of Furness and Scunthorpe and in the sub-regions of the North West Standard Region in selected years of the 1960s confirmed the existence of considerable hidden reserves of female labour even in regions with high overall female participation rates. See J. Taylor, 'Hidden Female Labour Reserves', *Regional Studies*, 2, 1968. Similar estimates of the extent of hidden reserves of labour can be found in G. Davies, 'Regional unemployment, labour availability, and redeployment', *Oxford Economic Papers*, 19, 1967, and F.J.B. Stilwell, 'The Regional Distribution of Concealed Unemployment', *Urban Studies*, July 1970. Since the latter ignores those persons who are not seeking work as a result of poor job prospects it does not fully detect the existence of hidden unemployment. The results of some recent estimates of the registration propensity of males and females are given below pp. 91–2.

The situation among women is more complex because of the factors influencing their propensity to drop out of the labour force and to register as unemployed.[52] Their registration patterns reflect the vagaries of the national insurance system and the need for or desire of certain age groups to supplement family income. Unmarried females are generally expected to register in a similar fashion to males since they pay full national insurance contributions. But since some fail to qualify for unemployment benefit or live unmarried in households where they are not the sole provider their level of registration tends to be lower than that of males. Women moreover, unlike men, cannot obtain increases on top of flat-rate benefit for dependants (husband and children) unless their husbands are mentally or physically infirm. A married man is therefore more likely to be the one to register if both he and his wife are unemployed. Given the low propensity to register of unemployed married women, it is clear that the registration behaviour of all unemployed females depends on the weight of each respective group in the total.

The Dimensions of Unregistered Unemployment

The unregistered unemployed are, by definition, excluded from administrative records. Some indication of their numbers can be obtained however from surveys of the population, namely the Census of Population and the General Household Survey.[53] Both of these adopt a different approach to the measurement of unemployment to that of the Department of Employment.[54] But the Department has suggested a method of adjusting the data in the Census, the General Household Survey and in its own official series to provide estimates of the extent of unregistered unemployment. The results, relating to the 1966 and 1971 Censuses and to the General Houshold Surveys of 1972 and 1973, were published in the *Gazette* in December 1976 and are worth summarizing in some detail.

Both the survey and registration data were modified for the purpose of this comparative analysis. The unemployed who were sick were

52. See S. Dex, 'Measuring Women's Unemployment', *Social and Economic Administration*, 12, Summer 1978.
53. This present discussion is limited to data on unregistered unemployment. For details of the more general information on unemployment obtained from the Household Surveys and from the Census see below pp. 126–61.
54. See above pp. 62–7.

excluded from the survey estimates. Because the survey data did not always distinguish between those seeking full-time or part-time work, about 1,000 males and about 8,000 females were added to the official figures to include those seeking part-time work. The number of 'occupational pensioners' included in the official registration figures (available from occasional estimates) were excluded for comparative purposes because many such persons would classify themselves in a survey as retired rather than unemployed. Since March 1976, students in full-time education who are registered for vacation work have been excluded from the official figures. In the Censuses students in full-time education were omitted from the main analyses of economic activity whereas, in the GHS, they were included. While students were omitted from past official figures when comparisons were made with Census data, they were included when comparisons were made with the GHS.

In order to make useful comparisons between the official monthly count and estimates derived from both types of survey it was necessary to make the official figures applicable to a reference week instead of a reference day. The difference between the numbers registered as unemployed in the reference week and on a reference day was, according to the 1966 census, approximately 9,000 males and 5,000 females. This represented about 25 per cent and 50 per cent respectively of those in the official count who had been unemployed for less than a week. Similar percentages were thereafter applied to the official data to determine the difference between the reference week and the reference day for the period 1971 to 1973.

The net adjustments needed to put the official count on a survey basis have been estimated as shown in Table 10 overleaf.[55]

With these adjustments in mind, the estimated extent of unregistered unemployment based on a comparison of the 1966 Census figures and the adjusted official count is shown in Table 11 overleaf.[56]

---

55. *Gazette,* December 1976.
56. Previous estimates of the numbers of unregistered unemployed which, however, could not include the statistical revisions based on later information, can be found in Department of Employment, *Historical Abstract,* Annex A, p. 412; Cmnd. 5157, op. cit., pp. 22–3; 'Statistics of Unemployment in the United Kingdom', *Gazette,* May 1974, and 'The unemployment statistics and their interpretation', *Gazette,* March 1975. In 1973 the OECD estimated that the proportion of unregistered unemployment amongst males in the United Kingdom was a little over 1 percentage point. *Economic Survey, United Kingdom,* January 1973, p. 31.

TABLE 10
COMPARABILITY OF UNEMPLOYMENT DATA,
REGISTERED AND BY SURVEY[a]

| | Total Adjustment 000s | |
	Males	*Females*
1966 Census	–6	+4
1971 Census	–15	+3
1971 General Household Survey	–9	+5
1972 GHS	–11	+2
1973 GHS[a]	–5	+4

NOTES

a. Persons working on only a few days a week but who were genuinely looking for full-time work could be counted as unemployed if they were registered for work on the day of the count but would be excluded from surveys adopting a reference week. No allowance was made for this category, however, since their numbers were unknown.

b. This modification includes those individuals seeking work through Jobcentres. They would be included as unemployed in a survey but excluded from the official count if they were not receiving benefit.

TABLE 11
ESTIMATED UNREGISTERED UNEMPLOYMENT:
DEPARTMENT OF EMPLOYMENT AND CENSUS DATA, 1966

	Males 000s	*Females* 000s
Census reference week beginning 18 April 1966		
Registered	192	63
Unregistered[a]	95	122
Adjusted official count, 18 April 1966	228	67

NOTES

1. People seeking part-time work are excluded in the official registered count (unless entitled to unemployment benefit). The official unemployment total would not be increased to the extent of the figures shown above and below in the text, even if all the unregistered unemployed decided to register, since many such persons are unemployed females seeking part-time work.

One immediate source of discrepancy is the difference between the total Census registration figures and those of the adjusted official count of the unemployed. The shortfall of about 36,000 males and 4,000 females is probably explained, for males in particular, by the inclusion in the official count of occupational pensioners, most of whom would have classified themselves as retired in the Census. In addition some 20,000 males and 8,000 females described themselves in the Census as registered but unable to work because of temporary sickness. Though they are thereby excluded from the Census returns for the purpose of this comparative analysis, such individuals may have been counted as unemployed in the official data because their spell of sickness had not been sufficiently long to exclude them from the count.[57]

The determination of unregistered unemployment using data from the 1971 Census was more difficult because the Census did not include a question on registration and referred only to a reference week. The number of unregistered unemployed could only be obtained, therefore, by subtracting an estimate of the registered unemployed from the total unemployed. This was achieved by taking the average of the two official counts on either side of the Census date (25 April 1971) and adjusting for comparison with the Census according to the procedure described above.

The 1971 Census results and the adjusted official registered count are shown in Table 12.

The raw data obtained from the General Household Surveys had to be adjusted by different means in order to arrive at some tentative estimates of unregistered unemployment. The questions adopted in the Surveys were addressed to those who in any particular reference week were looking for work, would have looked for work if they had not been temporarily sick, or were waiting to take up a job they had already obtained.[58] Estimates of unregistered unemployment can be obtained from such sample data by two methods:[59]

---

57. Normally spells of sickness of 3 days or less would not lead to a person's removal from the unemployment register.
58. The school-leaving age was raised to 16 from 1972/3. The GHS results for 1972 were based on interviews conducted with persons aged 15 and over, those for 1973 onwards with persons aged 16 and over.
59. Full details are in the special article on unregistered unemployment in the *Gazette*, December 1976.

(A) Because the GHS samples are small compared with Censuses and because they exclude the institutional population, e.g. those in schools, hospitals, hotels etc., it is necessary to obtain a 'grossing factor' for each year by comparing the appropriate sample numbers with the mid-year population estimate. These 'factors' are then applied to the sample numbers in each GHS category, e.g. 'seeking work—registered, unregistered'; 'waiting to take up a job—registered, unregistered'. Estimates of the registered unemployed can then be compared with the official figures.

(B) The ratio of unregistered to registered unemployed from the sample data is applied to the appropriate (adjusted) official count (i.e. the annual average, suitably adjusted for comparison with the GHS by the procedure outlined above).

The results for 1972–3 using both methods are shown in Table 13.

The sampling error on the GHS females figures has been put as high as 80,000 and the acceptable estimates of unregistered female unemployment at 175,000 (1972) and 160,000 (1973).[60] For males, the GHS registration figures (which include occupational pensioners) show a shortfall of about 90,000 in 1972 and 1973 from the adjusted unemployment counts. This may be explained by the treatment of the temporarily sick who were not asked the registration question. Because of this the better estimates of the unregistered males are probably those grossed by method (A). This suggests estimates of approximately 90,000 unregistered males in 1972 and 100,000 unregistered males in 1973.[61] The most recent estimates of registered and unregistered unemployment based on information from various sources including the Census, the EEC Labour Force Survey, the GHS, and the Family Expenditure Survey are given in Table 14 overleaf.[62]

60. According to the 1973 survey the incidence of non-registration was much higher for women than for men; the rate of non-registration among married women was twice as high as that for unmarried women.
61. Unadjusted estimates of the registered and in subsequent surveys the unregistered unemployed have been included.
62. *Gazette,* June 1977, p. 588. There is evidence of a marked reluctance among young West Indians to register as unemployed. See Home Office, *Unemployment and Homelessness: A Report,* Reference Division, Community Relations Commission, HMSO 1974.

TABLE 12
ESTIMATED UNREGISTERED UNEMPLOYMENT:
DEPARTMENT OF EMPLOYMENT AND CENSUS DATA, 1971

	Males 000s	*Females* 000s
Census unemployed (registered and unregistered)[a]	642	344
Adjusted official count	598	115
Difference (i.e the unregistered unemployed	84[b]	229

NOTES
a. The Census category 'out of employment (other than sick)' included prisoners who had been in detention for less than six months. The above data excludes 25,000 males in order to allow a comparison to be made with the official count figures. (The female numbers are negligible; the male total is based on an estimate for end-March 1971).
b. The official count includes a number of occupational pensioners, predominantly males, estimated at about 40,000, who would have classified themselves as retired in the Census. The number of male unregistered unemployed on the basis of the 1971 Census is therefore approximately the sum of the difference between the Census and the adjusted official count (44,000) plus 40,000.

TABLE 13
ESTIMATED UNREGISTERED UNEMPLOYMENT.
DEPARTMENT OF EMPLOYMENT AND GENERAL
HOUSEHOLD SURVEY DATA, 1972/3

	1972		1973	
	Males 000s	*Females* 000s	*Males* 000s	*Females* 000s
Official count of registered unemployed adjusted for comparison with GHS	694	141	494	103
GHS grossed up figures				
− registered (Method (A))	597	148	410	89
− unregistered (Method (A))	90	180	100	147
− unregistered (Method (B))	106	171	121	170

TABLE 14
ESTIMATES OF REGISTERED AND UNREGISTERED
UNREGISTERED* MALES AND FEMALES 1971–76
(in thousands)

	1971	1972	1973	1974	1975	1976
Registered unemployed males	589	647	461	439	680	972
Unregistered unemployed males	84	90	100	64	51	50
% males registering	88	88	82	87	93	95
Registered unemployed females	98	119	84	75	149	306
Unregistered unemployed females	229	175	160	150	143	175
% females registering	30	40	34	33	51	64

* Excluding sick and out of work

Unemployment and Underemployment

If the unemployment figures are adequately to reflect movements in excess labour supply then some measure of the under-utilization of employed labour (labour hoarding) has to be added to recorded unemployment and to estimates of hidden unemployment (those not in the labour force but looking for work).[63]

A firm's labour input is the result normally of the combination of the number of workers employed and the degree to which the potential service of such workers is used. In practice, however, there may be limits to the extent to which the simultaneous adjustment of the labour input to short run changes in output can be made. In the short run labour may be a quasi-fixed factor of production rather than a purely variable factor input for a number of reasons.[64] Contractual commitments may prevent an employer from discharging workers at short notice. Indivisibilities in the production process may give rise to a technical constraint. Where a production process is organized 'in series'

63. J. Taylor, 'Hidden Unemployment, Hoarded Labour and the Phillips Curve', *Southern Economic Journal,* XXXVII, 1970.
64. The following analysis of the meaning of labour hoarding relies heavily on J. Taylor, *Unemployment and Wage Inflation,* London 1974, chapter 3.

or where collective agreements specify the number of workers to be used on a particular process it may prove difficult to adjust the number of workers employed when output falls. It may, in addition, prove better to safeguard worker efficiency and union-management relations by resisting frequent changes in employment levels in response to short-run fluctuations in demand. The costs associated with dismissing skilled and experienced workers and of hiring and training may prove prohibitive, encouraging employers to minimize labour turnover. Expectations of future changes in demand may prove critical in determining the employer's willingness or otherwise to discharge or recruit workers. Finally, there may be a lagged response of the employment level to short-run demand variations because of the lags in the flow of information relating to current levels of output, sales, and inventories. Unplanned labour hoarding may occur as a result of discrepancies between actual and desired employment levels. Changes in the utilization rate of workers by, say, adjusting the length of the working week may also be precluded by existing collective agreements between management and men and the potential effects on workers' moral and efficiency of frequent changes in working hours.

The excess supply of labour is not directly observable but economists have suggested alternative measures which are felt to be more representative of it than are the official statistics of registered unemployment. Taylor, for example, has suggested a method of measuring the demand-deficiency component of unemployment which incorporates elements currently excluded from the published series. His 'unemployment gap'(U)—the sum of unemployment and under-employment—includes a deficient-demand component of registered unemployment (U_r), hidden unemployment arising from demand deficiency (U_h), and labour hoarding arising from demand deficiency (U_d). Thus $U = U_r + U_h + U_d$.

Taylor has calculated a quarterly series of labour hoarding in sixteen British industry groups during the years 1952-72; the rate of hidden unemployment in Great Britain, 1951-73, and by region 1951-66, and the frictional and demand-deficient components of registered unemployment in the production sector, Great Britain, 1953-73.[65] It

---

65. ibid., chapter 6 and appendix 3. See also Taylor, 'The unemployment gap in Britain's production sector, 1953–73', in G.D.N. Worswick (ed.), *The Concept and Measurement of Involuntary Unemployment*, London 1976, and 'A Regional Analysis of Hidden Unemployment in Great Britain, 1951–66', *Applied Economics*, 3, 1971.

is, however, extremely difficult to obtain a satisfactory measure of labour hoarding (or, incidentally, of underemployment by virtue of skill) and the assumptions on which Taylor's work is based have been seriously challenged.[66]

U, V Statistics and the Demand for Labour

The co-existence of statistics of unemployment and of unfilled vacancies[67] raises the question of how far the two series fairly reflect the pressure of demand for labour. The seminal work in this respect is that of Dow and Dicks-Mireaux, who in 1958 drew attention to the striking inverse parallelism between the seasonal swings of the series of unemployment and unfilled vacancies. Data for the period 1946–56 revealed that up to a point the two series, taken together, provided a fairly reliable indication of the pressure of demand, though not a direct measure of its magnitude. Even when seasonal movements were removed changes in demand still appeared to be reflected in the statistics. An index of net excess demand for labour was derived for all industries and for seven industry groups from 1946.[68] Dow summarized the approach thus:

However high the level of demand, unemployment will never fall to zero. Beyond a point, therefore, unemployment must become a decreasingly sensitive index of the pressure of demand; and beyond this point it is better to rely on the evidence provided by the vacancy statistics. The *index* is based on the idea that at some point net excess demand is zero, i.e. the excess demand for some types of labour equals

66. D. Leslie and C. Laing, 'The Theory and Measurement of Labour Hoarding', *Scottish Journal of Political Economy*, 25, 1978; D.I. MacKay, 'Labour Reserves. Some Problems of Measurement', in National Economic Development Office, *Labour Statistics*, May 1973. Other empirical studies of labour hoarding include S. McKendrick, 'An Inter-industry Analysis of Labour Hoarding in Britain 1953–72', *Applied Economics*, 7, 1975, and, for British engineering during 1964–71, G. Evans, 'The Labour Market Mechanism and the Hoarding of Manpower' in J.S. Wabe (ed.), *Problems in Manpower Forecasting*, Saxon House 1974.

67. For details of the nature and availability of such data see below pp. 162–6.

68. J.C.R. Dow and L.A. Dicks-Mireaux, 'The Excess Demand for Labour: A Study of Conditions in Great Britain, 1946–1956', *Oxford Economic Papers*, 10, 1958.

the excess supply for other types. Above the zero point, the index is based on the vacancy statistics; below it, on the unemployment series.[69]

Dow subsequently calculated indices of the pressure of demand for labour for the period 1946-60, revising the interpretation contained in the original 1958 study which had ignored the possibility of understatement by the unemployment statistics.[70]

Numerous attempts have since been made to remove the arbitrariness associated with the conventional classification of unemployment into structural, frictional, and demand-deficient components. Thirlwall, for example, has sought to separate out demand-deficient from non demand-deficient unemployment using as an objective dividing line the point of balance between the available supply of labour and the unsatisfied demand for labour, represented in the former case by yearly averages of a quarterly series of unfilled vacancies and in the latter case by unemployment as a percentage of the total workforce. The amount

69. J.C.R. Dow, *The Management of the British Economy 1945-60*, Cambridge 1968, p. 340. The index was derived thus:

let	v = recorded unfilled vacancies
	s = the proportion of true vacancies that is recorded
hence	v/s = true vacancies
	u = recorded unemployment
	t = the proportion of true unemployment that is recorded
hence	u/t = true unemployment
	m = maladjustment, which may be defined as the amount of unemployment (u/t) at that pressure of demand where u/t = v/s
	d = net excess demand for labour, being positive for excess and negative for deficient-demand

Assuming that m, s and t are constant, u will decrease and v increase as the pressure of demand increases. Because u is a decreasingly sensitive index of demand, a plot of u and v will lie on a curve convex to the origin. Assuming further that this curve can be approximated by a rectangular hyperbola, $\sqrt{uv/ts}$ will be constant, and may be taken to measure m.

The index measures excess demand (d) as true vacancies *less* maladjustments ($v/s - m = v/s - \sqrt{uv/ts}$ when excess demand is positive ($u/t < v/s$); and as maladjustment *less* true unemployment ($\sqrt{uv/ts} - u/t$) when excess demand is negative ($u/t > v/s$). It is further assumed that s = 0.5; that at or below the point of zero excess demand, t = 0.5 also.

The principles of construction are more fully set out in Dow and Dicks-Mireaux (1958), Appendix (1)—though no account was taken there of the possibility that recorded unemployment might understate the position. Dow, op. cit. (1968), p. 340.

70. ibid., pp. 337-43.

of unemployment in excess of the point of balance between the two series was identified as 'demand-deficient' and that amount at the point of balance (i.e. when aggregate unemployment is equal to aggregate unfilled vacancies) as non demand-deficient. A point in excess of the actual level of unemployment would represent net excess demand for labour, i.e. unfilled vacancies exceeding unemployment. On this conceptual basis average amounts of non demand-deficient unemployment have been calculated for the Standard Regions and for 24 Orders of the 1958 Standard Industrial Classification for Great Britain during the period 1949-66.[71]

The quarterly occupational data of wholly unemployed adult workers and unfilled vacancies available since 1958 classifies occupations according to the functions associated with the job and the skills, knowledge, and abilities required by the worker in order to perform these functions. Such information of the skill composition of both vacancies and the unemployed has been used to measure quarterly structural and frictional unemployment in Britain (males and females separately) between 1958 and 1972.[72] These estimates are based on the conceptual distinction between vacancies which are of the right or wrong type to absorb the unemployed. Workers are thereby classified as structurally unemployed if they do not possess the qualifications to fill a vacancy, and frictionally unemployed if they do possess the necessary qualifications.[73] Both structural and frictional unemployment were found to have increased in the period relative to total unemployment as the latter declined; in other words, both were 'more the product of the "good" times than of the "bad"'.

71. A.P. Thirlwall, 'Types of Unemployment with Special Reference to "Non Demand-Deficient" Unemployment in the U.K.', *Scottish Journal of Political Economy,* February 1969, pp. 22-7.
72. J.J. Hughes, 'The Use of Vacancy Statistics in Classifying and Measuring Structural and Frictional Unemployment in Great Britain 1958-72', *Bulletin of Economic Research,* 26, May 1974. (Equivalent data was not available for the time period analysed by Thirlwall.) Because the use of national occupational data masked structural unemployment due to regional immobility of labour Hughes provided an additional regional analysis for males during 1963-72. For a discussion of the incidence of structural unemployment by skill in the U.K. see D.J. Smyth and P.D. Lowe, 'The Vestibule to the Occupational Ladder and Unemployment. Some Econometric Evidence on United Kingdom Structural Unemployment', *Industrial Labor Relations Review,* 23, July, 1970.
73. Hughes, loc. cit., pp. 19-24.

Clearly the value of these empirical measures of the different components of total unemployment depends upon the reliability of the unemployment and vacancy data.[74] Thirlwall's estimates, for example, presuppose that the vacancy statistics are a fairly reliable proxy measure of the unsatisfied demand for labour. Where reported vacancies understate the true amount of the unsatisfied demand for labour the amount of 'demand-deficient' unemployment would be over-estimated and the amount of 'non demand-deficient' unemployment underestimated.[75] The exact relationship between the point where unemployment equals unfilled vacancies is uncertain and may change over time. The equality of true unemployment and vacancies may bear little relation to that suggested by the equality of recorded statistics. As Thirlwall notes:

It does not seem possible to make meaningful year to year estimates of non demand-deficient unemployment from data of unfilled vacancies and unemployment alone. . . . The most that can be done with the time series comparison of aggregate vacancies and unemployment is to observe points of intersection between the two series and to identify the periods of deficient, and net excess, demand for labour.[76]

There are a number of reasons why we should doubt the precise recording ratio of the existing vacancy data. There are always on the supply side groups of persons who are unemployable to some degree or other or available for work but unregistered, and on the demand side some over- and under- reporting of vacancies. Dow and Dicks-Mireaux pointed out in 1958 that the vacancy data 'neither record transactions nor register decisions, but represent a sort of queue. The size of the queue may be either more or less than the real unsatisfied demand: people may either duplicate orders or join several queues, or they may give up trying and not join a queue at all'.[77] Nevertheless they concluded that 'the positioning of the full employment or zero excess demand point (i.e. where vacancies equal unemployment) is probably not in error by more than about ± 0.25 per cent'.[78]

74. It is impossible to classify individual workers as suffering from frictional, structural, or demand-deficient unemployment since job vacancies are not reserved for individuals.
75. Thirlwall, loc. cit. (1969), p. 31.
76. ibid., pp. 38, 41.
77. Dow and Dicks-Mireaux, loc. cit., pp. 1–2.
78. ibid., p. 6.

It is doubtful, however, whether such acknowledged deficiencies in the measurement errors of the vacancy data fully represent the short-comings of the series. The most that can reasonably be claimed for vacancy statistics is that they show the direction in which the demand for labour is moving. The recorded total measures only a fraction of available jobs and considerably understates the true demand for labour. Moreover the ratio of notified to true vacancies is likely to vary significantly over the trade cycle and to contain an occupational and skill bias.[79] As demand increases and unemployment falls, employers may be more prepared to use official agencies to obtain labour and even over-represent vacancy notifications in the hope of increasing their share of the available allocation. But the ratio of notified to true vacancies may equally fall as demand increases. As unemployment falls the ratio of skilled/unskilled unemployed tends also to decline and employers seeking skilled workers may consider the Exchanges inadequate for meeting their demands; there may, in addition, be serious doubts as to the suitability of an Exchange recruit. Furthermore if a large number of firms believe that competitors will over-report vacancies there may be no gain in them following suit. In reality, therefore, the positioning and perhaps the slope of the U/V relation may be far different from that postulated under Thirlwall's assumptions and the evidence that observed unemployment is demand-deficient may refer instead to the existence of structural unemployment requiring an entirely different armoury of policy correctives.[80]

The value of the ratio of notified to actual vacancies depends to a large extent on the effectiveness of the employment service in the job-finding process compared with other available means. Traditionally, the service has had a poor reputation among both employers and employees, leading to an unwillingness to use the facilities offered save in exceptional circumstances.[81] The situation has improved in recent

79. A survey by the Manpower Services Commission put the employment service's share of total unfilled vacancies on 6th May 1977 at 36 per cent. The variation of the ratio of notified to true vacancies by skill on the same day showed 24 per cent for non-manual occupations and 47 per cent for manual. *Gazette,* June 1979, p. 558.

80. A. Woodfield, 'Job Search Costs and the Measurement of Structural Unemployment', *Scottish Journal of Political Economy,* XXII, 1975.

81. G.L. Reid, 'The Role of the Employment Service in Redeployment', *British Journal of Industrial Relations,* IX, 1971; H.R. Kahn, *Repercussions of Redundancy,* London 1964; F. Herron, *Labour Market in Crisis,* London 1975.

years because of the extensive modernization of the available services, especially with the separation of the employment function (carried out by Jobcentres) from the payment of unemployment and related benefits (by the Department of Employment).

As far as the employment service's work itself is concerned, it is evident that a substantial proportion of registrants in recent years, even among those on the register for up to and over six months, have not been submitted to a vacancy during their spell of unemployment.[82] This itself reflects on the overall level of notified vacancies made to the Exchanges. Currently, about two thirds of all vacancies notified to the employment service are filled by it and this proportion is fairly static from year to year. It is not entirely clear to what extent this is due to the personal and labour force characteristics of the registrants themselves.[83] McGregor's study of the 'matching' of registrants and vacancies in one employment office in the west of Scotland in January 1975 indicated that although those persons under the age of 30 and the semi-skilled were less likely to be placed in employment in general there was little evidence that characteristics associated with a high submission probability had a similarly high placement probability. Thus he wrote that:

although we found that registrants with short durations of unemployment were significantly less likely to be submitted to a vacancy than longer term registrants *once submitted* the short-term registrant may be more likely to receive a job offer from the employer. This may simply reflect a preference among employers for men who have not been out of work for long periods. With respect to age it may be that variations across age groups in the probability of a successful placement result from a greater preparedness on the part of older workers to accept offers of work that are made to them.[84]

There is no accurate means of calculating the effect of the reorganization of the public employment service on 'placing share', i.e. the ratio of the flow of placings over a specified period to the flow of total

82. 'Vacancy Study', *Gazette,* March 1974; 'Characteristics of the Unemployed: Sample Survey Results', *Gazette,* March 1974; A. McGregor, 'The Placement Activity of the Employment Service Agency', *British Journal of Industrial Relations,* XVI, 1978.

83. See Alison Donaldson, *United Kingdom Unemployment Statistics,* International Institute of Management, Berlin, September 1978.

84. McGregor, loc. cit., p. 314.

engagements in the labour market as a whole. The National Survey of Engagements and Vacancies conducted by the Manpower Services Commission during April to July 1977 put the overall placing share of the employment service at 23 per cent. This may be an under-estimate of current performance in as much as the survey excluded all placings made by the Careers Service and by offices of Professional and Executive Recruitment and because of the subsequent expansion of the Jobcentre programme.[85] The annual General Household Survey records the various means by which people seek jobs and indicates a much lower placing shown by the public employment service than that indicated above. Its figures are derived, however, from jobseekers who had changed their job at least once during the year prior to their inter-view. Engagements by the unemployed and multiple job changes by the same job seeker are thus omitted.[86] There is no reason to believe that informal job-search techniques are necessarility inefficient or likely to produce less satisfactory results than would reliance on more formal methods.[87]

The campaign to raise the degree of notified vacancies does not necessarily make them any more reliable as an economic indicator. To the extent that the employment service works to a target of notified vacancies and for administrative reasons proves zealous in its enquiries concerning available jobs the number of registered vacancies at given levels of unemployment might appear more buoyant than would other-wise have been the case.[88] Moreover, changes in the duration of vacancies over the trade cycle tend to invalidate inter-period comparisons of vacancy data, even on an ordinal basis. Little is known, however, about the duration of registered vacancies despite the fact that they are the important link between the stock of unemployment and the flows of unemployment on and off the register. The major part of all cyclical

85. For details of the National Survey see *Gazette,* November 1978 and June 1979. See also Manpower Services Commission, *Job Centres: an evaluation,* March 1978.
86. The extent to which informal job–search/finding methods are important over varying geographical areas is discussed in P. Beaumont, 'The Means of Finding Jobs beyond Local Labour Market Conditions', *Industrial Relations Journal,* 8, Spring 1977.
87. G.L. Reid, 'Job-search and the Effectiveness of Job-Finding Methods', *Industrial and Labour Relations Review,* 25, 1971–2; C.A. Pissarides, 'Job Matchings with State Employment Agencies and Random Search', *Economic Journal,* 89, December 1979.
88. MacKay in *Labour Statistics,* op. cit., pp. 95–6.

change in the stock of unfilled vacancies in Britain during the early 1970s was accounted for by changes in vacancy duration.[89]

The Interpretation of Unemployment and Vacancy Data

Criticism of the published unemployment data developed with remarkable rapidity after 1966 when the official registered unemployment series appeared to assume peculiar characteristics. Between 1952 and 1965 the unemployment (U) and vacancy (V) series for men displayed a general inverse relationship with a rise in unemployment normally accompanied by a fall in the number of unfilled vacancies as both responded to changes in the demand for labour. This apparently stable relationship[90] began to shift outwards after the third quarter of 1966, i.e. for any value of unfilled vacancies the level of unemployment appeared higher than would have been expected from the observed inverse relationship of the U/V curve.[91] The shift in the relationship between unemployment and vacancies during the period 1966–74 was equivalent to an increase of about 300,000 in the level of unemployment corresponding to a given level of vacancies.[92]

The reasons advanced to explain this shift concentrate particularly on the role of supply and demand factors. They are of particular relevance here because the 'breakdown' in the U/V relationship casts doubt on the unemployment figures in general and on the male unemployment rate in particular as reliable measures of unused labour resources.

89. Some interesting work in this field is reported by P.B. Beaumont in 'The Duration of Registered Vacancies: An Exploratory Exercise', *Scottish Journal of Political Economy*, 25, February 1978 and in 'Some Evidence of the Speed of Filling Registered Job Vacancies', *Bulletin of Economic Research*, 21, 1979.

90. There is reason to believe that the U/V relationship had been basically unstable since the 1950s but the discussion has centred very much on post-1966 experience. G. Evans, 'A Note on Trends in the Relationship between Unemployment and Unfilled Vacancies', *Economic Journal*, 85, 1975. For more detailed analysis see D.J. O'Dea, *Cyclical Indicators for the Postwar British Economy*, Cambridge U.P. 1975.

91. J.K. Bowers, P.C. Cheshire and A.E. Webb, 'The Change in the Relationship between Unemployment and Earnings Increases: A Review of Some Possible Explanations', *National Institute Economic Review*, 54, November 1970. cf. J. Taylor and S. McKendrick, 'How Should We Measure the Pressure of Demand?', *Lloyds Bank Review*, 115, January 1975.

92. *Gazette*, October 1976, p. 1093.

Supply Factors

The substantial increase in the measured unemployment rate after 1966 has been ascribed to a shift in the labour supply function following changes in the level of unemployment compensation. More specifically, the existence of relatively high tax-free social benefits, redundancy pay, and tax rebates supposedly increased 'voluntary' unemployment by reducing the economic incentive of the unemployed to seek jobs. Thus, the argument runs, higher unemployment benefit has lowered the cost of leisure in terms of income foregone, and has encouarged the unemployed to become more selective in their job-search, thus helping to increase the total number out of work at any one time.

This general thesis is often couched in terms of indifference curve analysis of income and substitution effects. Thus the benefits from remaining unemployed (increased leisure and the opportunity to obtain a job with special characteristics) are traded off against the costs of being out of work (loss of current income and loss of status, for example). The argument is that increased benefits will, via sub-stitution and income effects, shift the optimum towards more unemployment, especially for those who become unemployed involuntarily. Fixed-sum redundancy payments are felt to work in the same direction only via an income effect.[93] The increase in standard social security benefits together with the effects of the PAYE Scheme in providing income tax repayments to skilled manual workers when they lose their jobs could have similar potential effects though there is less direct evidence available in this respect. Nor is it certain to what extent the unemployment figures are affected by the willingness of husbands

93. J.S. Cubbin and K. Foley, 'The Extent of Benefit-Induced Unemployment in Great Britain: Some New Evidence', *Oxford Economic Papers*, 29, March 1977, pp. 128–9. Note for example the following statements:

'What matters for the purpose of studying the measurement of unemploy-ment is that the supply price of labour must have been changed by the increase in financial help to the unemployed since 1966', (Wood (1972), op. cit., p. 59).

'The shift in the meaning of the unemployment figures is partly due to redundancy payments and higher unemployment benefits, which give people more time to look for jobs and make it less urgent for them to take whatever turns up', *Financial Times*, September 1971, cited in MacKay and Reid, loc. cit., p. 126.

For details of the availability of statistics on entitlement to benefit see below pp. 173–8.

to spend longer looking for a job because their wives are in paid employment.

Despite Keynes's emphasis on the extent to which deficient demand for labour causes 'involuntary' unemployment, the 'supply' thesis lends support to the popular notion that there exists among the unemployed a substantial body of persons who are 'work-shy' or who are at least voluntarily unemployed without admitting it.[94] (It is very rarely suggested that people actually leave their jobs because it pays to be unemployed). Gujarati has suggested that the introduction of the Redundancy Payments Act (1965) and earnings-related unemployment benefit in October 1966 created an 'artificial' increase in registered unemployment as workers engaged in more extensive and time consuming job-search.[95] He maintains that to 'correct' actual unemployment (U_t)[96] for the effects of these legislative changes it should be divided by a corrective factor of 1.44 in each quarter since the end of 1968 to the middle of 1971 and of $1.12 + 0.4_t$ in each quarter from 1966-IV to 1968-IV, where t is the number of quarters since 1966-IV. Similarly, Maki and Spindler suggested in 1975 that earnings-related supplement (ERS) was the main factor in inducing changes in measured unemployment rates, claiming that on average the overall and male unemployment rates between 1967 and 1972 were 30 per cent and 33 per cent higher, respectively.[97] Although they have since come to recognize the inherent difficulties in estimating the effect and in evaluating the explanatory power of the benefit/income ratio, they nevertheless maintain a belief in the positive influence of unemployment insurance on the observed level of unemployment.[98] MacKay and Reid's analysis of male redundancy in the West Midlands during 1966-8

94. The public outcry against alleged abuses of social security benefits was particularly acute during 1976/7. See A. Deacon, 'The Scrounging Controversy: Public Attitudes Towards the Unemployed in Contemporary Britain', *Social and Economic Administration*, 12, Summer 1978.

95. D. Gujarati, 'The Behaviour of Unemployment and Unfilled Vacancies: Great Britain, 1958–1971', *Economic Journal*, 82, March 1972.

96. Gujarati's unemployment rates are percentages of the working population and not of total employees, the official Department of Employment deflator.

97. D. Maki and Z.A. Spindler, 'The Effect of Unemployment Compensation on the Rate of Unemployment in Great Britain', *Oxford Economic Papers*, 27, 1975.

98. Z.A. Spindler and D. Maki, 'More on the Effects of Unemployment Compensation on the Rate of Unemployment in Great Britain', *Oxford Economic Papers*, 31, March 1979.

established a significant relationship between the amount of unemployment benefit and the duration of unemployment.[99] Hill's random sample of unemployed men in Newcastle, Coventry, and Hammersmith in October 1971 appears, after more detailed analysis, to suggest a stronger association between benefit income and prolonged unemployment than was first believed. Moreover, the association appears in part to be independent of those strong correlates of prolonged unemployment, namely advanced age and low skill.[100]

The results of recent and more fully-specified research do indicate a positive connection between unemployment and related payments and the incentive to work. But they relate to particular groups of people in special circumstances and do not support the notion that the increase in the level and duration of unemployment can be explained in general by the conscious decision of a large proportion of the unemployed to remain out of work because of generous welfare provision. Data on male unemployment in 1972 suggest that, holding constant family size and the availability of jobs, a 10 per cent increase in the 'replacement ratio', i.e. the net family income where the man is unemployed relative to the net family income when the man is in work[101] would increase

99. MacKay and Reid, loc. cit. They suggested that an increase in unemployment benefit of £1 per week tended to increase the length of unemployment by almost half a week. See also D.I. MacKay, 'Redundancy and Re-engagement: A Study of Car Workers', *Manchester School*, 40, 1972.

100. M.J. Hill, 'Can We Distinguish Voluntary from Involuntary Unemployment?', in Worswick (ed.), *The Concept and Measurment*, op. cit.

101. The average replacement ratio has been used in most recent research into the possible effects of benefit on duration of unemployment. It is not necessarily the best yardstick since the net income attributed to a man in work is associated with a full year's earnings, while the income when unemployed ignores tax rebates and the effect of unemployment on subsequent tax liability. Ideally, the marginal net earnings for an extra week's work ought to be compared with the tax-free unemployment benefits. On 1977 tax and insurance levels, such comparisons would suggest a greater disincentive problem than is indicated by average replacement ratios. A. Atkinson and J. Flemming, 'Unemployment, Social Security and Incentives', *Midland Bank Review*, Autumn 1978, pp. 10–13.

Moreover the use of average earnings (net of income tax) ignores the extent to which unemployment is experienced by those with less than average earnings. It can also distort the effective replacement ratio over time because the tax threshold has been falling since 1959 and the first rate of income tax rising while the rate of income tax at average earnings has remained relatively stable. M. Scott and R. Laslett, *Can We Get Back to Full Employment?*, London 1978, pp. 123–4.

the unemployment rate by *c.* 5 per cent of itself.[102] The effect seems, however, to be concentrated on those who have been unemployed for under six months. Nickell, using data on duration from the 1972 General Household Survey, finds an elasticity of unemployment duration with respect to the replacement ratio of between 0.6 and 1.0. The significant effect of overall benefits on incentive appears limited, moreover, to those unemployed for under 20 weeks and is greater for the low paid and for those with large families; the impact of benefit levels on the conditional probability of obtaining work in any given week seems negligible for the long-term unemployed (26 weeks or more).[103] The minority who tend to be noticeably better off when unemployed are often so disadvantaged in other respects that many would find it difficult to compete successfully in the labour market even if they were positively seeking work.

As far as ERS is concerned, it is noticeable that only a small proportion of the benefits received by the unemployed between 1965-72 was accounted for by ERS, that there has been no appreciable increase in the proportion of male claimants in the 2 to 26 weeks duration category during which the benefits are payable,[104] and that the size of the benefits relative to net earnings have not increased since 1967. It is possible, though as yet not certain, that some of those induced to become or remain unemployed by the prospect of ERS might subsequently have been denied it and that, alternatively, actual ERS recipients may have supported additional unemployed workers.[105] But Maki and Spindler's claim that the introduction of ERS increased male unemployment rates by 33 per cent is probably an exaggeration— more recent research suggests an induced increase in the rate of unemployment from this source of the order of 10 per cent.[106]

Gujarati's claim that the recorded unemployment levels during 1968-71 were 44 per cent higher than expected is based on a statistical analysis of absolute levels of unemployment and vacancies and

102. Royal Commission on the Distribution of Income and Wealth, *The Causes of Poverty*, by R. Layard, *et al.*, Background Paper No. 5, London, HMSO 1978, pp. 80–82.
103. S. Nickell, 'The Effect of Unemployment and Related Benefits on the Duration of Unemployment', *Economic Journal*, 89, March 1979.
104. See M.C. Sawyer, 'The Effects of Unemployment Compensation on the Rate of Unemployment in Great Britain: A Comment', *Oxford Economic Papers*, 31, March 1979.
105. Spindler and Maki (1979), loc. cit., p. 157.
106. Nickell, loc. cit., pp. 46–7.

does not allow for the extent to which the two variables were time-dependent. Analyses based on changes in the data rather than the levels between 1966-IV and 1971-II suggest a much smaller degree of 'excess unemployment' and little evidence of any substantial inflation of the official series.[107] There is little indication either of any noticeable increase in unemployment resulting from changes in the amount and availability of redundancy payments after 1965. Although the size of such payments was correlated with the length of time taken to find a new job, cause and effect have been largely discounted because it was older people[108] who formed the largest proportion of redundant workers, who received the larger sums by way of compensation, and who had most difficulty in obtaining fresh employment.[109]

An increase in the amount and range of unemployment compensation does not necessarily lead to a substantial improvement in benefit

107. D.T. Llewellyn and P. Newbold, 'The Behaviour of Unemployment and Unfilled Vacancies', *Industrial Relations Journal*, 4, 1973.

108. There are no detailed statistics of the age of people made redundant before redundancies became notifiable after the 1965 Act. The best available source of detailed statistical information about officially notifiable redundancies in relation to age is a 10 per cent sample taken by the Department of Employment of all redundancies in the year 1975/76. See *Gazette*, September 1978. Daniel's national survey of the unemployed in October 1973 found that redundancy played a larger part in the unemployment of older age groups than people in their twenties. W.W. Daniel, *A National Survey of the Unemployed*, Political and Economic Planning, 1974.

109. MacKay and Reid, *Economic Journal* (1972), loc. cit., failed to find any significant relationship between the length of unemployment and the size of redundancy payments. This raises the interesting point as to whether duration of unemployment could not be reduced on aggregate by a greater emphasis on the lump-sum unconditional element in unemployment compensation. See D.S. Hameresh, 'A Note on Income and Substitution Effects in Search Unemployment', *Economic Journal*, 87, June 1977.

A report by the Social Survey division of the Office of Population Censuses and Surveys (*Effects of the Redundancy Payments Act*, HMSO 1971), noted that those persons who received redundancy payments did not appear more selective in obtaining new jobs nor did they remain longer on the unemployment register than other unemployed persons. Similar conclusions emerged from a detailed study of redundant workers in Woolwich. See W.W. Daniel, *Whatever Happened to the Workers in Woolwich? A Survey of Redundancy in S.E. London*, London, PEP 1972. Perhaps it is not altogether surprising that the effects of a fixed capital sum on the job-search activity of the unemployed seem somewhat different to the alleged effects of the continuing cash flow benefits from unemployment pay, tax rebates, and social security payments.

income relative to past earnings. There are wide variations in the spending power of the unemployed depending on their family composition, their previous income,[110] and on when and for how long they are out of work. Only a small proportion of unemployed claimants have been found on investigation to be drawing income greater than they might reasonably be expected to obtain in work.[111] Nor should the power of the work ethic in Britain be ignored. Daniel, surveying the disincentive effects of out-of-work payments on the unemployed, writes that 'the overwhelming weight of evidence pointed to the conclusion that it was the physical, social and psychological characteristics of workers: their age, stage in the life cycle, number of dependants, strength, state of health, and level in society when working, that determined how keen they were to work, and that the level of social benefits played a very small part in the overall picture'.[112] If the income effect of changes in permanent income are taken into account increases in unemployment benefits appear to have a negligible effect on the level of unemployment.[113] An increase in recorded unemployment from 1966 as the result of a response by individuals to a general easing of financial pressure, does not accord either with the wide variation in the regional and industrial shift of the U/V curve that seems to have occurred. Differences in regional and sectoral labour demand may, in reality, have proved to be more determinant influences on job-search behaviour.[114]

110. This is not to deny that for certain individuals there could be a positive connection between the level of benefit income and the minimum earnings sought from fresh employment (varying with previous earnings) which could affect duration of unemployment.
111. Department of Employment, 'Characteristics of the Unemployed: Sample Survey June 1973', *Gazette,* March 1974; D. Donnison, Chairman Supplementary Benefits Commission, 'The Poverty Trap', lecture delivered at North London Polytechnic, 7 December 1976, cited in F. Field (ed.), *The Conscript Army,* London 1977, p. 41.
112. W. Daniel, (PEP 1974), op. cit., p. 151.
113. Cubbin and Foley, loc. cit.
114. J.I. Foster, 'The Behaviour of Unemployment and Unfilled Vacancies: Great Britain, 1958-1971—A Comment', *Economic Journal,* 83, March 1973. Cf. Cheshire's conclusion that if the new benefits made a difference 'they did not do so all at once, but over a period of years; also they operated either at rather different rates in different regions, or to the accompaniment of influences peculiar to particular regions that in varying degrees masked or accentuated their effects'. P.C. Cheshire, 'Regional Unemployment Differences in Great Britain', in NIESR, *Regional Papers II,* Cambridge 1973.

There are good reasons to doubt, therefore, whether recent changes in unemployment compensation have made the proportion of those actually better off when out of work than in work large enough to make a substantial difference to the published figures. Most contrary arguments are based on 'representative' case studies—normally a married couple with two children where the wife does not work—which often bear little relation to the actual situation and income receipts of the vast majority of the unemployed. By late 1977, for example, only one in six of those out of work was receiving ERS and fewer than half were in receipt of basic national insurance benefit.[115] Moreover, the replacement ratio (as defined above) tends to fall with the duration of unemployment and more so when families fail to claim the statutory benefits available to them.

A more fundamental problem is that cross-section studies among different types of people are basically inadequate as a means of testing the effects over time of the introduction of new benefits. Earnings-related benefit, for example, is not paid for the first six weeks to those who leave their jobs voluntarily, who are sacked for disciplinary reasons, or who are not entitled to such payments because of the regularity of past employment or their previous level of earnings. As Brittan notes: 'The sort of people who receive benefit tend to be those who are in any case more attractive to potential employers and/or keener to find work than those who do not. A cross-section study among *different* types of people cannot show the effects over time of the introduction of new benefits for *comparable* groups of people.'[116] Until more sophisticated and reliable statistical methods are found for measuring the magnitude and direction of insurance-induced unemployment, other than by using aggregate time-series data, it will remain extremely difficult to assess the relative importance of 'supply' factors in affecting measured unemployment rates or even to evaluate the significance of the various explanations advanced in support of such a basic hypothesis. It is, moreover, extremely difficult to isolate supply effects on the volume of unemployment. 'Voluntary' unemployment which appears to arise from the free choice of individuals may be more a reflection of the existence of structural factors which prevent jobs matching the unem-

115. Atkinson and Flemming, loc. cit. In any event the ratio of flat-rate and earnings-related benefits to disposable earnings for a married couple with two children early in 1976 was about the same as it had been in 1967.
116. Brittan, op. cit., p. 59.

ployeds' skills, training, and expected earnings from being available.[117]

One additional and related factor worth considering relates not to the level of social security benefits as such but to the system within which they are administered. The Manpower Services Commission maintains that reorganization of the employment services has benefitted all groups of job-seekers, including those with particular difficulties, and that whatever the period of unemployment, the chance of being submitted for a job are greater for those served by Jobcentres than for those served by old-style employment offices.[118]

Some labour economists, however, maintain that by virtue of the reorganization far fewer people are being denied benefit on the grounds that they are work-shy and that the pressure to maximize the number of placements has made employment advisers reluctant to submit those with doubtful prospects or questionable enthusiasm to prospective employers. Layard, for example, has argued that the division of function between benefit-paying and job-matching has probably been responsible for a fraction of the increase in recorded unemployment since 1973.[119]

Demand Factors

Those who contend that unemployment compensation has had, at most, only a limited impact on the prospective supply of labour emphasize instead the effects of a 'shake-out' of labour from the mid-1960s as employers engaged in extensive dishoarding of labour.[120] Thus as firms laid off previously hoarded workers both unemployment and the degree of utilization of the employed labour force increased.[121]

117. See B. Showler, 'Incentives, Social Security Payments and Unemployment', *Social and Economic Administration,* 9, Summer 1975.
118. Manpower Services Commission, *The Employment Service in the 1980s,* London 1979.
119. R. Layard, 'Have the Jobcentres increased Unemployment?', *The Guardian,* 5 November 1979.
120. This followed the introduction in July 1966 of restrictionist economic measures aimed at 'shaking-out' labour so that it could be redeployed to more essential, especially export-orientated, sectors.
121. J. Taylor, 'The Behaviour of Unemployment and Unfilled Vacancies: Great Britain, 1958–71. An Alternative View', *Economic Journal,* 83, December

The rise in unemployment was not accompanied by the usual fall in vacancies, partly, it is claimed, because the surplus labour thus disgorged was not necessarily that being required to fill vacancies. More specifically, demographic changes in labour supply (notably an abnormal increase in young, inexperienced labour of low productivity) and the effects of redundancy legislation during the late 1960s are claimed to have encouraged among employers 'a polarisation of redundancies towards very young and very old, less efficient employees'.[122] Legislation relating to national insurance and selective employment tax and a general pessimism about British growth potential are likewise thought to have increased the fixed cost to the employer of hoarding labour (by under-utilizing man-hours or retaining more workers than required) relative to the cost of adjusting output via hoarded hours (i.e. utilizing hoarded labour whose working week had been below that which they desired and were prepared to offer). At the same time redundancy legislation is claimed to have reduced the costs of dishoarding workers in those firms where redundancy payment agreements already existed. This was felt to affect in particular older men who, because of their length of service, stood to gain most. Thus not only was total hoarding by firms reduced but also, it is suggested, the proportion of the total for which the firm normally incurred a cost. The effect of these changes was to alter the pattern of labour hoarding in favour of adjusting labour by reducing the numbers employed, thus causing a much greater proportion of the slack in the economy to be reflected in registered unemployment. The shift was, it is maintained, partially offset by an increase in average hours of work by those who remained employed as firms took up the internal slack of under-utilized labour.[123]

1972; A.J. Brown in Worswick (ed.), op. cit., pp. 142–3; J. Taylor, 'Incomes Policy, the Structure of Unemployment and the Phillips Curve: the United Kingdom Experience 1953–70', in M. Parkin and M.T. Sumner, *Incomes Policy and Inflation,* Manchester 1972, pp. 188–9; J.K. Bowers, P.C. Cheshire, A.E. Webb and R. Weedon, 'Some Aspects of Unemployment and the Labour Market, 1966–71', *National Institute Economic Review,* 62, November 1972.

122. J. Foster, 'The relationship between unemployment and vacancies in Great Britain (1958–72): some further evidence', in D. Laidler and D. Purdy (eds.), *Inflation and Labour Markets,* Manchester 1974.

123. K.G. Knight and R.A. Wilson, 'Labour Hoarding, Employment and Unemployment in British Manufacturing Industry', *Applied Economics,* 6, 1974; K. Holden and D.A. Peel, 'The Determinants of Unemployment and the

There is evidence to suggest that there was a decline in labour hoarding during the 1971-2 recession and no more hoarding during the 1972-3 upswing than in the past, resulting in less hoarding over the trade cycle and more marked cyclical swings in registered unemployment for a given amplitude of fluctuation in output.[124] The emphasis on an alleged 'shake-out' of labour, moreover, adds weight to the claim referred to earlier that labour hoarding is in reality an important component of the excess supply of labour and must be added to registered unemployment if changes in pressure of demand in the labour market are to be adequately measured. To this extent a shift in the U/V curve outwards (a rise in unemployment relative to vacancies) would result in a rise in the proportion of measured unemployment to 'true' unemployment, since part of the change would result from shifts between surplus labour (fall) and measured unemployment (rise).[125]

The influence of demand could, of course, work in the opposite direction, suggesting a possible 'shake-in' of labour. Both the fall in manufacturing output and the reduction in man-hours worked were stronger during the 1974-5 downturn than in previous cycles. Employers may have been reluctant to make skilled workers redundant. At the same time the rise in the level of statutory redundancy payments and the fact that longer-serving employees tend to comprise an increasing proportion of those made redundant as a recession deepens may have deterred a bigger shake-out of labour. There is as yet insufficient evidence to determine in which direction employers are likely to move in response to labour market fluctuations. As far as the period

---

"UV" Relationship', *Applied Economics,* 7, 1975; Holden and Peel, 'The 'Shake-out' Hypothesis: A Note', *Oxford Bulletin of Economics and Statistics,* 38, 1976; R.A. Sleeper, 'Manpower Redeployment and the Selective Employment Tax', *Bulletin of the Oxford Institute of Economics and Statistics,* 32, 1970.

A fall in labour hoarding could be as comparable with a supply shift as a demand shift for labour. Employers may have chosen to run down their labour stocks or have been unable to obtain the labour they needed as a result of increased voluntary quits. To the extent that dis-hoarding was involuntary, one would not expect unfilled vacancies to have fallen in line with the rise in unemployment. Bowers, in Worswick (ed.), op. cit., p. 113.

124. S. Brittan, 'Full Employment Policy: A Reappraisal', in ibid., pp. 256-7.
125. Llewellyn and Newbold, loc. cit., pp. 34-5.

from the mid-1960s to the early 1970s is concerned the OECD concluded in 1973 that:

On balance it would seem that the dominating factors behind the change in unemployment behaviour lie with the demand for labour. The change may have reflected some combination of lack of confidence in future output prospects, rapid rates of wage increase and a stronger reaction than in the past to fluctuations in output ... while less resistance to redundancies because of redundancy payments and improved unemployment benefits and easier recruitment prospects suggested by the large pool of unemployed labour suggested smaller-than-usual costs of shedding labour.[126]

The situation has been complicated in recent years by the operation of a number of special government measures designed to counteract the effects of industrial recession. It is reasonable to assume that the array of tax-financed job creation schemes, employment subsidies, and employment protection laws introduced at various intervals since the mid-1970s have brought about short-term decreases in the aggregate unemployment register and made the overall situation look better than it would otherwise have been. The available evidence is not sufficiently conclusive, however, for us to determine precisely the degree to which the recorded unemployment rate would have been different in the absence of such measures. It is not clear how far management has been inhibited by employment protection legislation from taking on new labour where they otherwise would have done so. Nor is it altogether certain how far employment subsidies, by reducing the relative costs and prices of firms receiving them, have reduced consumption of the goods of non-subsidized firms and increased unemployment within them. The total number of persons assisted by the various schemes of subsidizing and creating jobs does not necessarily represent the number kept off the unemployment register. Some people on the schemes would not previously have registered themselves as unemployed. The new initiatives have probably had only a limited influence on the overall demand for labour, tending to delay unemployment rather than prevent it altogether.

The preponderant bias towards demand or supply explanations of the changing relationship between unemployment and vacancies during

126. OECD, *Economic Surveys, United Kingdom*, February 1973, p. 27.

the period 1966-71 in particular, has obscured other plausible methods of investigating labour market activity. Only recently has the relationship between female vacancies and unemployment been investigated.[127] It appears, for example, that female unemployment did not rise relative to vacancies in 1966 and 1967 and that there was an unnoticed downward shift in the female U/V relationship between 1961 and 1966.[128]

The dominant factor influencing the U/V curve for both sexes between 1966 and 1971 may have been a change in the proportion of the unemployed registering. Thus the inward shift of the female U/V curve between 1961 and 1966 could have resulted from a fall in the proportion of unemployed females registering as unemployed, many of whom, having opted out of the national insurance scheme, would have had less incentive to register when unemployed than would males. Though both the total and the male U/V curve moved outwards during the period 1966-8 the female curve either did not shift or shifted slightly inwards. This explanation is neither a 'demand side' one (that more have been made unemployed) nor a 'supply side' one (that more want to remain unemployed for longer periods) but merely one that argues that 'the changes in benefits have caused more men who have become unemployed to register as unemployed'.[129]

It may be, therefore, that while the 'true' U/V relationship has not really changed the measurement of it has.[130] By contrast, the significant rise in the proportion of the total registered unemployed accounted for by women since 1974 must bring into sharper focus all those influences, autonomous or otherwise, which affect female activity rates and the propensity to register.[131]

'Demand and supply' explanations of the post-1966 unemployment situation are based on assumptions about the relationship between unemployment and vacancies which may themselves be suspect. The labour demand thesis, for example, implicitly assumes that there were no structural shifts in the economy in the chosen periods and that the

127. This will be impossible to repeat in the future since from 1 January 1976 it has been illegal, in most cases, to discriminate between the sexes in advertising vacancies.
128. A. Evans, 'Notes on the Changing Relationship between Registered Unemployment and Notified Vacancies: 1961–66 and 1966–71', *Economica*, 44, May 1977.
129. ibid., p. 193.
130. Llewellyn and Newbold, loc. cit., pp. 37–8.
131. Cf. comments on registration patterns above pp. 91–2.

specification of the U/V relationship was correct. Recent evidence suggests that the true movement of the U/V curve during 1969 to 1973 was obscured by the influence of a structural shift in employment— a fall in manufacturing employment during the period 1969–73 matched from 1971 by a rise in non-manufacturing employment.[132]

Analyses of the relationship between aggregate levels of unemployment and vacancies depend a great deal on the assumption that the 'U/V' relationship is a meaningful concept, especially in view of the extent to which the understatement of the true demand for labour seems greater for vacancies than for unemployment. It cannot be assumed that the effects of a change in the ratio would be the same irrespective of whether it resulted from a change in V or an opposite change in U. A given change caused by a change in V is likely to reflect a more substantial shift in employment conditions than the *same* change in the ratio caused by a change in U.[133] Hughes has indicated how calculations of structural and frictional unemployment (U_s and U_f) can be biased by virtue of unrecorded unemployment and the non-notification and duplication of vacancies. The effects of the official data on estimates of U_s and U_f have been summarized as shown in Table 15.[134]

TABLE 15
THE EFFECT OF UNRECORDED UNEMPLOYMENT, NON-NOTIFICATION AND DUPLICATION OF VACANCIES ON THE MEASURES U_s AND U_f

	Effect of Unrecorded Unemployment		Effect of non-notification of vacancies		Effect of duplication of vacancies	
	U_s	U_f	U_s	U_f	U_s	U_f
Slack labour market ($U_t > V_t$)	Over-estimate	Under-estimate	Under-estimate	Under-estimate	Over-estimate	Over-estimate
Tight labour market ($V_t > U_t$)	Under-estimate	Under-estimate	Over-estimate	Under-estimate	Under-estimate	Over-estimate

132. Bowers in Worswick (ed.), loc. cit., pp. 118–29.
133. MacKay, (1971), op. cit., p. 100.
134. Hughes, (1974), loc. cit., p. 28.

The two variables, U and V are in essence measures of the same phenomenon—the vacancy rate does not determine the unemployment rate. Both are endogenously determined and it is questionable how far any expected general relationship between the two can be an important explanatory variable of general economic change. There need be no presumption of a fixed association between the two variables over time. Evidence of a 'mismatch' between unemployment and vacancies at any time or for the degree of such a mismatch to change over time as demand for labour fluctuates tells us very little. The duration of vacancies appears to vary inversely with changes in the level of unemployment: falling unemployment tends to lengthen the duration of vacancies and contribute to a rise in the level of vacancies. Each variable moreover is subject to specification errors over different phases of the trade cycle. There are still differing opinions as to whether an equilibrium relationship actually exists between unemployment and unfilled vacancies on which any meaningful discussion of a shift in the U/V curve can be based.[135]

Clearly the evidence of the recent past casts serious doubt upon the reliability of unemployment statistics as a labour market indicator. What is less certain, however, is the relative importance one should attach to the plethora of available explanations. Bowers noted in 1970 that given 'the similarity of their expected consequences, and the virtual similarity of their appearance, an eclectic position is the only one at present tenable'.[136] There seems little reason to disagree with him in this respect and every reason to concur with his view that the real problem lies not with faulty data but with faulty labour market models.[137]

135. In this context see Holden and Peel (1975), loc. cit.; A. Parikh, 'The Relationship between Unemployment and Vacancies: a Comment', *Applied Economics*, 9, 1977, pp. 77–8; R.S. Warren, 'The Behaviour of Unemployment and unfilled Vacancies in Great Britain: a Search-turnover View', loc. cit.; R.A. Bewley, 'The Dynamic Behaviour of Unemployment and Unfilled Vacancies in Great Britain: 1958–1971', *Applied Economics*, 11, 1979.
136. Bowers, *et. al.*, (1970), loc. cit., p. 60.
137. Bowers, in *Labour Statistics*, op. cit., p. 118.

4

Census and Survey Data

Official Surveys of the Unemployed

(a) Pre-1914

Several attempts were made before the First World War to supplement the regular if partial material available on unemployment. Some merely provided detailed case studies of particular aspects of the problem, often during a critical phase of the trade cycle, while others sought to calculate the extent of unemployment on a very much wider basis than usual or to relate it to other variables.[1] Dr. William Ogle, the Registrar-General's Superintendent of Statistics, attempted to count the unemployed in certain selected districts of London in 1887.[2] It proved impossible, however, to attach any definite meaning to the vague and inaccurate statements made by the workmen, many of whom connected the survey with the prospect of public relief. Ogle himself concluded that the returns were 'of very small statistical value'. Neither the pioneering work of Charles Booth on the condition of the poor in London[3] nor a proposal from W.T. Stead and H.C. Burdett in 1895 to conduct a house-to-house inquiry into the social and industrial condition of the people of London convinced government statisticians that the results of such inquiries warranted an

---

1. The study by Bowley in 1912 has already been referred to. See p. 27.
2. *Tabulation of the Statements Made by Men Living in Certain Districts of London in March 1887*, C. 5228, 1887. The word 'unemployed' was added to the occupational description of persons ordinarily engaged in some industry but out of work at the time of the 1871 and 1881 Census but no reference to unemployment was made in any subsequent Census until 1931. See below pp. 130–8, 152–61.
3. C. Booth, *Life and Labour of the People of London*, London 2 vols, 1889 and 17 vols, 1903.

116

official 'census of the unemployed'. 'It is doubtful if the State could undertake with propriety to assess the value of the impressions left on the minds of a number of persons by certain facts, and make a statistical record of these impressions', wrote Llewellyn Smith in 1895, 'Government statistics as a rule must be records of facts or statements derived first-hand, and resting on a perfectly definite and tangible basis . . . and it is partly because in the case of the unemployed such a basis is quite untrustworthy, that a census in the true sense is not possible'.[4]

It was because the 'factual' basis of Edwardian unemployment data was itself limited to inquiries of particular groups of people, such as trade union members, Labour Exchange registrants, and applicants to distress committees, who were not necessarily typical of the whole class, that more general investigations were sometimes undertaken of those out of work. Rowntree and Lasker, for example, attempted to quantify for the first time the extent of unemployment over the entire city of York on 7 June 1910. Their investigators 'called on every working-class house in York, and ascertained whether any person residing there was out of work, and desirous of finding it . . . whether the unemployed person was male or female, and the occupation which he or she was seeking'.[5] The results obtained were of limited value since they referred only to individuals unemployed on one day of the year. They could not reveal, therefore, the total number of those who suffered from unemployment or under-employment even in 1910.

Periods of exceptional distress and industrial dislocation occasionally prompted the government to examine the available evidence of the state of employment in greater detail and to undertake fresh inquiries where statistics were lacking. In October 1908 Churchill presented the Cabinet with a detailed report on unemployment and short-time working in the United Kingdom based upon confidential information from employers, returns from local correspondents of the Labour Department (which included estimates of the proportion of non-

---

4. PRO, Cab. 37/38, 'The Unemployed', 23 January 1895.
5. S. Rowntree and B. Lasker, *Unemployment. A Social Study*, London 1911, p. x. The working definition of unemployment adopted in the survey was as follows: 'A person is unemployed who is seeking work for wages, but unable to find any suited to his capacities and under conditions which are reasonable, judged by local standards', ibid., p. xii. As such it excluded those at school, the temporarily sick, and those persons mentally deficient or chronically ill or infirm.

unionists out of work), and the reports of Distress Committees and relief agencies such as the Salvation Army and the Church Army.[6] A month later the Local Government Board reported on the state of pauperism and unemployment in each of its fourteen districts in England and Wales during September 1907–October 1908.[7]

A general impression of the effect of the outbreak of war on employment after 1914 can be obtained from special reports compiled by the Board of Trade. They were based on returns received from industrial firms employing over 4 million people (representing about 43 per cent of the industrial population) providing details, among other things, of the total number of males and females estimated to be employed in each group of trades according to the Census of 1911 and the proportion of workpeople who had left their employment since the outbreak of war. In the case of males extra information was obtained of the percentage of those employed in July 1914 who were known to have joined the military or naval forces and the extent to which there had been a net displacement of workpeople over and above those who had joined the forces.[8] The 'net displacment' figure for any trade was not, however, necessarily the same as the proportion of people actually unemployed. The figure merely indicated the per-centage of workers who had been displaced from a particular trade and it could differ considerably from the unemployment figures. The majority of those so displaced were likely to obtain other employment easily while there would be a certain number of persons who would enlist after losing their job unknown to their employers and who would not therefore be returned as having joined the forces.

None of the individual efforts to widen the scope of enquiry into the problem of unemployment produced such radically new methods

6. PRO, Cab. 37/95, 'Report on Unemployment in the United Kingdom in September 1908', 10 October 1908. The following industries were included in the survey: building, coalmining, iron and steel, engineering, shipbuilding, shipping and docks, transport, cotton, other textiles, hosiery and lace, boot and shoe, furniture, minor metals, printing, glass, chemicals, pottery, food and drink, fishing. A special account was also given of unemployment among women workers in London.

7. PRO, Cab. 37/96, 'Pauperism and Unemployment', 3 November 1908.

8. *Report of the Board of Trade on the State of Employment in the United Kingdom in October, 1914*, Cd. 7703, 1914; ibid. etc. . . *in December, 1914*, Cd. 7755, 1915; ibid. etc. . . *in February, 1915*. Cd. 7850, 1916. See also A.L. Bowley, *The War and Employment*, Oxford Pamphlets 1914–1915.

of analysis or results of sufficiently general application to overcome the deficiencies in the official returns. In 1895 Charles Booth suggested to the *Select Committee on Distress from Want of Employment* that an indication of unemployment trends could be got from 'a combination of statistics, such as those relating to revenue and traffic, banking and pauperism'[9] but no such exercise was undertaken. Wood made a pioneering attempt in 1899 to relate the level of unemployment to the consumption of basic commodities[10] and in 1907 Beveridge tried to chart the 'pulse of the nation' by correlating figures relating to unemployment and pauperism, interest-rates, marriage, and crime.[11]

(b) Between the Wars

Although the introduction and subsequent expansion of unemployment insurance increased the availability and range of official statistics, especially after 1923, they remained inadequate in many important respects as previous chapters have shown. They were particularly deficient in reflecting the changing composition of the unemployed. Some relevant information of this type emerged, however, from the practice of the Ministry of Labour after 1923 of making special investigations by sample of the personal characteristics, economic state, and insurance record of unemployed persons. It would be ponderous to list the detailed results of each sample here. The information is contained in Appendix I to this chapter and the bracketed figures below refer to the relevant inquiries listed there. The emphasis here is upon the particular approaches adopted in the use of sampling techniques and upon the more important statistical information they provided.

The Ministry conducted its first sample inquiry early in 1923 and confined it to the information contained in every current third claim to unemployment benefit [1]. Later in the year the need was felt for more detailed analysis of the 1¼ million people returned each week as 'insured workpeople unemployed'. It was obviously impracticable to examine and codify each separate case in the detail required. The inquiry proceeded, therefore, on the basis of a 1 per cent sample after ensuring that the cases selected were evenly distributed, and without

9. Q. 10520, 14 June 1895, H. C. (365), IX, 1895.
10. G.H. Wood, 'Some Statistics relating to Working Class Progress since 1860', *Journal of the Royal Statistical Society*, LXII, 1899.
11. W.H. Beveridge, 'The Pulse of the Nation', *Albany Review*, 2, 1907. Cited in Harris, op. cit., p. 372.

bias[12] [2]. Both of the 1923 inquiries related solely to claimants to unemployment benefit and therefore excluded those who, though unemployed, were not for any reason claiming benefit. One should be cautious in drawing from their results conclusions as to the composition of the unemployed population in general.[13] Disqualifications for and exhaustion of benefit varied in their incidence according to age and personal circumstances. Because, for example, females in industry were in general much younger than males in industry the disqualification affecting young persons fell with greater frequency upon females and there was likely to be proportionally more unemployed insured females who did not figure among claimants to benefit than was the case with males.

The most frequently repeated feature of the one per cent sample inquiries represented investigations into the personal circumstances and industrial history of claimants to benefit [2, 4, 7]. The principal statistics obtained analysed claimants according to their age distribution, degrees of employability, physical health and defects, early training, mental state, number of dependants, number on poor law relief, age of entry into insurance, and contribution and benefit record since entry into insurance. By cross-tabulation of the statistical data information previously lacking as to the relation of one set of characteristics to another in the incidence of unemployment was obtained.

Another 1 per cent sample inquiry conducted in 1929 [10], though it provided less comprehensive information than others of its type, examined the number of days of unemployment experienced during each week of the preceding twelve months by claimants aged 18-64. The information it provided enabled the insured claimants to be classified according to the total amount of unemployment experienced during the period of the investigation and to separate the numbers of those unemployed for long periods from those who were out of work for comparatively short stretches of time. Separate figures were obtained

---

12. For a discussion of the statistical difficulties which this task presented see J. Hilton, 'Enquiry by Sample: An Experiment and its Results', *Journal of the Royal Statistical Society*, LXXXVII, July 1924. A discussion of the experience gained in sampling techniques to 1928 is in J. Hilton, 'Some Further Enquiries by Sample', *Journal of the Royal Statistical Society*, XII, 1928.

13. This qualification also applied to most of the sample studies conducted in later years.

on this occasion of persons employed in the coalmining industry.[14] The remaining 1 per cent sample studies carried out in 1930 related specifically to married women claimants to benefit and to an investigation of the extent to which there had been a movement among claimants between the ordinary benefit and transitional benefit classes [12, 14].

Until 1925 the sample inquiries conducted by the Ministry were concerned exclusively with unemployed persons. It was equally important to have corresponding information as to the composition and insurance record of the whole body of insured persons. The first sample inquiry of this sort was made in April 1926 on the basis of 1 in every 218 accounts held by the Ministry, (i.e. records of contributions, age, industry etc.) [6]. From this data details were obtained of the age distribution of all insured persons by industry, the transfer of insured persons from one industry to another, the number who had drawn benefit at some time or other and who had not drawn benefit at all, and the relative number of contributions paid and benefit drawn in various industries. The inquiry enabled the entire insured population to be classified according to the total number of contributions paid and benefit drawn, thus providing a record of the extent and duration of both employment and unemployment. It also furnished data from which could be calculated for the first time the rate of unemployment of men and women according to age, not only among the insured population as a whole but also among those persons engaged in particular industries.[15] Although 'persons insured against unemployment' was not a Census category the results of the inquiry served to some extent as inter-censal data concerning a large section of the occupied population. Two further sample inquiries yielding similar information were concluded in the early 1930s [13, 18].

Although each official sample survey of the unemployed was conducted with a stringent regard to statistical technique and trustworthiness no claim was made that the varied data, so carefully assembled, represented an adequate reflection of either the character or the extent of unemployment. The statistical information contained in each analysis was fairly regarded as an acceptable indication of the particular

14. Similar information was obtained on the basis of a number of 10 per cent samples. See appendix I [3, 5, 8, 9, 11, 15] and from a ½ per cent sample [16].
15. See also the later inquiries relating to the age distribution of the unemployed appendix I to this chapter, [21, 22, 23, 24].

aspect of unemployment under consideration but exact comparisons of the results of most of the sample studies proved virtually impossible because of the differences in the particular type of data collected. For example, the studies made in April 1926 and April 1927 [6, 7] covered only days on which benefit was received, while the two investigations in March and September 1929 [10] included days on which those with current claims to benefit were unemployed, regardless of whether benefit was received. In addition the 1926 and 1927 studies included persons aged 16 and 17 and persons over 64; the two 1929 samples included only persons 18–64. The inclusion of persons of 16 and 17 years of age tended to shorten the average duration of unemployment; the inclusion of those over 64 tended to increase it. Moreover because of the particular statutory provisions in force at the time concerning the duration of extended benefit, the proportion of the total unemployment period covered by the maximum benefit in individual cases, as set forth in the two earlier studies, cannot be compared with that portion of the total period of unemployment under which those in the two 1929 samples were able to receive benefits. In the two earlier studies the proportion of the total period of benefit was restricted by statutory provisions as well as by the actual duration of unemployment. The two 1929 studies referred to the duration of recorded unemployment among those with current claims to benefit.[16]

(c) Since the Second World War

Despite the increased specification of a number of important unemployment series after 1948, regular sample surveys of the characteristics of the unemployed were totally neglected in the official data of the Department of Employment until the 1960s. Once it became more generally recognized, however, that the regular statistics were an inadequate reflection of the state of the labour market sample surveys of the registered out of work were conducted at irregular intervals from 1961, providing information not normally collected in the unemployment count.

Of particular relevance was the failure of the published data to distinguish sufficiently between those who were unemployed mainly as a result of some personal characteristics and those who, because of some special deficiency, could be difficult to place whatever the

---

16. For further details see Mary Gilson, op. cit., p. 177 *passim*.

demand for labour. Much of the discussion of the problem of unemployment in the 1950s and earlier had been based on certain assumptions about the characteristics, experiences, behaviour, and attitudes of the unemployed which had never been tested by frequent empirical research on any large scale.

The regular unemployment statistics available by the early 1960s provided information about the unemployed in terms of their age, the duration of their unemployment, and their occupational and industrial distribution. The sample surveys of the characteristics of the unemployed which became available thereafter introduced fresh information of the prospects of the unemployed securing work. The information was obtained, it is true, from the subjective assessments of local employment staff based on registration records and, where applicable, on knowledge of just those personal characteristics of the registrants that appeared to have some bearing on the duration of unemployment. Details became available, too, of the total amount of unemployment experienced over a given period[17] and of wide variations among the sample unemployed in the prospects of obtaining long-term work and in the attitudes to work. Full details of the range of data supplied by the surveys can be found in Appendix II to this chapter.

The results of the separate surveys are not strictly comparable. There were differences, for example, in the coverage of the 1976 sample compared with that of 1973. Since 1974 unemployed people had been free to register either at careers offices or employment offices and a small number of those aged 18 and over chose the former (only 8 per cent of those aged 18 to 19 and negligible numbers aged over 19). Furthermore, 'temporary registrants' were excluded in 1973 but included in 1976. These were registrants who were expected to get jobs quickly and for whom less information was recorded under the temporary registration procedure; in 1973 they accounted for less than 2 per cent of the unemployed total and in 1976 only about ½ a per cent of the sample. Again in 1973, but not in June 1976, adult students registered for vacation employment were included in the unemployed. A small number, about 1 per cent of the sample, were included in the

---

17. i.e. as distinct from the length of a person's current spell of unemployment as indicated in the official duration series. The Department of Employment's data would measure a current period of unemployment of a worker who had previously been unemployed but had left the register through sickness only from the time the worker re-registered as unemployed after his illness.

1973 data. However, these were seeking short-term work and were excluded from certain analyses in the *Gazette* articles, including those showing prospects of obtaining long-term work.

There are other points to consider when using such survey data apart from details of coverage. Some surveys were drawn up at different times of the year from others and at different levels of prevailing unemployment. (The 1973 and 1976 surveys were both conducted in June, though the previous ones—1961 and 1964—were in different months). The lack of comparability in this respect does not appear, however, to be as great as one might expect since the characteristics of the unemployed have been found not to differ widely over time or at different levels of unemployment. The point is worth elaborating never- theless in connection with the subjective analysis adopted by the Department of Employment in assessing the characteristics of the unemployed. Given the imbalance in the regional distribution of unemployment it is quite conceivable that in a high unemployment region the same persons classified as deficient in some respects could actually obtain work in a region of low unemployment and thereby escape classification. Local officials may be influenced by prevailing conditions and by the general 'character' of the local unemployed in their assessments of suitability for placing.[18] Certainly the Ministry of Labour was aware in the 1960s of the non-uniformity in standards of classification and of the difficulties of applying the classification used in the surveys to some standard level of demand rather than to the regional level of demand. But it does not appear from more careful scrutiny of the data that demand variations distorted the classifications to any very large extent.[19]

But that is not to say that regional levels of demand do not exert some influence on the number of the unemployed judged difficult to place on personal grounds. As Cheshire has pointed out, 'the pro- portion of a region's labour force (thus) identified ... (is) as much a function of the unemployment rate in the region as of the number of less easily employed in the region's labour force as a whole.'[20] What is equally significant is that although surveys of characteristics of the

18. L.C. Hunter, 'Unemployment in a Full Employment Society', *Scottish Journal of Political Economy*, X, 1963.
19. Cheshire, *Regional Unemployment Differences*, op. cit., appendix 'The Ministry of Labour Survey of the Characteristics of the Unemployed'.
20. Cheshire, op. cit., pp. 38, 40.

unemployed reveal variations in the proportions of regional male labour forces judged likely to find difficulty in getting work on personal grounds, the results do not appear to reflect such differences in the quality of regional labour forces as to explain in any determinate way inter-regional variations in total unemployment rates.[21]

As with the regular unemployment statistics (apart from flow statistics) the results of the various surveys relate only to those adults who bother to register as unemployed on a particular day. They do not, therefore, reflect conditions prevailing at different times of the year nor do they indicate the large degree of turnover on the register. Of those who constitute the monthly inflow onto the unemployment register, many remain there for only a short time and include a high proportion of those people submitted to vacancies by the employment service. The sample inquiries, therefore, covered a group of registered workers who were not necessarily the same as those who would be registered over a period of time; over the space of one year for instance the proportion of those who are unemployed for only a short time is higher, relative to the long-term unemployed, than it would be at any particular time, when the longer-term unemployed have a greater chance of being selected than the shorter-term unemployed. Neither the questions asked nor the group of registrants involved were common to the inquiries and until more work is completed on the inter-relationship of the great variety of results obtained they can be of only partial, if nevertheless valuable, use.

An important and independent sample survey of the unemployed was carried out for PEP in autumn 1973 by W. Daniel.[22] A follow-up survey was subsequently conducted in late 1976.[23] The October 1973 survey covered a nationally representative sample of 1479 registered unemployed in a period of relatively low unemployment. The two reports together provide (with the June 1976 DE sample) a useful commentary on the variety of employment and unemployment experiences of people over a three-year period when unemployment rose to a comparatively high level. Although like the DE surveys the samples related only to specific periods, they nevertheless presented an impressive range of information of substantial potential value to students of the

21. Cf. Brown, *Framework of Regional Economics,* op. cit., pp. 226–32.
22. Daniel, *National Survey of the Unemployed,* op. cit.
23. W.W. Daniel and Elizabeth Stilgoe, *Where Are They Now?,* PEP Broadsheet No. 572, October 1977.

dynamics of the labour market. The 1973 inquiry sought to determine for example:

the characteristics of the unemployed, the proportion of those registered who were effectively not in the labour market, the costs that unemployed workers endured both while out of work and when back in jobs, owing to the quality of their new jobs in relation to the ones they had lost; the circumstances under which they had lost their own jobs and the implications that these had for their subsequent experiences; their experience and behaviour while seeking new jobs and the effectiveness of the public employment service in helping them; the factors which influenced the length of time they were out of work and the effect of different types of financial benefit on their job-seeking and job choice; and their attitudes and experiences in relation to engaging in retraining to fit themselves for a new job and to move house to find a new job.[24]

(d) The General Household Survey
In view of the time lag between decennial population Censuses and the need for information not normally included in the official unemployment series, details of an individual's economic activity status (including registered/unregistered unemployed and economically inactive) have become an essential part of the government's General Household Survey (GHS). Following the 1972 report of the working party on unemployment statistics, the GHS itself became officially regarded as a useful means of supplementing the count of the registered unemployed. It was never the intention, of course, that the Survey should replace the register. The GHS is a continuous multi-purpose survey, begun in 1971, covering between 12,000–15,000 private households each year in Great Britain. It is conducted by personal interview but excludes the institutional population (in hotels, boarding houses, hospitals, boarding schools, halls of residence, military barracks, and prisons), estimated to be about 1½ per cent of the economically active population.[25]

The GHS and the Census of population use slightly difference concepts because the former relies on an interview survey and the latter on

24. Daniel, *National Survey,* op. cit., p. 3.
25. So far six surveys have been completed. The data year and date of publication are as follows: 1971 (July 1973), 1972 (June 1975), 1973 (March 1976), 1974 (August 1977), 1975 (February 1978), and 1976 (June 1978). The data is only published for Great Britain as a whole.

self enumeration. In the GHS the unemployed consist of those who, in the week prior to the interview, were looking for work, would have looked for work if they had not been temporarily sick, or were waiting to take up a job they had already obtained. These definitions applied whether or not the person was registered as unemployed.[26] (By indicating which of those persons unemployed according to the survey definition are registered as unemployed and which are not the data can be used to analyse the extent of 'hidden' unemployment).[27] The sampling errors in such small surveys (compared with the Census) are by no means negligible.[28] There may be differences, too, in the accuracy with which respondents answer interview questions compared with the information they might impart in self-completed Census forms. This is especially true of an individual's own assessment of whether he or she is looking for work. The GHS sample is also more likely than is the official series to understate the proportion of the registered unemployed aged 55 and over. In so far as it is aimed at those persons out of work and seeking work but unregistered it will tend to omit those workers aged 55-64 who are registered as unemployed but are not actively seeking employment.

Overall unemployment rates based on the GHS naturally differ from those of the Department of Employment. The latter are based on the total number of employees available to take up work, and exclude the self-employed and the temporarily sick[29] but include those who are registered and who would describe themselves in a survey as economically inactive. GHS figures are based on the whole labour force, including the self-employed and the unregistered unemployed, but exclude the economically inactive, even though registered. A comparison of the two sets of data is given in Table 16. The National Institute of Economic and Social Research has estimated that had data been collected on a household survey basis the published unemployment rate for all

---

26. The 1971 GHS inquiry was restricted to those who were actually looking for work.
27. See above, pp. 86-92.
28. See R. Barnes, 'Estimating the Characteristics of Non-Respondents in the General Household Survey', *Statistical News*, 30, August 1975.
29. The inflation of the GHS data by the inclusion of the temporarily sick may have been offset to some extent by the fact that some persons experiencing short spells of sickness may also have been registered at an Employment Exchange and included in its figures.

TABLE 16
MALE UNEMPLOYMENT RATES, 1971–76 (GREAT BRITAIN)

	1971	1972	1973	1974	1975	1976
	%	%	%	%	%	%
GHS data	4.0	4.7	3.5	2.8	4.0	5.4
D/E data	4.6	5.0	3.5	3.6	5.4	7.1

workers between 1960–70 would have been about 50 per cent higher each year.[30]

The other principal source of information on unemployment collected in the GHS relates to the time spent out of work. Since 1973 respondents have been asked to state how long they had been unemployed but wanting work (less than a week, 1 week but less than 1 month, 1 month but less than 3 months, 3 months but less than 6 months, 6 months but less than 1 year, 1 year or more). Apart from such periods, information was sought from 1974 as to whether during the previous twelve months individuals had been looking for work or waiting to take up a job they had already obtained as well as the number of times over the year they had been unemployed but wanting work. The results of these inquiries are not published in the GHS annual report but are available in tabulations held by the Social Survey Division of the Office of Population Censuses and Surveys.

Despite the intrinsic usefulness of using household surveys to obtain data not normally available from official sources (on unregistered marginal workers, for example), they present particular problems of their own. They do not necessarily relate to the total number of persons who are prepared to take up paid employment. The conditions and terms under which job search would be undertaken by the unregistered unemployed are many and varied. The mere counting of heads would not indicate the extent to which the offers of secondary workers were alternatives to the employment of primary workers.[31] Moreover, such

---

30. 'Notes on Statistics of Manpower Costs and Unemployment in Major Industrial Countries', *National Institute Economic Review,* May 1971, p. 67.
31. J.K. Bowers, 'Unemployment Statistics 1966–70: A Note', *British Journal of Industrial Relations,* XI, July 1973. See above, pp. 80–6.

surveys are subject to considerable sampling errors and though they throw some light on the operation of the labour market they do not provide an adequate coverage of it, especially at local area level.

Since 1973 Great Britain has participated in the EEC Labour Force Survey. A biennial sample survey of 80,000 private households (i.e. excluding institutions) has been conducted to determine the various characteristics of the unemployed—defined generally as all persons declaring themselves to be unemployed and seeking a paid job. This includes the temporarily stopped but excludes students. The data available classify persons by sex, whether seeking employment, the method and duration of job search, including whether registered at an official employment exchange and the cause of unemployment and its percentage distribution by age group.[32]

The Labour Force Survey adopts international definitions for the purpose of analysis which are felt most likely to provide results comparable between countries. The many intractable problems associated with the international comparison of unemployment data need not be discussed here.[33] What is clear is that the Survey results do not always agree with data assembled in accordance with national definitions. Unemployed persons according to the Community Survey definition include persons having worked as employees and no longer having a contract of employment, persons having worked as self-employed or family workers and seeking a paid job, persons never having worked and seeking their first paid job, persons having interrupted their careers for a period of over one year and seeking a paid job, and persons laid off either temporarily or for an indefinite period without pay. Those excluded include persons who declare themselves as unemployed but are not seeking employment or proposing to work as self-employed, persons normally having a job but not working during the reference week for any particular reason (partially unemployed), non-active persons (housewives, students) who declare themselves as seeking a job, and persons having a principal occupation and seeking another job.

32. Statistical Office of the European Communities, *Labour Force Sample Survey 1975*, 1976, *Labour Force Sample Survey, 1977*, 1979.
33. For a recent discussion of some of the problems involved see Organisation for Economic Co-operation and Development, *Measuring Employment and Unemployment*, Paris 1979.

The Census of Population

It was only in 1931 that statistical returns of the unemployed were separately identified in the Census for England and Wales and for Scotland. Nevertheless the 'unemployed' have been included explicitly and implicitly in the returns since 1841, subsumed in the data of the total working population. From 1881 inmates of workhouses over the age of 60 and patients in lunatic asylums who were unlikely to return to their former occupations were excluded from the count of the working population; but paupers under 60 were coded to their former occupations before and after 1881 and are likely to have included many of the unemployed. The unemployed over 60 not in the work-house were equally coded to their former occupations. All the unemployed, therefore, except those over 60 in the workhouse were included in the returns of employment after 1881.[34] In 1871 and again in 1881 the word 'unemployed' was added to the occupational descriptions of persons ordinarily engaged in some industry but out of work on 3 April but no separate statistics were made available in this respect.

The format of the Census schedule was common to each decennial Census between 1921-51.[35] Persons out of work could, therefore, have been included in or excluded from occupation and industry tabulations. The out of work were included in data relating to the total occupied population in the 1921 Census but were not separately enumerated. The impact of economic depression and the existence of heavy structural unemployment, however, led to a direct effort in 1931 to identify the scale of the problem by the Census method, despite the fact that this was not the most appropriate approach to adopt. Unemployment varied according to the time of year and between occupations: a snap picture taken on a particular day in April could be quite unrepresentative of conditions during the year as a whole and of the normal incidence of unemployment among the various occupations listed. Moreover the general concept of unemployment was sufficiently ambiguous to make it difficult to frame a question on such a subject in a way that would ensure a uniform reply. Certain degrees of unemployment, like partial or temporary unemployment, could not be con-

34. Buxton and MacKay, op. cit., chapter 1. For a general discussion of the practices and problems of the population Census see B. Benjamin, *The Population Census,* London 1970.
35. No Census was taken in 1941.

sidered in the same category as the chronically and unavoidably 'out of work'. One of the inherent difficulties in collecting data by means of the household schedule was that of gauging the reliability of the respondents' answers to questions and this was particularly so in the context of whether or not they regarded themselves as unemployed.

The direct question adopted in 1931 to which a positive reply was expected in respect of every person aged 14 or over who was following or had previously followed some occupation or calling for profit was as follows:

State occupation or calling followed. If out of work or wholly retired add "Out of Work" or "Retired" as the case may be after the statement of occupation.

The following instructions were added:

Subject to the special cases mentioned below, the usual occupation should be stated. A person does not cease to have an occupation solely because he is for the time being unemployed. A carpenter remains a carpenter, even though he is temporarily out of work ... but cases may occur where a man has not been employed at his original occupation for a very long time. The question is—what is the occupation by which he is seeking to earn a livelihood. If he is still seeking a living at his original occupation, he should enter that occupation (adding "out of work") even if he has been for a long time unemployed at it. If, on the other hand, he has no prospect of making a living by that occupation and is getting and relying upon some other work for his means of livelihood, he should state the occupation by which he at present is getting a livelihood. But if a man has done no paid work of any kind since he ceased to be employed at his original occupation he should in any case state that occupation adding "out of work" if still seeking to earn a living, or "retired" if no longer seeking to work for a living.[36]

The separate identification of the unemployed was repeated in 1951 with the schedule question directed to those out of work but seeking work (including young persons over 15 who had never had a job) on the appointed day. Unemployment data were published in advance of the full Census reports as a result of the decision in 1951 to institute for the first time a 1 per cent sample inquiry of the entire Census

36. Census of England and Wales 1931, General Report, London 1930, p. 156. The fact that the unemployed were separately tabulated meant that the basic Industry and Occupation Tables were not strictly comparable with those of the 1921 Census.

records of Great Britain. Though this produced information far more quickly than ever before the sample was so small that the reliability of the results are open to serious doubt.

The emphasis in the 1961 Census was on counting the 'economically active' of which those out of work were a part. Two significant differences of enumeration were adopted. First, the Census questions on industry or occupation were addressed only to a 10 per cent sample. Second, the unemployment question was to be completed by those aged 15 and over who at the end of the week before the Census were not in employment but intending to get work, including those unemployed during the whole week before the Census or ceasing to be employed during the week, distinguishing those who were sick from others. No such time reference had been adopted before. Those holding a job but temporarily absent from it 'because of holidays, sickness, strikes, etc. . .' were counted as in employment if their jobs were being kept open for them.

Estimates of the unemployed in the 1966 Census were derived entirely from a 10 per cent sample enquiry.[37] They related to those out of work during the week preceding the Census date 28 April[38] (distinguishing those registered and those unregistered) and those not in employment on Monday, 18 April. In the latter case a distinction was made between the registered (temporarily sick, others) and the unregistered (temporarily sick, others), the main purpose of which was to reconcile the Census returns with the Ministry's unemployment figures which related to a Monday.[39] Further information was sought

37. The holding of a Census in 1966 broke the traditional ten yearly cycle although the Census Act of 1920 permitted a Census to be held every five years subject to Parliament's approval. In 1951 the 1% sample related to the completed tabulations of every householder. In 1961 only 10% of all households were involved in the statistical exercise.

38. People holding a job but absent from it because of holidays, sickness, or industrial disputes were again regarded as being employed.

39. A quality check on a selection of the 1966 Census returns has cast doubt on whether this particular exercise achieved its purpose in view of the confusion among respondents in answering the relevant question, the errors of the General Register Office in assigning individuals to particular categories, and the dubious distinction made between those unable to seek work because of temporary sickness and others. See P. Gray and F.A. Gee, *A Quality Check on the 1966 Ten Per cent Sample Census of England and Wales,* Office of Population Censuses and Surveys, Social Survey Division, London 1972, Part IV. In any event it was too much to hope that the Census would produce results sufficiently accurate to permit a full reconciliation with Ministry of Labour estimates of the unemployed labour force.

from those out of work for the whole of the preceding year. Also included in the count were those who, though not at work, had found a job and were waiting to start work after the Census day.

Persons classified as 'out of employment' in the 1971 Census (in both the 100 per cent and 10 per cent returns) comprised all those who throughout the week ended 24 April were out of work but seeking work or waiting to take up a job already obtained and those who were out of work throughout the week but prevented by temporary sickness or injury from seeking work.

For various reasons the Census figures of persons returned as unemployed have never been regarded as strictly comparable with the unemployment statistics published by the Department of Employment and its precedessors because they were compiled on a different conceptual basis. When Census estimates of the unemployed became available in 1931 the official unemployment series referred to persons registered at the Employment Exchanges as unemployed whether in receipt of unemployment benefit or not. The Census figures related to persons returned as 'out of work' and included a number who, although unemployed, were not registered at an Employment Exchange, and therefore excluded from the Ministry of Labour statistics. These were mainly persons outside the State scheme of unemployment insurance. On the other hand the Ministry's statistics, which included persons temporarily unemployed as well as those wholly unemployed, embraced a certain number not shown in the Census figures as 'out of work'. Although there were references in the Census instructions to a person being 'temporarily out of work' and 'out of work at the time' the effect appears to have been that persons who were only temporarily suspended at the end of April 1931, but expected to return to work with the same employer, did not record themselves as out of work. Moreover some persons may have been reluctant to state that they were out of work, e.g. females engaged in domestic duties pending re-employment in their own particular occupation, while other elderly persons willing to accept work if offered may have included themselves in the Census returns as 'retired' rather than 'out of work' because of the absence of any reasonable prospect of future employment.[40]

By combining Census and unemployment insurance returns Feinstein has shown that both sets of data were inadequate in their raw state as indicators of the full extent of unemployment, Table 17 overleaf.

---

40. Feinstein, op. cit., p. 220.

TABLE 17
COMPARISON OF CENSUS OF POPULATION AND UNEMPLOYMENT INSURANCE STATISTICS OF UNEMPLOYMENT IN GREAT BRITAIN, 26-27 APRIL 1931*

(Thousands)

	Census of Population		Unemployment Insurance[a]		Deficiency	
	All ages (1)	Aged 16-64 (2)	Wholly unemployed[b] (3)	Total[b] (4)	Census (4)-(2) (5)	U.I. (2)-(4) (6)
A. Industries with deficiency in Census data						
Coal mining	218.9	205.8	182.1	279.3	73.5	
Other mining and quarrying	18.6	17.1	17.4	22.4	5.3	
Manufacturing	1,098.6	1,032.0	966.7	1,381.4	349.4	
Building and contracting	204.6	185.8	206.7	214.9	29.1	
Shipping, docks, canals etc.	84.5	79.3	104.3[c]	106.0[c]	26.7	
Distributive trades	217.2	202.0	194.3	203.7	1.7	
Central Government and defence	10.5	9.9	10.9	11.4	1.5	
Catering, hotels etc.	62.7	60.1	62.6	64.0	7.6[d]	3.7[d]
Laundries, dry cleaning etc.	11.7	10.9	11.8	13.4	2.9[d]	0.4[d]
B. Industries with deficiency in Unemployment Insurance data						
Agriculture and forestry	64.6	51.7		5.4		51.7
Fishing	10.0	9.2	5.3			3.8

Railways, road transport, Post

Office etc.	79.6	75.2	60.2	63.5	11.7
Insurance, banking and finance	18.2	17.0	11.8	12.0	5.0
Local government	86.1	79.6	39.9	41.5	38.1
Professions	30.1	28.5	6.7	6.9	21.6
Entertainment and sport	34.1	32.3	17.4	18.0	14.3
Private domestic service	116.7	105.9			105.9
Other miscellaneous services	13.7	13.0	43.8	46.0	71.9
Industry not stated	123.9	104.9			
Adjustment				1.9	1.9
TOTAL	2,524.7	2,339.3	1,955.9c	2,504.5c	499.6	334.4

* Adapted from Feinstein, op. cit., p. 219. A separate estimate by Colin Clark puts the full extent of unemployment in 1931, combining Census and unemployment insurance returns, at 3,289,000. C. Clark, *The Conditions of Economic Progress*, London 1951, pp. 30–1. Cf. E. Brew, 'The "Out of Work" Enquiry of 1931', *Manchester School*, X, 1939. For a discussion of the relative rates of unemployment among the insured and the workforce as a whole see pp. 58–61.

a. Persons aged 16–64 insured under the Unemployment Insurance Acts and recorded as unemployed.

b. Separate figures for wholly unemployed (including casual workers) and temporarily stopped are not given for Great Britain and in each industry the wholly unemployed are assumed to represent the same proportion of the total as in Great Britain and Northern Ireland.

c. Excluding 11.0 dockers. The reduction is made to allow for the fact that prior to 1932 certain classes of dock workers were counted as unemployed if they were out of work on any of three consecutive days, rather than one day only. See above pp. 43–4.

d. The amount shown in column (6) and included in column (5) is an adjustment made to allow for the fact that certain workers in these industries were excluded from the unemployment insurance scheme.

Comparisons between Census returns and the Department of Employment series in more recent years are complicated by the adoption of different definitions as to who are the 'unemployed'. The 1971 Census showed striking discrepancies between the registered figures of unemployment and those who said they were unemployed on their Census forms. The published Census figures showed 1,365,775 people out of work in the week before the Census. Registered unemployment in April 1971, when the Census was taken, stood at 773,800. The major area of discrepancy related to the figures for women.[41] In the Census persons who believe themselves to be capable of work, without seriously seeking work or being capable of regular work, could nevertheless describe themselves as being out of work. Census figures are more subjective than are registration figures and now normally refer to a reference period rather than to a specific date. The population Censuses taken in April 1966 and April 1971 counted the number of persons unemployed, defined as looking for work, or waiting to take up a job already obtained, or unemployed but prevented from looking for work through temporary sickness. In 1961 and 1971 the unemployed referred to those persons who were out of a job at the end of the Census week; in 1966 it referred also to those out of a job on the Monday of that week—the latter date coinciding with that of the official monthly registered count. The question about unemployment registration was only asked in 1966.

The Census definition of 'looking for work' includes those persons who may limit themselves merely to scanning newspaper advertisements for jobs and who would not in other countries be regarded as part of the 'economically active' population. Though persons were classified in the Census as unemployed if they were intending to get work this did not necessarily mean that such persons actively sought work. Persons such as students about to leave full-time education to start a job in the near future but who in the meantime took a holiday, as well as school leavers and young persons just entering the country, were regarded as unemployed ('waiting to take up a job') even though they were not strictly part of the economically active population until the job had been taken up. In addition, the Census data from 1966 included those who would have looked for a job but for temporary sickness. Anyone registered at the Exchanges as unemployed is removed from the official register after three days of sickness because they are not regarded

41. For a discussion of the value of Census data in estimating the probable extent of unregistered unemployment see above, pp. 86–92.

as available for work. The following relatively small groups are also included in the Census count as unemployed but excluded from registration figures:- severely disabled persons who are unlikely to obtain employment except under special conditions; trainees at Government training centres and industrial rehabilitation units who have no employer and do not receive wages and are therefore not in employment; and persons not claiming unemployment benefit or social security but seeking part-time work.

Moreover the unemployment count relates to a particular day of the week and so includes some persons who did not have a job that day but who were employed at some other time during the same week. On the other hand, recent Census figures generally exclude persons who were unemployed at the beginning of the week but were in employment at some time later in the week (the exception being the specific count of the unemployed at the beginning of the Census week in 1966). They also count some married women as economically inactive even though they might register as unemployed. Those, in addition, who do not seek work because they believe that it is unavailable will be counted in the Census as inactive and not as unemployed. The temporarily stopped are regarded as employed and all students as economically inactive, whether they are actually employed or unemployed.

Because Census data are derived from sampling techniques the results are open to greater potential inaccuracy than those arising from the administrative activities of the Department of Employment. Sampling techniques cannot avoid the errors in coverage of the population and those arising from the response rate, from inaccurate replies to questions, and from the coding and punching of documents. The data can only be used over a number of decades if full account is taken of the detailed changes which have occurred in the industrial and occupational classifications in use. An explicitly occupational classification was first adopted in the Census in 1921 and was used again in 1931 and 1951 with some changes in details to provide a consistent occupationally classified time-series during that period. A different classification based on the International Standard Classification of Occupations was adopted in 1961, and used in the Census of that year. The classification of occupations used in the 1966 and 1971 Censuses differ and are, although comparable, different from that used in 1966.[42]

42. The classifications used are described in three volumes published by HMSO. 'Classification of Occupations 1960', 'Classification of Occupations 1966' and 'Classification of Occupations 1970'.

There is no satisfactory means, however, of bridging the gap in classification between 1951 and 1961. The industrial classification of Census
data first adopted in 1921 was used with slight modification in 1931.[43]
The entirely new Standard Industrial Classification used in 1951 was
itself subsequently revised in 1958 and again in 1968. Buxton and
MacKay have provided full details of the precise relationship between
the series over the post-war period.[44]

A summary of the data on unemployment provided in each Census
since 1931 is given in Appendix III to this Chapter.

43. Details are in the Census, *Industry Tables,* table C, 714.
44. Buxton and MacKay, op. cit., chapter 5.

Appendix I

Sample Surveys of the Unemployed Conducted by the Ministry of Labour, 1923–1940.

1. Analysis of Claims to Unemployment Insurance Benefit. Analysis of a sample of over 370,000 claims to unemployment benefit current in Great Britain on 27 January 1923. Representative of about 30 per cent of the total number of claims current at Employment Exchanges on the date mentioned. *Gazette,* November 1923.

2. Ministry of Labour, *Report on an Investigation into the Personal Circumstances and Industrial History of 10,000 Claimants to Unemployment Benefit, November 5th to 10th, 1923.* 1924. For details see pp. 120–21.

3. Unemployment Insurance. Analysis of Claims to Benefit During the 'Fourth Special Period'. Analysis of a 10 per cent sample of all the claims to benefit made between 2 November 1922 and 17 October 1923. Its principal object was to ascertain the gross number of persons who during the period of about 11½ months had been claimants to unemployment benefit and to analyse the total according to sex, age, and industry and according to the amount of benefit the claimants had received in the period. *Gazette,* July 1924.

4. Ministry of Labour, *Report on an Investigation into the Personal Circumstances and Industrial History of 10,903 Claimants to Unemployment Benefit, November 24th to 29th, 1924.* 1925. All claimants were individually interviewed. Provided some minor details not hitherto ascertained by sample, e.g. whether or not claimants were casual workers and whether or not the claims were authorized in respect of 'standard' or 'extended' benefit.

5. Ministry of Labour, *Report on an Enquiry into the Personal Circumstances and Industrial History of 3331 Boys and 2701 Girls Registered for Employment at Employment Exchanges and*

Juvenile Employment Bureaux, June and July 1925. 1926.   Represented 10 per cent of the juveniles aged 14 to 17 registered for
employment. Analyses were made of age distribution, physical
characteristics and appearance, home circumstances, school career,
first situation on leaving school, industrial history, contributions
and benefit, and employability.

6. Ministry of Labour, *Report of an Investigation into the Employment and Insurance History of a Sample of Persons Insured Against
   Unemployment*. 1927.   Related to April 1926. For details see
   pp. 121–2.

7. Ministry of Labour, *Report on an Investigation into the Personal
   Circumstances and Industrial History of 9748 Claimants to
   Unemployment Benefit, April 4th to 9th, 1927*. 1928.   For
   details see pp. 120, 122.

8. Unemployment Insurance Benefit. 30 Contributions Qualification.   Sample analysis of those over 18 with claims authorized
   for benefit on 28 January 1929. Estimated the number of such
   persons who had paid fewer than 30 contributions in the two years
   preceding that date and who would therefore have been disqualified had the 30 contribution rule been fully in operation when
   the analysis was made. *Gazette*, March 1929.

9. Unemployment Insurance Benefit. 30 Contribution Qualification.   A further analysis as in item 8 above on the basis of a 10
   per cent sample of adults with claims authorized for benefit on
   14 October 1929. *Gazette*, January 1930. Both samples provided
   Divisional data and separate information for the more important
   industries, for the depressed mining areas, and for various age
   groups.

10. Analysis of the Unemployment Record of Claimants aged 18 to
    64 on the Registers of Employment Exchanges.   In order to
    analyse the record of unemployment over the previous 12 months
    samples were taken on 18 March and 16 September 1929 rep-
    resenting 1 per cent of the number of insured persons aged 18 to
    64 inclusive with current claims to benefit on the registers of
    Employment Exchanges. For each claimant information was
    obtained as to age, industry, number of spells of unemployment
    recorded in each week of the previous 12 months, and number of
    days for which unemployment benefit was paid. *Gazette*, January
    1930. For further details, see pp. 120–22.

11. Wholly Unemployed Persons Receiving Transitional Benefit.   On
    17 February, 26 May 1930 samples were taken of those adults on
    the Live Register who had current claims on the wholly unemployed
    and casual files and had paid fewer than 30 contributions in the
    preceding 2 years and those who had no current claims for benefit

(whether insured or uninsured). The dates on which the samples were taken were just before and just after the coming into operation of the 1930 Unemployment Insurance Act. *Gazette*, October 1930.

12. *Royal Commission on Unemployment Insurance, Memorandum of Evidence, No. 2*. (Ministry of Labour).   One per cent sample of married women claimants to benefit, July 1930.

13. *Analysis of Persons Insured Against Unemployment in Great Britain at July 1930. Royal Commission on Unemployment Insurance, Appendices to Minutes of Evidence, Part V, Appendix XXVI*, London 1932. Ministry of Labour sample of 1 per cent of persons insured at the beginning of July 1930, exclusive of persons insured under the special schemes for the banking and insurance industries. This inquiry was similar to the one conducted in April 1926 (6 above) and provided details of the employment and insurance record of those insured, including contribution and benefit record by sex, age, and industry.

14. One per cent sample of claimants for ordinary and transitional benefit, November 1930.   *Gazette*, 1931.

15. Seasonal Workers on the Registers of Employment Exchanges in Great Britain.   Special analyses by 10 per cent sample were made on 8 September 1930 and 19 January 1931 regarding seasonal workers on the Live Registers of Employment Exchanges. The principal object was to determine to what extent insured persons took up seasonal work for a limited period each year, and remained unemployed and in receipt of benefit for the whole, or the greater part, of the remainder of the year. For this purpose particulars were obtained showing the amount of seasonal work performed since January 1928, the amount of non-seasonable work, together with the number of insurance contributions paid and the amount of benefit drawn in each of the preceding 3 years. In addition to this general survey a detailed analysis was made for each week of the preceding year showing the number of days of unemployment, the number of days for which benefit was paid and whether or not contributions were paid. *Gazette*, August 1931. A similar analysis appeared in the *Gazette*, October 1932.

16. *Persons on the Registers of Employment Exchanges in Great Britain at 2nd February 1931. Royal Commission on Unemployment Insurance, Appendices to Minutes of Evidence, Part V, Appendix XXVII*, London 1932.   Half per cent sample covering all adults on the register and not merely claimants to benefit. Particular emphasis on duration and frequency of spells of unemployment in addition to the standard form of information as collected in previous samples of this kind, e.g. November 1923 and 1924, and April 1927. The information given included, as did

that of 1924 and 1927, figures as to the 'employability' of the men and women included in the sample, distinguished in terms of the number and proportion who were placed in each of the special categories of employability.

A similar analysis of employability was made of a random selection of 7,705 persons on the registers at 1 October 1934. The results are in PRO, Cab. 58/24, Economic Advisory Council Committee on Economic Information, Sub-Committee on the Trend of Unemployment, July 1935.

17. Personal Circumstances and Industrial History of nearly 5 per cent of Juveniles under 18 on the Live Register 16 February 1931. *Gazette*, September 1932. Information was obtained on age distribution, unemployment insurance and benefit record, percentages unemployed at ages 16 and 17, education, employment record, and employability.

18. Persons Insured Against Unemployment in Great Britain at July 1932. A sample representing 1 in 300 of those insured to obtain information similar to that provided for the *Royal Commission on Unemployment Insurance* (13 above). *Gazette*, September 1933.

19. Seasonal Workers Engaged in Salmon Fishing. Regulation 2 of the Anomalies Regulations, 1931 as amended in 1933 provided that a seasonal worker could only receive unemployment benefit during the 'off-season' if, in addition to satisfying the other requirements of the insurance acts, he was able to prove that he had had insurable employment to a substantial extent in two out of the three consecutive off-seasons which included the off-season in which his claim was made. The suggestion that salmon fishers did not receive any appreciable amount of unemployment benefit or transitional payments when they were unemployed was investigated for the period September 1932 to November 1933. *Gazette*, January 1934.

20. Seasonal Workers–Unemployment During Normal Working Season. An investigation was made at the end of 1933 representing one third of all claims disallowed under Regulation 2 of the Anomalies Regulations, 1931 as amended by the Anomalies (Amendment) Regulations 1933 (see 19 above) July, September, October, and November of that year. Its purpose was to discover the extent to which persons whose claims were disallowed under this Regulation during the subsequent off-season had drawn unemployment benefit. *Gazette*, February 1934. See also 15 above.

21. Age Distribution of Unemployed Men and Women at 13 May 1935. A detailed analysis of the age distribution of adult persons on the registers of Employment Exchanges who were wholly unemployed, temporarily stopped or seeking casual employment,

nationally and by Ministry of Labour Divisions. *Gazette,* July 1935. Comparable data were collected for those persons registered on 4 November 1935, 18 May 1936, 2 November 1936, 3 May and 1 November 1937 and summarized in the *Gazette* in February, August, and December 1936, July 1937 and January 1938 respectively. The last sample was compiled in accordance with the revised procedure for counting the unemployed introduced in September 1937 under which persons subsequently found to be in employment at the date of the count were excluded from the figures. Unlike the others it did not distinguish types of unemployment.

22. Ages and Industries of Persons Unemployed for a Year or More at 29 July 1935. A specific analysis of part of the regular information published in the *Gazette* of the insured persons who were applying for insurance benefit or allowances according to the length of their last spell of unemployment. *Gazette,* October 1935.

23. Persons Registered as Unemployed. Analysis by Age and Duration of Unemployment, 28 February 1938. Purpose was to obtain information as to the relation between age and duration of unemployment among registered adults. *Gazette,* June 1938. Ditto for those registered on 1 May 1939. *Gazette,* July 1939. In each survey the age and duration categories adopted were different from those normally published by the Ministry.

24. Age Distribution of Persons Insured Against Unemployment. Special analysis of a random sample of *c.* 2 per cent of the total number of persons insured against unemployment at July 1937, including those insured under the agricultural as well as the General Scheme but excluding those in the special schemes for banking and insurance. Included a special analysis of the age distribution of those aged 18 to 64 registered as unemployed on 28 February 1938. By relating the figures to the estimated number in insurance by age at July 1937 details were given of variations in the percentage rate of unemployment at different ages. The analysis related only to persons registered as unemployed and so excluded those in the Two Months file. Consequently the percentage rates of unemployment obtained by relating this analysis to the estimated number of insured persons are not strictly comparable with those given in the monthly *Gazette,* which related to unemployment among insured persons generally (including those in the Two Months file). *Gazette,* August 1938. This age distribution of insured unemployment was also classified by industrial groups in the *Gazette,* September 1938.

25. Analysis by age and duration of unemployment, of unemployed men and women applicants for insurance benefit and unemploy-

ment allowances on 1 January 1940 who had been continuously on the registers of Exchanges for a year or more. In the case of men, a further analysis by occupation was obtained (this was not available in the similar surveys conducted in February 1938 and May 1939—see 23 above). Includes Divisional data. *Gazette,* February 1940.

26. Age and Occupation of the Unemployed. Analysis according to age and occupation of the men aged 18 years and over who were registered at Exchanges as wholly unemployed at 11 March 1940. Similar analyses according to age had been made at frequent intervals since 1935 but no complete analysis had previously been obtained giving particulars according to both age and occupation except for the survey of January 1940 (see 25 above) relating to persons applying for benefit or allowances who had been on the registers for twelve months or more. Includes Divisional analysis. *Gazette,* May 1940.

Appendix II

Surveys of the Characteristics of the Unemployed Conducted by the Department of Employment, 1961-1977

NB: Figures for 1961 and 1964 are grossed up totals; those for 1973 are sample numbers; those for 1976 are sample numbers, in many cases with grossed-up totals.

NATURE OF SAMPLE (GREAT BRITAIN)	INFORMATION COLLECTED	SOURCE OF PUBLICATION
1961 4 per cent of all claimants to unemployment benefit over the age of 18 registered at Employment Exchanges as wholly unemployed on 21 August (219,000 persons)	Amount of unemployment in year ended August 1961 (men, married women, single women—including widowed and divorced). Amount of unemployment by numbers of spells of unemployment in year ended August 1961 (men, married women, single women—including widowed and divorced). Amount of unemployment by number of jobs in year ended August 1961 (men, married women, single women—including widowed and divorced). Normal occupation by amount of unemployment in year ended August 1961 (men, married women, single women—including widowed and divorced). Suitability for placing (men, married women, single women—including widowed and divorced). Normal occupation by age (men—distinguishing registered disabled persons; women).	*Gazette*, April 1962 (Further details about the employment, training, re-habilitation and unemployment record in the four years up to August 1961 of the people covered in the enquiry were given in the *Gazette*, September 1962.)

145

NATURE OF SAMPLE (GREAT BRITAIN)	INFORMATION COLLECTED	SOURCE OF PUBLICATION
	Industry of last employment by age (men, women).	
	Suitability for government vocational training and for industrial rehabilitation (men, married women, single women—including widowed and divorced).	
	Training received (men, married women, single women—including widowed and divorced).	
	Type of schooling (men, married women, single women—including widowed and divorced).	
	Mobility group by age (men, married women, single women—including widowed and divorced, distinguishing in each case registered disabled persons and others).	
1964 10 per cent sample of the wholly unemployed over the age of 18 registered at Employment Exchanges on 12 October (313,000 persons). Unlike the 1961 survey this included those people on the register who were not claiming unemployment benefit.	Prospects of securing employment relating to (1) sex and marital status; (2) duration of current spell since last employment; (3) region (U.K.). Women by age and region (married, single—including widowed and divorced). Women: placing prospects and mobility. Women: by suitability for vocational training and region (married, single—including widowed and divorced).	*Gazette*, April and July 1966.

1973

1 in 30 of the wholly unemployed over the age of 18 registered at Employment Exchanges on 26 June (16,641 persons). Includes those registrants not claiming unemployment benefit. The survey was monitored by the working group on studies of the characteristics of the unemployed established on the recommendation of the inter-departmental working party on unemployment statistics (Report, Cmnd. 5157 November 1972).

Sex and marital status.

Age last birthday (also for men by region and by occupation).

Duration of current spell of registered unemployment (also for men by occupation and by region).

Number of spells of registered unemployment in previous 12 months (including current spell) (also for men by occupation and by region).

Availability for long-term, short-term or full-time work, and reason if short-term.

Number of jobs in last 12 months (also for men by occupation and by region).

Number of recorded introductions to prospective employer in current spell.

Attitude to work.

Prospects of obtaining long-term work (also for men by occupation).

Attitude to work and prospects of obtaining long-term full-time work.

Attitude to work and prospects of finding work by: (1) age and duration of unemployment; (2) region (men, excluding those seeking short-term or part-time work).

Attitude to work by region: (men).

Prospects of obtaining long-term work by region (men).

Gazette, March, May and June 1974. In order to reduce the element of subjectivity, a follow-up survey was carried out in January 1974 to establish whether the persons employed in June 1973 were still out of work and whether or not they had been in employment at any time in the intervening period.

NATURE OF SAMPLE (GREAT BRITAIN)	INFORMATION COLLECTED	SOURCE OF PUBLICATION
	Follow-up survey: Percentages (men) by:–	
	(1) Prospects of obtaining long-term work at June 1973–whether unemployed in January 1974; whether in employment at any time in June 1973–January 1974.	
	(2) Attitude to work at June 1973–by prospects of obtaining long-term work, whether unemployed and whether in employment at any time in June 1973–January 1974.	
	(3) By occupation–whether unemployed or in employment at January 1974.	
	(4) By region–whether unemployed or in employment at January 1974 (also by prospects at June 1973).	
	Whether registered disabled person (also for men by region).	
	Willingness to work beyond daily travelling distance (also for men by region).	
	Unemployment benefit and credit position (also for men by region).	
	Number of dependants for whom dependants benefit had been authorized (Unemployment Benefit claimants only) (also for men by region).	
	Total weekly benefit to which currently entitled (also for men by region).	

1 in 60 sample of persons aged 18 and over registered at Employment Offices as wholly unemployed on 29 June (18,231 persons).

Sex (some details for women only available on request).

Industry in which last employed—details only available on request.

Main occupation for which registered (men), by age, duration of current spell of unemployment, attitude to work, prospects of obtaining long-term work, reason for leaving the register and by region.

Age last birthday (and also for men by region).

Duration of current spell of registered unemployment (and for men by region).

Number of spells of registered unemployment in previous 12 months (including current spell) (and also for men unemployed up to three months by age, occupation and region).

Claimant (non-claimant).

Disablement status (and also for men by region).

Country of birth.

Availability for short or long-term work and reason (if short-term).

Whether available for full-time work (over 30 hours per week).

Number of recorded submissions for jobs in current spell of unemployment (excluding self-service submissions).

Prospects of obtaining long-term work by attitude to work (men).

with cross-classification by age, reasons for leaving the register, duration of unemployment and by region.

Gazette, June, September, October 1977. As with the 1973 survey, a follow-up enquiry was arranged. Information was collected as registrants in the survey left the register in the six months following the main enquiry and from the remainder still on the register in January 1977.

NATURE OF SAMPLE (GREAT BRITAIN)	INFORMATION COLLECTED	SOURCE OF PUBLICATION
	Local area unemployment percentage rate by region (men).	
	Whether registration had lapsed by January 7, 1977 and why	Follow-up questions
	Registration ceased or transferred to another employment office—month in which left the register.	
	Those remaining on or leaving the register and reason for leaving by age and duration (men) (also for men reasons for leaving by region).	
	Those leaving the register for employment, analysed by prospects and attitude: variation by age and duration (men).	
	Those leaving the register by month of leaving and those still unemployed on January 1, 1977: by age and duration of unemployment (men).	
	Whether registrants served an apprenticeship in the occupation for which registered if under age 30 or had applied for or completed a training course under the Training Opportunities Scheme or the Training Services Agency.	
	Pension (per week), if any, from previous employer (men, women aged 55–64) (and also for men by region).	

Whether in receipt of Unemployment Benefit, Supplementary Allowance or National Insurance credits (men, women aged 55–64 only).

Benefit and credit position by pension from previous employer (men aged 55–64).

Weekly wage likely to be obtained if placed. (Also for men by total weekly benefit to which currently entitled).

Pension (per week), if any, from previous employer (men aged 55–64 only) and by region and by benefit and credit position.

Occupation for which registered by benefit and credit position (men).

Appendix III

Unemployment Returns in the Census of Population, 1931–1971

CENSUS DATE & DATA COLLECTED	AREAS	AGE GROUP
1931		
Total number of occupied population out of work. Males, females.	England and Wales; Scotland.	14+15; 16+17; 18–20; 21–24; 25–29; 30–34; 35–44; 45–54; 55–59; 60–64; 65–69; 70–74; 75+over (70 and over in Scotland).
Total out of work by occupation. Males, females; marital condition.	England and Wales; Scotland.	as above.
Percentage of occupied population out of work by occupation. Males, females.	England and Wales.	as above.
Total number and percentage of occupied population out of work. Males, females.	England and Wales; Regions; Administrative Counties; County Boroughs; and other Urban Areas with populations exceeding 50,000; Scotland; and its Cities, Counties and Large Burghs.	14+
Total number of the occupied population out of work. Males, females.	Urban Areas with populations not exceeding 50,000 and Rural Districts (England and Wales).	14+

Total number of occupied population out of work by occupation. Males, females.	England and Wales; Regions; Administrative Counties; County Boroughs and Urban Areas with populations exceeding 50,000; Scotland; its Cities, Counties and Large Burghs.	Juveniles aged 14–20.
Total number and percentage of population out of work by industry group. Males, females.	England and Wales.	as identified in the 13 age groups above.
Total number of occupied population out of work by industry group. Males, females.	England and Wales; Regions; Administrative Counties; County Boroughs and other Urban Areas with populations exceeding 50,000; Scotland.	14+
Number out of work as a percentage of number in work by industry group. Males, females.	England and Wales.	14+
1951 Number of total occupied population out of work by occupational group. Males, females.	England and Wales; Scotland.	15+
Number of total occupied population out of work. Males, females; marital condition.	England and Wales; Scotland.	15, 16, 17, 18–19; 20–24; 25–29; 30–34; 35–44; 45–54; 55–59; 60–64; 65–69; 70–74; 75+over.
Percentage of occupied population out of work. Males, females; marital condition.	England and Wales.	Under 25; 25–44; 45–64; 65+over.

CENSUS DATE & DATA COLLECTED	AREAS	AGE GROUP
Number of occupied population out of work by occupation. Males, females; marital condition.	England and Wales.	Under 20; 20–24; 25–29; 30–34; 35–44; 45–54; 55–59; 60–64; 65–69; 70–74; 75+over.
Number of occupied population out of work. Males, females.	England and Wales; Regions; Wales, Conurbations, Administrative Counties, County Boroughs, Metropolitan Boroughs, and Urban Areas with 50,000 population or more. Conurbation Divisions and Sub-Divisions, Urban Areas with populations of less than 50,000, Rural Districts and New Towns. Scotland—Central Clydeside, Conurbations, Cities, Counties, Large Burghs.	15+
	Great Britain 1% sample.	
	England and Wales	15+
	Great Britain (1% sample)	15, 16–19; 20–24; 25–34; 35–44; 45–54; 55–59; 60–64; 65–69; 70+over, and for each age group 60, 61, 62, 63, 64, 65, 66, 67, 68, 69 (males) and aged 55, 56, 57, 58, 59, 60, 61, 62, 63, 64 (females)

Number out of work by selected occupational group. Males, females; marital condition.	Great Britain (1% sample).		15+ and for age groups 15, 16–19; 20–24; 25–34; 35–44; 45–54; 55–59; 60–64; 65–69; 70+over
Number of occupied population out of work. Males, females.	England and Wales; Scotland; Regions of England; Wales; Large Areas (Conurbations; Counties and Cities (England and Scotland separately); Medium Areas (England and Wales (total 42) and Scotland (total 7) separately).	1% sample	15+
Number of occupied population out of work by industry group. Males, females.	England and Wales; Scotland.		15+

1961 (10% sample only).

Number out of work (including sick) by occupational group. Males, females; marital condition.	England and Wales; Scotland.	Under 20; 20–24; 25–29; 30–34; 35–44; 45–54; 55–59; 60–64; 65–69; 70–74; 75+over.
Number out of work (distinguishing sick, other). Males, females.	Scotland.	15, 16, 17, 18–19; 20–24; 25–29; 30–34; 35–44; 45–54; 55–59; 60–64; 65–69; 70–74; 75+over.

CENSUS DATE & DATA COLLECTED	AREAS	AGE GROUP
Number of total economically active population out of work (including sick). Males, females.	England and Wales.	Under 20; 20–24; 25–34; 35–44; 45–54; 55–59; 60–64; 65+over.
Number out of work (distinguishing sick, other). Males, females; marital condition.	Scotland.	Under 20; 20–24; 25–29; 30–34; 35–44; 45–54; 55–59; 60–64; 65–69; 70–74; 75+over.
Number out of work (distinguishing sick, other). Males, females.	Scotland, Regional Divisions and Sub-Divisions; National and Regional Burghal/Landward aggregates.	15+
Number out of work (including sick) by industrial group. Males, females.	England and Wales; Scotland.	15+
Number out of work (including sick). Males, females.	England and Wales; Scotland.	15, 16–17; 18–19; 20–24; 25–29; 30–34; 35–44; 45–54; 55–59; 60–64; 65–69; 70–74; 75+over. as above to 60–64; 65+over only for females (England and Wales; and for each sex in Scotland).
Number out of work (distinguishing sick, and others) by employment status and age. Males, females. – self-employed without employees	England and Wales; Scotland.	Under 20; 20–24; 25–29; 30–34; 35–44; 45–54; 55–59; 60–64; 65–69; 70–74; 75+over.

self-employed with employees
(small establishments)
managers (large establishments)
managers (small establishments)
foremen and supervisors (manual)
foremen and supervisors (non-manual)
apprentices, articled clerks and
formal trainees
professional employees
other employees.

Number out of work (including sick). Males, females.

Regions; Conurbations; National and Regional urban/rural aggregates; Scotland; Northern Ireland; Counties; County Boroughs; Metropolitan Boroughs; Urban areas with population of 50,000 or more; County Remainders; Conurbation Centres; New Towns (published in County Leaflets for England and Wales distinguishing sick, and others). Scotland: Regional Divisions and Sub-divisions; National and Regional Burghal/Landward aggregates.

15+

Number out of work (including sick) of residents born outside of England and Wales and Scotland by country of birth or nationality. Males, females.

England and Wales; Scotland.

15+

Number out of work (including sick) of residents born outside of England and Wales and Scotland and whether born in the UK and whether Commonwealth Citizen or Alien. Males, females.

England and Wales; Regional Divisions and Sub-Divisions of Scotland.

15+

CENSUS DATE & DATA COLLECTED	AREAS	AGE GROUP
1966		
Number out of work during the whole week ending 23 April 1966 (distinguishing those registered and those not registered; those out of employment during the whole year ending 23 April 1966; those in employment part of the year ending 23 April 1966); not in employment on Monday 18 April 1966 (distinguishing those registered (sick and others) and those unregistered (sick and others)). Males, females; married females (*see note (b)).	Great Britain; *England and Wales; Scotland; Regions of England and Wales; Conurbations. (*details for regions of Scotland available on request).	15, 16, 17, 18, 19, 20, 21–24; 25–29; 30–34; 35–39; 40–44; 45–49; 50–54; 55–59; 60–64; 65–69; 70+over.
Number out of employment during whole of the week ending 23 April 1966. Males, females; married females.	Sub-divisions of Regions in England and Wales; Economic Planning Sub-Regions of Scotland.	as above.
Number out of work by occupational group. Males, females; marital condition.	Great Britain* (*details for Scotland and regions of Scotland available on request).	as above.
Number out of work (distinguishing those registered and unregistered). Males, females; marital condition of unregistered females (distinguishing single, married, widowed, and divorced).	Great Britain* (*data for Scotland; regions of England and Wales; regions of Scotland; Conurbations of Great Britain available on request).	15+
Number out of work by industrial group.	Great Britain*	15+

...country of Birth for Great Britain.

Residents born outside of Great Britain by place of birth for Regions of England and Wales; Scotland; Conurbations.

Cities; Counties; Counties (excluding Large Burghs); Large Burghs, Districts of Counties with populations of 50,000 or more; New Towns, and Conurbation Centres of Scotland.   15+

Total number out of work. Males, females.

(a) *Unpublished Data* Available on request.

Table 42U Persons out of employment on Monday, 18 April 1966. Occupation and Industry Orders by Registered, Not Registered (Sick) and Not Registered (Others) by Sex and Age. Available for Great Britain.

Table 43U Persons out of employment on Monday, 18 April 1966. Occupation and Industry Orders by Registered, Not Registered (Sick) and Not Registered (Others) by Sex. Available for Great Britain, Regions, and Conurbations.

(b) Details of the number of married females in private households out of work (distinguishing between those with and without children and by age of youngest or only child) can be found in Department of Employment, *1966 Sample Census of Population Paper No. 7. Females Not At Work*, n.d.

1971

Number out of work (distinguishing number who were sick). Males, females; married females.

Great Britain*; England and Wales; Scotland; Regions/Conurbations/sub-divisions of Regions of England and Wales; Central Clydeside Conurbation; Remainder of Scotland; planning sub-regions of Scotland (*data for regions of

15, 16, 17, 18, 19, 20, 21–24; 25–29; 30–34; 35–39; 40–44; 45–49; 50–54; 55–59; 60–64; 65–69; 70+over.

CENSUS DATE & DATA COLLECTED	AREAS	AGE GROUP
	Scotland and all separate areas available on request). Counties; County Boroughs; Urban areas with populations over 50,000; Conurbations and New Towns (England and Wales in County Volumes).	
Number out of work (10% sample). Males, females.	Great Britain; England and Wales; Scotland. Regions; Conurbations (England and Wales); Central Clydeside Conurbation; Remainder of Scotland.	15+
Number out of work (distinguishing those who were sick) (10% sample). Males, females; married females.	Great Britain; England and Wales; Scotland; Regions; Conurbations (England and Wales); Central Clydeside Conurbation; Remainder of Scotland.	Sub-divisions of age as above.
Number out of work by occupation (10% sample). Males, females; marital condition (total number married only).	Great Britain.	Sub-divisions of age as above.
Number out of work (sick, others) (10% sample). Males, females.	Sub-divisions of Regions (England and Wales).	15+
Number out of work (sick, others) (10% sample). Males, females; married females.	Sub-divisions of Regions (England and Wales).	Sub-divisions of age as above.
Number out of work (sick, others) (10% sample). Males, females; married females.	New Towns; England and Wales; Scotland.	15+ (Scotland—data by sub-divisions of age as above).

Number out of work resident in the area (10% sample). Males, females.

New Towns; England and Wales.

15+

Number out of work (sick, others) (10% sample). Males, females; married females.

Scotland: Planning Sub-Regions, Cities, Counties, Large Burghs, County Remainders, Conurbation Centres.

15+

Number out of work. Analysis by year of birth. Males, females.

Scotland: Conurbations, Remainder of Scotland–Planning Sub-Regions; Cities; Counties.

Year of birth between:
1971-1966; 1965-1961;
1960-1956; 1955-1951;
1950-1946; 1945-1941;
1940-1936; 1935-1931;
1930-1926; 1925-1921;
1920-1916; 1915-1911;
1910-1906; 1905-1901;
1900-1896;before 1896.

5

Miscellaneous Series

Statistics of Placings and Vacancies[1]

(a) Before 1947

Until the passing of the Labour Exchanges Act (1909), Labour Bureaux conducted by voluntary organizations and local authorities were the only intermediaries between employers and employees in the labour market. From 1885 they reported their activities to the Board of Trade.[2]

By 1906 there were ten bureaux maintained by metropolitan borough councils under the Labour Bureaux (London) Act (1902). They were later subsumed in the larger organization of the Central (Unemployed) Body for London, exercising functions under the Unemployed Workmen Act (1905). The monthly returns of voluntary labour bureaux in the provinces and elsewhere were published in the *Gazette* from 1894 to 1910, including details of the number of fresh applications by workpeople, the number of jobs offered by employers and the numbers for whom work was found, with a broad occupational analysis. Separate tables were published in respect of the Central (Unemployed) Body for London after its establishment in 1906 and, until July 1915, of a number of Women's Employment Bureaux. Annual figures of the work of labour bureaux appeared in *First* to *Fourteenth Abstract of Labour Statistics*. Figures for Women's Bureaux continued up to *Seventeenth*

---

1. This section is concerned primarily with sources of data. The problems of interpreting vacancy figures are discussed above pp. 94–115.
2. For details of their early activities see Board of Trade, Labour Department, *Report on Agencies and Methods for Dealing with the Unemployed*, C. 7182, 1893. This also provides evidence of the official classification of types of unemployment. See also E.J. Urwick, 'The St. Pancras Labour Bureau', *Economic Review*, III, 1893.

Abstract. The early exchanges were limited in their geographical and industrial scope and were too often adjuncts to Distress Committees. As such they often became the resort of casual unskilled workmen and failed to attract a sufficiently varied range of employers or workmen to make their returns reliable.

With the establishment of Employment Exchanges on a national basis in 1910 the available statistical data regarding the registered unemployed became more plentiful and comprehensive. Regular monthly publication of the work of the Exchanges, analysed by trades and districts, began in the *Gazette* in April 1910. For some years after the National Insurance Act of 1911 came into operation separate figures were given for insured and uninsured trades, the figures for each being analysed by occupational groups and sex. Details were given of the numbers registered and for whom work was found and of vacancies notified and filled.[3] This information continued to be published in the *Gazette* on broadly similar lines until the end of 1924 (though the occupational analysis was discontinued after August 1922).

From January 1925 to September 1939 the information given in the *Gazette* was limited to a short table of the total number of vacancies filled and vacancies unfilled (or notified). During the period 1932-8, in order to determine the proportion of the total number of engagements which could be attributed to the placing activities of the Ministry, the number of placings each year was related to the total number of wholly unemployed persons going off the unemployment register during the year. The results were published under the title 'Placing Indices'.[4] To some extent the placing index figures were boosted by the inclusion of industries largely under public control—national government, local government, public works contracting, and gas, water, and electricity supply. Yet in another respect the influence of the Exchanges was understated since a large proportion of all engagements were re-

3. Detailed figures for 1910-14 are in *Report on the Proceedings of the Board of Trade under the Labour Exchanges Act, 1909, and under Part II of the National Insurance Act, 1911, to July, 1914.* This report was not published but is available for reference from the Department of Employment.

4. The best sources for all aspects of the work of the Exchanges between the wars are their *Annual Reports.* See also 'The Use of the Employment Exchange Service in Great Britain as a Labour Clearing House', *International Labour Review*, 24, 1931; R.G.D. Allen and B. Thomas, 'The London Building Industry and Its Labour Recruitment Through Employment Exchanges', *Economic Journal*, XLVII, 1937.

engagements by the same employer made otherwise than through the Employment Exchange.

(b) Since 1947

Figures of the total number of vacancies filled and unfilled were discontinued during the 1939–45 war and the immediate post-war period. Publication was resumed in October 1947 on much the same conceptual basis as had existed before, with two exceptions. Persons with professional and other academic or equivalent qualifications were allowed to register for employment at special offices (until March 1959). Similar provisions were made for nurses (until April 1962) and for those with technical and scientific qualifications (until March 1962). Thereafter the activities of each group became part of the routine work of the local Exchanges.[5] With the introduction of the Disabled Persons (Employment) Act (1944) the Ministry of Labour undertook to publish separate figures of the number of disabled persons placed in ordinary employment and the number of severely disabled persons placed in sheltered employment.[6]

The current series relate to those vacancies for adults which were notified by employers to the Employment Exchanges and those vacancies for young persons under 18 years of age which were notified to the responsible juvenile or youth agency. They ignore all those vacancies which were not so notified. The placing figures exclude those persons who were engaged without the direct assistance of the offices and do not claim to represent the total demand for labour.[7] Vacancies notified to employment offices could include some that are suitable for young persons. Similarly vacancies notified to careers offices could include some for adults. Because of possible duplication the two series should not be added together.

5. Monthly figures of the work of the Appointments Offices and Technical and Scientific Register are in the *Gazette* from 1946, showing the number of vacancies notified, filled, cancelled, and unfilled. Annual figures in *Annual Reports* from 1947. Quarterly figures of the work of Nursing Appointments Offices are in the *Gazette* (February, May, August, and November) since 1948, showing the number of vacancies filled and unfilled. Annual figures in the *Annual Reports* from 1947.
6. Figures in the *Gazette* quarterly 1949–52 (March, June, September, and December) and half-yearly since 1953 (March and September). Annual figures in the Ministry's *Annual Reports* from 1947.
7. See above pp. 97–101.

The nature and scope of the available data have been affected over time by changes in the organization of the employment services and other administrative details. Until March 1950, Control of Engagements Orders required the majority of labour engagements to be made through the local offices. In February 1952, the Notification of Vacancies Order re-introduced statutory controls and required all engagements within its scope to be made either through a local office or a scheduled employment agency. The Order remained in force until May 1956. Consequently the number of vacancies notified to Exchanges and those unfilled on any particular day were higher than they would otherwise have been.[8]

Returns were made every four weeks (i.e. thirteen times a year) until January 1957 after which they were made monthly on the Wednesday prior to the monthly unemployment count on an industrial and regional basis for each sex. (Following the introduction of the Sex Discrimination Act vacancies are no longer recorded separately for males and females).

Two discontinuities in the monthly count figures for the period after July 1958 were removed by making modification to the data before analysis. Before May 1962, the special Nursing Appointments Offices, responsible for the nursing section of the Ministry of Labour employment services, were not regarded as unemployment Exchanges for statistical purposes. Vacancies notified to those offices were not, therefore, included in the statistics of vacancies notified to Exchanges. Counts of unfilled vacancies from May 1962 have thereafter included vacancies in nursing occupations. Notional additions of 3,200 vacancies for men and 16,000 for women were made to the actual count figures for each month from July 1958 to April 1962. The second modification was to deduct from the count of figures for men, month by month from July 1958 to February 1960, those notifications to the Exchanges by agricultural workers who, when national service was in force, could be granted deferment for call-up until they were replaced.[9]

8. For a comparison of activity between the periods October 1950–September 1951 and October 1953–September 1954 see E. Cleary, 'The Placing Service of the Ministry of Labour', *Sociological Review*, 4, 1956.
9. See 'Vacancies Notified and Remaining Unfilled, Monthly 1948–1968' and 'Numbers of Persons placed in Employment by the Employment Exchange and Youth Employment Services 1948–1968', National and Regional analysis, tables 179, 180, 182, *Historical Abstract*. Details thereafter in appropriate *Year Books*.

From February 1970 figures of persons placed in employment were replaced by a quarterly occupational analysis of placings and cancelled vacancies for adults. Figures for unfilled vacancies continued as before.

Statistics of vacancies unfilled have been collected nationally and by region for those registered at employment offices only, at quarterly intervals on an occupational basis since 1956.[10] Analyses by region were conducted monthly as were those by industry up to June 1976 after which they became available on a quarterly basis. There are no published data on age-specific vacancies.

The current series is adjusted for seasonal variations by the same method as that used for the principal unemployment series,[11] with one notable exception. In contrast to adults, vacancies for young persons are often notified well in advance of the end of school terms in the hope of attracting school leavers. Such jobs may be offered to and accepted by boys and girls several months or weeks before work commences; assuming always that the offer of a job is actually taken up. The vacancy is regarded officially as unfilled until such work starts. The demand for young persons is influenced, not only by prevailing economic conditions, but also by the volume of the outflow from various educational institutions and by the number in this particular age group of the population. As a result of the conceptual and other differences between the data for adults and young people, school leavers have been ignored in the seasonally-adjusted vacancy data.

10. Details for 1956–68 are in table 181, *Historical Abstract* and in *Year Books* thereafter. From December 1961 to June 1976 the quarterly occupational analysis of unfilled vacancies has related to the same day as the monthly industrial analysis. Previously the analyses related to different days in the quarter month. The data are subject to the changes in occupational classification and problems of interpretation referred to above pp. 101–15.

11. See pp. 00–00. For the purpose of seasonal adjustment the vacancy data from July 1958 to June 1967 were based on figures for the period beginning March 1952. It was assumed throughout that the seasonal movements in the figures between March 1952–May 1956 were not affected to any marked extent by the operation of the Notification of Vacancies Order. This had required all engagements within its scope to be made through an Employment Exchange. As the frequency of statistical returns of vacancies was changed early in 1957 from a four-weekly to a calendar month period, a notional series of monthly figures for seasonal adjustment purposes was compiled for the period 1952–7 by interpolation.

Persons in Receipt of Poor Relief and Unemployment Benefit

(a) Poor Relief Returns to 1939.

Statistics of the number of workmen who sought relief before 1914 offer another potential source of unemployment data, on the basis that changes in the proportion of persons out of work will be reflected in the changes in the proportion who are driven to seek public aid. Under the Unemployed Workmen Act (1905) Distress Committees were established in all the main industrial centres to register and investigate unemployed persons applying to them for assistance. Details of the numbers relieved and the cost in relation to total income are available in the *Annual Distress Committee Returns* for the period 1905-14.[12]

The returns are of limited use since they include only an uncertain proportion of the unemployed. In some areas of the country there was no registration at all and elsewhere errors of computation and consistency frequently arose. Few of those who registered belonged to a trade union giving unemployment benefit. Official efforts were made to make the totals of registered unemployed more precise by requesting Committees to exclude all who were known to have found work or to have left the locality since registering but the returns cannot, and were never intended to, provide an accurate count of the total number actually out of work.

The records refer in the main to the casual and unskilled groups in large commercial and urban centres who were unrepresentative of the working class as a whole. The number given relief could easily be greater or less than the number in distress or unemployed. The large proportion of persons unemployed for a short time felt little inducement to apply for relief as destitutes, whether skilled or unskilled, unionist or non-unionist. At the same time many who were in distress because of casual or irregular employment, perhaps aggravated by personal deficiencies, were not necessarily entirely unemployed. Want

---

12. *Return as to the Proceedings of Distress Committees under the Unemployed Workmen Act, 1905 in England and Wales, up to 31 March 1906*, 1906, (392), civ, 507 and annual thereafter to 1909. *Return as to the Proceedings of Distress Committees in England and Wales and of the Central (Unemployed) Body for London during the year ended 31 March 1910*, 1910, (268), lxxiv, 623 and annually thereafter. *Report by the Local Government Board for Scotland as to the Proceedings of Distress Committees in Scotland from the Date of their Appointment to 15 May 1906*, Cd. 3431, 1907 and annually thereafter.

of funds or the lack of suitable employment for applicants often influenced total relief expenditure, while changes in the number remaining on the registers would often reflect no more than the feeling that there was a greater or less prospect of obtaining work through the Distress Committees in one year than in another.

The returns do, however, provide partial information for the first decade of the twentieth century of the age, occupational status, and duration of unemployment of those covered.[13] Distress Committees in London often registered female applicants for relief, though few elsewhere did so, thus accentuating the comparative neglect of the trend of female unemployment in the available data before 1913.[14] In a more general sense, however, the distress returns were useful because they related to a class of unskilled workmen generally excluded from the trade union returns. To quote Beveridge: 'The applicants to Distress Committees, if they are not all the unemployed, are the unemployed for immediate practical purposes. They are those in urgent need of relief.' They were, in addition, 'of a class to which information has hitherto been wanting—an industrial stratum intermediate between the skilled trade unionists recorded in the *Labour Gazette* and the paupers and vagrants known to Board of Guardians'.[15]

A more regular source of information are the returns on the number of able-bodied paupers in receipt of outdoor and indoor relief.[16] Their reliability as indicators of unemployment (in the generally accepted sense) is limited by the fact that not all persons in receipt of outdoor relief were ordinarily engaged in some regular occupation or necessarily being relieved solely on account of unemployment. Wide local variations existed too in the concept of 'able-bodied'. Moreover the number of paupers included in the returns was not necessarily equivalent to the

---

13. See below pp. 183–4. Details of the age and occupation of applicants to Distress Committees can also be found in Cd. 4795, op. cit., *Royal Commission on the Poor Laws and Relief of Distress, Appendix, Volume XIXA,* Cd. 5073, 1910; ibid., etc. *Appendix XIXB,* Cd. 4890, 1909; G.B. Morrison, 'Age and Unemployment', *Journal of the Royal Statistical Society,* LXXIV, 1911 and S.J. Chapman and H.M. Hallsworth, *Unemployment,* Manchester 1909, chapter V, 'Age, Trade and Past Work of the Unemployed'.
14. J. Tawney, 'Women and Unemployment', *Economic Journal,* XXI, 1911.
15. Beveridge, *Unemployment,* op. cit., pp. 24–5.
16. Details are in Local Government Board *Annual Reports* for England and Wales, Scotland, and Ireland.

number who had actually received relief in the year or at any time in their lives. The returns did, nevertheless, reflect cyclical fluctuations, usually reaching their highest point slightly more than a year after the nadir of a trade depression.[17]

The administration of poor relief until 1930 was essentially a local service subject to the general supervision of a central department. Until 1919 this central body was the Local Government Board; thereafter its poor law functions were transferred to the newly created Ministry of Health. The poor law functions of the Boards of Guardians, the local units of administration, were transferred in 1930 to the councils of Administrative Counties and County Boroughs in England and Wales. Poor relief was thereafter known as public assistance.

In Scotland public relief was not legally available to able-bodied persons before 1921. Following heavy and unprecedented unemployment at the end of 1920 provision was made to authorize public relief for able-bodied persons who were 'destitute and unable to obtain employment'. As in England the system was locally administered.

In order to compare the relative importance of the insurance and residual relief system in Great Britain before 1939 it is necessary to modify the poor relief statistics because of the differences in the classifications used in the several series available and because the statistics for Scotland and for England and Wales were reported separately and include different information.

Both England and Scotland distinguished between outdoor (domiciliary) and indoor (institutional) relief. From 1920 the figures relating to poor relief or public assistance given to able-bodied persons in England and Wales were usually derived from data concerning recipients of outdoor relief alone. (After 1920 the number of persons receiving indoor relief remained fairly steady in spite of increased unemployment. The degree of under-statement involved by the exclusion of institutional cases cannot be very large.) From May 1922 published Scottish statistics, unlike their English counterparts, distinguished among both indoor and outdoor relief recipients those who received aid on account of unemployment.

---

17. See *Royal Commission on the Poor Laws and Relief of Distress,* 'Statistics of Labour Bureaux for 20 years or so long as available distinguishing between those managed by Distress Committees under the Unemployed Workmen Act and those not so managed', *Minutes of Evidence, Appendix XXI(1).*

As far as England and Wales are concerned, it is necessary to bear in mind the precise composition of poor law relief statistics. Whenever relief was granted in respect of *any* member of a family, the head of the family was included in the statistics, even though he may not himself have received the relief. The statistics of insured persons on poor law relief included not only a number of persons whose claims to unemployment insurance benefit had been disallowed, but also those in the 'waiting period', those actually in receipt of benefit, and those persons whose claims to benefit had been disallowed but for which, on subsequent revision of the decision, unemployment benefit had been used to repay the guardians any poor law relief in respect of the period up to the date of revision.[18]

Between 1922 and 1926 the Ministry of Health published statistics of the number of persons (including dependants) in receipt of outdoor relief, indicating which persons were ordinarily engaged in some regular occupation. Another series classified the ordinarily engaged into those (including dependants) insured under the unemployment insurance acts and all others normally engaged in some occupation. This second series included some persons who should not be counted as being relieved on account of unemployment, namely an unknown number of employed persons, those of the unemployed who were granted relief for reasons other than unemployment, e.g. sickness, and others whose families were in need because of an industrial dispute.[19]

It is possible, however, to exclude such groups from the figures since returns are available for January in each year from 1922 of the number of persons in receipt of outdoor relief on account of unemployment. From October 1926 the Ministry of Health, in conjunction with the Ministry of Labour, revised the basis on which the outdoor relief returns from local authorities were classified in the hope of providing more precise and meaningful figures. Statistics of unemployed insured persons on poor relief in England and Wales became available in a form which enabled a more accurate comparison to be made with unemployment insurance figures. Previously the poor law figures had included wives and dependants, for whom relief was being paid, in the same total with heads of families and did not give separate figures for heads of families.

18. *Memorandum on Certain Points Concerning the Statistics of Unemployment and of Poor Law Relief,* Cmd. 2984, November 1927, pp. 2-3.
19. Burns, op. cit., p. 350.

Recipients of poor relief (and their dependants) were thereafter divided into four classes (corresponding figures were not available for Scotland):

Class I: Persons insured under the unemployment insurance acts who were unemployed and who had lodged their unemployment book with an Employment Exchange.

Class II: Persons not insured under the unemployment insurance acts who were unemployed.

Class III: All other persons ordinarily engaged in some regular occupation.

Class IV: All other persons in receipt of outdoor relief.

Although this classification was adopted in order to indicate the extent to which unemployed persons were in receipt of outdoor relief it did not necessarily follow that all the persons in the first two classes were actively maintaining registration at Exchanges on the date to which the returns relate. The number of persons in receipt of outdoor relief in respect of unemployment who were not actively maintaining registration was comparatively small though a proportion of them in Class I could have been included in the statistics of unemployment among insured persons derived from lodged unemployment books, e.g. the Two Months file. A Ministry of Health enquiry in 1934 revealed that in four 'test periods'—July, September, November, and December— the expenditure on account of unemployment alone amounted to 90.7 per cent of the total for Class I recipients and 98.2 per cent for Class II recipients.[20] It is unlikely, however, that the over-statement of numbers relieved would be very great even if it is assumed that the whole of Classes I and II were unemployed persons relieved on account of unemployment.

It is not known how many of the persons reported in Class III were normally wage-earners not registered at an Employment Exchange but who were receiving relief on account of unemployment. Their number is unlikely to be large since the majority of poor relief authorities

20. Ministry of Health, *Annual Report*, 1935-6, p. 140, cited in Burns, op. cit., p. 353. No other data on unemployment relief expenditures for the different classes were compiled by the Ministry. Even when statistics became available after April 1937 differentiating unemployment from other causes of relief they related to a period when the relief authorities could give only medical relief and emergency aid to persons falling within the scope of the unemployment insurance and assistance schemes (i.e. to all of Class I and the majority of Class II).

made registration at an Employment Exchange a condition for the receipt of relief by able-bodied persons.[21] Most of the persons normally engaged in some regular occupation would therefore, if uninsured, appear in Class II.[22] From June 1937 the quarterly statement of *Persons in Receipt of Poor Relief (England and Wales)* began, however, to show the number of persons receiving public assistance on account of unemployment.[23]

Estimates of the total number of persons in receipt of relief on account of unemployment are still not comparable with the number of those in receipt of unemployment insurance since the former includes dependants. No statistical segregation is available in this period for Class III and the breakdown for the remaining classes between wage earners and their dependants occurred at different times after 1926. Only rough methods of segregating dependants from main recipients can be used for the period prior to 1926. Nevertheless calculations are available of the number of wage-earners alone in each class receiving relief on account of unemployment in England and Wales between 1922 and 1939.[24]

21. To this extent of course a considerable part of the poor law figures represent persons already included in Ministry of Labour returns rather than being additional to them.
22. Burns, op. cit., p. 354. In 1934 it was found that in the four test periods previously mentioned, expenditures on account of unemployment alone accounted for only 6.1 per cent of the total expenditure for Class III.
23. Burns, op. cit., pp. 354-6 provides an estimate of the number of wage earners and their dependants in Class III in receipt of relief on account of unemployment in England and Wales 1929-39 by applying to the English figures the more precise Scottish returns which distinguished able-bodied unemployed persons from others in Class III. See also *Special Returns from Poor Law Authorities in Respect of Unemployed Persons in Receipt of Domiciliary Poor Relief During the Week Ended 7th February, 1931, Royal Commission on Unemployment Insurance, Appendices to Minutes of Evidence, Part II, Appendix XXI*, London 1931.
24. Burns, op. cit., pp. 355-7. Data of the number of claimants to unemployment benefit in receipt of poor relief were contained in a number of sample inquiries conducted by the Ministry of Labour. See pp. 139-44. The periodic returns of the Boards of Guardians to the Ministry of Health did not distinguish persons receiving and those not receiving unemployment benefit.
   Some indication of the relative importance of poor law relief compared with other means of support for those denied unemployment benefit can be found in *Royal Commission on Unemployment Insurance, Appendices to Minutes of Evidence Part III. Appendix XXII. Enquiry into the Personal*

Poor law data for Scotland are less troublesome. From 1922 the Scottish statistics reported for three days in each year (January 15, May 15, September 15) the number of destitute able-bodied unemployed receiving relief on account of unemployment. Neither the employed nor the unemployed relieved for reasons other than unemployment were included and the figures for dependants were shown separately from the main wage-earners.[25]

(b) Persons in Receipt of Unemployment Benefit and Supplementary Payments

Between the Wars[26] The statistics available of the operation of the extended unemployment insurance scheme in the interwar period are somewhat difficult to interpret. With the onset of industrial recession and protracted unemployment after 1921 it was necessary to meet the needs of those persons out of work whose rights to benefit under the insurance scheme were exhausted. From March 1921 to July 1924 such persons received uncovenanted benefits. From August 1924 'extended benefit' became available for the same purpose, a provision which continued until April 1928. Thereafter, those persons who had exhausted their rights to standard benefit received 'transitional benefit' on satisfying certain conditions. This benefit ended in November 1931 only to be replaced by a scheme of 'transitional payments', subject to an investigation of needs by local authorities. Such payments were

---

Circumstances of Persons Whose Unemployment Benefit is Disallowed. London 1931. See also *Unemployed Persons in receipt of Domiciliary Poor Law Relief in England and Wales during the week ended 18th June, 1927.* Cmd. 3006, 1927; 1928–29 Cmd. 3218; 1929–30 Cmd. 3433.

25. Another series of Scottish statistics, beginning in September 1929, paralleled the English data. Persons ordinarily engaged in some regular occupation in receipt of relief were separated into the three groups corresponding to the English classification. As in the English statistics, however, dependents were shown separately only for Classes I and II. Class III included some persons relieved for reasons other than unemployment. See *Twenty-Second Abstract of Labour Statistics,* p. 201. The number in Class III relieved for reasons other than unemployment can be determined since monthly figures were published for Scotland in the *Gazette* from October 1928 indicating the number of persons other than the insured and uninsured unemployed registered at Exchanges in receipt of relief due to unemployment.

26. Details of some of the sources of data on trade union unemployment benefit payments before 1914 can be found on pp. 15–16.

themselves superseded from December 1934 by 'unemployment allow-ances' payable after a similar investigation of needs by the Unemploy-ment Assistance Board.

The possible confusion arising from the different terminology used to describe the type of benefit available is compounded by changes in the meaning of 'claimants' and 'applicants' as they appear in official statistics. Until October 1931 people drawing either standard or transitional benefit were termed 'claimants' since their claim was associated with the notion of payment as of right. From 1931 a formal distinction was made between 'claimants' for benefit proper and 'applicants' for transitional payments, a procedure which continued when transitional payments were replaced by unemployment allowances—however, in the statistical analyses of duration of unemployment, the term 'applicants' was used to include both classes. Before April 1937 claimants and applicants were always insured persons but thereafter a change in unemployment assistance regulations admitted to assistance unemployed persons irrespective of their insurance contribution record.[27] The total of claimants and applicants therefore included a proportion of the uninsured persons on the unemployment register.

A primary distinction in the unemployment totals would seem to be between persons in receipt of benefit and persons not in receipt of benefit, but statistically speaking it was not possible to make such a precise distinction between the wars, because basic unemployment statistics referred to the position on the day of a particular count. The total number of persons receiving benefit at that time could not be determined exactly however since benefit was paid only on certain days of the week. Nor could it be said that a particular number of persons were entitled to benefit on the day of the count for on that day many claims would still be under consideration, not to be paid until later. Moreover the payment of benefit on a particular day was frequently dependent on proof of unemployment on one or more subsequent days.

Figures of claims to benefit to the end of 1931 refer to claims current rather than to claims authorized and as such tend to overstate the number of actual beneficiaries because they include persons with undecided claims, those serving the 'waiting period', and those with claims disallowed who still maintained registration. Claims under consideration and claims authorized were reported separately from

27. See pp. 51-2.

December 1931. The number of authorized claims is known specifically for only ten dates between 1922 and 1929 as a result of Ministry of Labour sample surveys.[28] Only on these ten dates was it also possible to distinguish between standard insurance beneficiaries and persons claiming uncovenanted, extended, or transitional benefits.

From January 1926 the *Gazette* published details of 'claimants disqualified but maintaining registration' and of those with 'claims admitted or under consideration'. But it is not possible to determine the proportion of the latter group that represented persons actually in receipt of benefit. To do so would necessitate deducting the total of those persons who had applied for benefit but whose entitlement was not yet known and those persons who had been deemed eligible for benefits but who were still in the 'waiting period' (6 days, prior to 1937).[29]

From December 1931 the Ministry of Labour separated total claims under consideration from total claims admitted, but it did not distinguish insurance claims admitted until December 1936. The number of claims admitted for insurance benefit is, however, in each annual report of the Unemployment Insurance Statutory Committee. Other statistics relating to claims for benefit etc. regularly published in the *Gazette* include: recommendations of Local Committees on claims for extended benefit, monthly January 1926 to May 1928; decisions of Insurance Officers and Courts of Referees on claims, monthly June 1928 to August 1939; numbers claiming insurance benefit or transitional payments, monthly December 1931 to January 1935 (or unemployment allowances instead of transitional payments, monthly February 1935 to September 1939).[30]

---

28. Burns, op. cit., appendix II. The dates are June, July, October, November 1922, April 1923, December 1924, June 1925, March 1927, December 1928 and September 1929. The sources of the precise figures are 1922-3, *Report on National Unemployment Insurance to July 1923;* 1924, *Report on an Investigation into the Personal Circumstances and Industrial History of 10,903 Claimants to Unemployment Benefit, November 24 to 29, 1924;* 1925, *Gazette,* June 1925; 1927, *Report on an Investigation into . . . History of 9,748 Claimants to Unemployment Benefit, April 4 to 9, 1927;* 1928 and 1929, *Gazette,* March 1929, January 1930. Details of the benefit record of unemployed persons included in other sample surveys are on pp. 139-44.
29. Burns, op. cit., pp. 344-5.
30. For further information on unemployment expenditures see *Royal Commission on Unemployment Insurance, Final Report,* Cmd. 4185, 1931-2; *Report of the Statutory Committee on the Financial Condition of the Unemployment Fund on 31 December 1934,* 1934-5 and annually thereafter

Since 1948 The comprehensive scheme of national insurance introduced in July 1948 provided a source of detailed statistics of payments
of unemployment benefit to those with a recent record of employment (other than the self-employed, those not normally gainfully
occupied, and married women and widow beneficiaries who chose not
to pay insurance contributions). The conditions of entitlement to
unemployment benefit and the rates of and periods during which such
benefit (and other allowances) are paid have changed frequently since
1948 and it is not necessary to recount such details here.

The local offices of the Department of Employment and its pre-
decessors have acted as agents of the central social security department
since 1948 for the purpose of payments arising from unemployment.
Each office made frequent detailed returns to headquarters of the
benefit and allowance situation of those registered as unemployed on
which the official published series were based. Details of the number of
claims to unemployment benefit made each year from July 1948 for
Great Britain, England, Wales, Scotland, and Regions, and of the number
of persons by sex receiving benefit are in the *Annual Reports* of the
social security ministry.[31]

to 1947–8; Unemployment Assistance Board, *Report for the Period ended
31st December, 1935,* Cmd. 5177, 1935–6; 1936–7 Cmd. 5526; 1937–8
Cmd. 5725; 1938–9 Cmd. 6021; *Return of the Number of Payments made
at Local Offices of the Ministry of Labour in the week ended Friday, 26th
June 1936, by way of Unemployment Benefit . . . and of Unemployment
Allowances . . . ,* Cmd. 5240, 1935–6.

31. The titles of the departments responsible for social security have changed
since 1948. In 1953 the Ministry of National Insurance, established in 1944,
was merged with the Ministry of Pensions, established in 1917, to form the
Ministry of Pensions and National Insurance. The National Assistance Board,
which had existed separately from 1948 to 1965, was merged with the MPNI
to form the Ministry of Social Security, national assistance benefit becoming
supplementary benefit under the oversight of a Supplementary Benefits
Commission (which published its own annual report). In 1968 the Ministry of
Health and the Ministry of Social Security were combined to form the Department of Health and Social Security. The DHSS is responsible for social
security for the whole of Great Britain but deals with health matters only
for England and Wales.

Full details of the relevant annual reports of the various ministries and of
changes in the rules and regulations governing the payment of unemployment
benefit and national assistance to 1960 are in Interdepartmental Committee
on Social and Economic Research, *Guides to Official Sources: No. 5. Social
Security Statistics,* HMSO 1961.

From November 1960 the *Gazette* published the results of a quarterly analysis of all persons on the unemployment register on the first Monday in the quarter showing separately those who received unemployment benefit and supplementary allowance (formerly national assistance), those who received supplementary allowance (national assistance) only, and those who received no payment.[32] The statistics previously included in the *Annual Reports* of the central social security department have been included since 1973 in a more comprehensive annual digest entitled *Social Security Statistics,* published by the DHSS. Apart from details of the nature and current rates of unemployment benefit and other supplementary allowances the most recent edition (1978 relating to the year 1976) includes the following statistical returns:- claims to unemployment benefit made in various periods and analysed by region[33] (1971-6); persons by sex receiving unemployment benefit on selected monthly dates (1966-76) and by region (1971-76); unemployed persons by sex registered on the first Monday in May and November analysed by benefit entitlement, (1969-76); unemployed persons by sex registered on 3 May 1976 analysed by benefit entitlement and region by benefit entitlement and age and by dependancy condition and age (males only), males receiving unemployment benefit on the first Monday in May and November, analysed by dependancy condition and whether receiving supplementary allowance, (1969-76); unemployed persons receiving earnings-related supplement on the first Monday in May and November, analysed by weekly amount paid, (1970-76). In addition, detailed classifications are made separately of the unemployed in receipt of supplementary benefit.

32. The current series provide for Great Britain details (February, May, August, November) of the numbers of unemployed persons (the wholly unemployed, casual workers, and, until November 1972, temporarily stopped workers) analysed by the type of unemployment benefit and/or allowances received distinguishing men, single women (including widowed and divorced), married women and, as a joint group, boys and girls under 18. Details from 1960 are in the *Historical Abstract,* table 176, and appropriate *Year Books.* The 'benefit situation' of the unemployed was also included in the Department of Employment's surveys of the characteristics of the unemployed. See pp. 145-51.
33. The regional boundaries for social security purposes are slightly different from those of Standard Regions. For details as at 11 February 1976 see *Social Security Statistics 1976,* DHSS 1978, appendix 4.

Despite the increased availability in recent years of detailed statistics of social security payments and of registered unemployment it is still difficult to draw firm conclusions from direct comparisons of the two sets of data. The Interdepartmental Working Party on unemployment statistics summarized the problem thus:[34]

Although everybody getting benefit must be on the unemployment register, it does not follow that everybody who is on the register must be getting benefit or even credits. There are a number of reasons why there is always a difference between the numbers on the unemployment register and the numbers getting benefit. One of those is technical and derives from the method of obtaining a count on a particular day. At any point in time there will always be some people who are registered as unemployed, and are so counted, and who will eventually get benefit but whose claims for benefit on the day of the count have not yet been decided or who are not yet entitled on that day to unemployment benefit (because of waiting days) or supplementary benefit (because they still have resources in the shape of their last wages).

Although the great majority of workers qualify for unemployment benefit when they lose their job, some groups do not—such as certain married women, young people and people from abroad with insufficient contributions to qualify for benefit, and those persons over pensionable age who are looking for work while in receipt of a retirement pension. Other unemployed workers not receiving benefit include those who have exhausted their entitlement and those who before being recorded as unemployed were working on their own account or were not gainfully occupied. Problems of interpreting unemployment and benefit data are particularly acute, therefore, in regions employing a significant proportion of persons who because of their loose attachment to the labour force may or may not be on the unemployment register, and where, in general, precise or regular information is lacking of the number of unemployed people disallowed benefit; of the number of those unemployed who may not be claiming benefit for fear of being disqualified; and of those who do claim, then suffer disqualification but remain registered as unemployed even though they are not entitled to benefit.

34. Cmd. 5157, op. cit., para. 3.13.

Unemployed Minority Groups

The three major sources of data about the level of unemployment among racial minority groups compared with the general population are: the statistics published by the Department of Employment, the results of the PEP survey of racial minorities, and the Census returns for 1966 and 1971 (advance analysis). In 1974 PEP conducted a national survey of the Asian and West Indian racial minority groups, including their experience of unemployment during 1970-74 and the previous ten years.[35] Figures by country of birth of the number of residents born outside Great Britain who were out of work in April 1966 are in the main Census returns for that year; the advance analysis of the 1971 Census also included returns of the proportion of the economically active who were unemployed in April analysed by birthplace. The Census and survey returns are, however, of somewhat limited value for comparative analysis since they are not based on any agreed definition of the minorities or of the unemployed and relate only to two specific periods.

Official statistics of unemployment among registered coloured workers in Great Britain first became available in June 1971 and related to quarterly counts from February 1963 onwards.[36] The data first referred to the registered wholly unemployed born in, or with a parent or parents born in, certain Commonwealth countries.[37] Adult immigrants were counted in total for each administrative region of

35. For details of the sampling technique adopted and of the statistical results obtained, see D.J. Smith, *The Facts of Racial Disadvantage*, PEP, Volume XLII, Broadsheet No. 560, February 1976.
36. Statistics had been collected in previous years but were not published. R.B. Davison used previously unpublished Home Office, Ministry of National Insurance and Ministry of Labour figures to assess the incidence of unemployment among coloured immigrants from Commonwealth Territories registered for employment between August 1960–May 1962. The returns included those temporarily stopped and both claimants and non-claimants to unemployment benefit. A separate analysis was made of coloured unemployment by Ministry of Labour Region and by country of origin. See 'Immigration and Unemployment in the United Kingdom, 1955–62', *British Journal of Industrial Relations*, 1, 1963.
37. The statistics related to three groups of countries: Group 1: Australia, Canada and New Zealand; Group 2: Cyprus, Gibraltar and Malta; and Group 3: Africa, India, Pakistan, the West Indies, and all other Commonwealth territories. Details of the countries included in the latter Group and in those of Africa and the West Indies are in the *Gazette*, July 1971, p. 616.

Great Britain. The figures were further analysed to show the regional total of unemployed men and women by country of origin. The basis on which such statistics were collected changed in 1970 as a result of the report of the Select Committee on Race Relations and Immigration into the problem of coloured school leavers.[38] From November of that year the count of unemployed Commonwealth immigrants was limited to those born in Africa, the West Indies, India, Pakistan, and the other territories previously specified, largely on the grounds that it was the employment position of coloured people as such and not of immigrants from, say, Australia, Canada, or New Zealand that warranted careful scrutiny. The count was at the same time extended to include unemployed adults, and from May 1971 young persons under 18, one or both of whose parents were born in one of the listed Commonwealth countries to the exclusion of those unemployed coloured workers born in this country whose parents were also born here. The data continued to be published at quarterly intervals and for each administrative region of Great Britain.[39]

The Department of Employment is the only source from which to obtain some idea of the long-term trend of unemployment among minority groups.[40] In general, however, there are no adequate time-series data of minority group unemployment by duration, occupation, or by industry although March issues of the *Gazette* provide an age analysis of minority unemployment for the previous month. The employment status of particular ethnic groups is tabulated in the annual General Household Survey and in the Department of the Environment's, *National Dwelling and Household Survey* but neither these nor other sample surveys[41] provide statistical returns of sufficiently substantial value to monitor the true extent of unemployment among the indigenous minority population.

38. *Report from the Select Committee on Race Relations and Immigration. The Problems of Coloured School-Leavers,* London, HMSO 1969.
39. Total numbers are given for each region and for Great Britain, (men, women, young persons) as well as estimates of all unemployed immigrants as a percentage of all unemployed (immigrants and others).
40. See 'Unemployment among Workers from Racial Minority Groups', *Gazette,* September 1975.
41. J. Taylor, 'High Unemployment and Coloured School-leavers: the Tyneside Pattern', *New Community,* 2, 1972/3; Shirley Dex, 'Job Search Methods and Ethnic Discrimination', ibid., VII, Winter 1978/9; Commission for Racial Equality, *Looking for Work: Black and White School-Leavers in Lewisham,* London 1978.

Part II

The Nature of Unemployment

6

The Duration of Unemployment

Official Statistics to 1939

Official published statistics of the duration of unemployment relate mainly to the period after 1930. The information available before 1914 is extremely selective, providing only limited data of duration in particular trades during the last quarter of the nineteenth century[1] and among a sample of the unemployed in York in 1911.[2] In addition there is evidence for the Edwardian period of the length of time for which individuals were unemployed before applying for relief from Distress Committees[3] and, later, at Labour Exchanges.[4]

By the time regular unemployment insurance statistics were available it was clearly recognized that the change in the Live Register total between any two dates was the net effect of a large number of separate

---

1. Results of an analysis of the vacant books of the Amalgamated Society of Engineers (Leeds and Manchester branches) during 1877, 1895, and the Amalgamated Society of Carpenters and Joiners and of the documents of the Compositors', Operative Plumbers', and Woodcutting Machinists' Unions are in *Royal Commission on the Poor Laws and Relief of Distress, Appendix XXV*, Cd. 5077, 1911.

2. Rowntree and Lasker, op. cit.

3. See *Royal Commission ... Relief of Distress, Appendix, Volume VIII*, Cd. 5066, 1910; E.V. Brichall, 'The Conditions of Distress', *Economic Review*, XX, 1910; C.W. Alington, 'Aspects of Unemployment in West Ham', *Economic Review*, XVI, 1906; Chapman and Hallsworth, op. cit.

4. Report on the Proceedings of the Board of Trade under the Labour Exchanges Act, 1909 and under Part III of the National Insurance Act, 1911 to July 1914 (unpublished).

changes, some of them increases and some of them decreases, in the
various parts of the country. In 1930, when the average number on the
Live Register stood at about 1¼ millions, the total number of separate
individuals who had been included in the figures in the course of a year
was about 4½ millions.[5] It was this flow onto and off the unemployment register of individuals experiencing varying durations of unemployment that was to provide the basis of more sophisticated duration
analysis in the 1960s.[6]

Regular monthly data on the duration of unemployment only became officially available in 1930. Selective information over the previous
five years was included in a number of sample surveys.[7] From June
1930 a monthly return was published in the *Gazette* classifying the
number of wholly unemployed claimants to benefit according to the
length of time they had been continuously on the register up to the
date of the count.[8] This was the only source of information of its type
until 1932. Thereafter a new monthly classification was adopted and
retained until August 1939. It related not to all the insured unemployed,
but only to those persons who were registered as unemployed on one

---

5. PRO, Cab. 58/146, 'Economic Advisory Council. Committee on Unemployment Statistics. Unemployment Returns as now Published', 22 March 1930,
   pp. 10–11.
6. See below pp. 192–6.
7. Ministry of Labour, *Report on an Investigation into the Employment and
   Insurance History of a Sample of Persons Insured Against Unemployment in
   Great Britain*, April 1926, ibid., *Report on an Investigation into the Personal
   Circumstances and Industrial History of 9,748 Claimants to Unemployment
   Benefit*, April 1927. Analyses of the unemployment experience during the
   previous twelve months of 1 per cent of benefit claimants were made in
   March and September 1929. *Gazette*, January 1930. Details of a similar
   sample survey are in *Royal Commission on Unemployment Insurance,
   Appendices to Minutes of Evidence, Part V*, 2 February 1931. Until 1931
   the Ministry of Labour collected data of the number of claimants to benefit
   who had been on the register for less than one month. However the special
   return from which the figures were derived was abolished in 1931 'as a measure
   of economy'. PRO Lab. 2/1597, 'Publication of New Statistics in the Ministry
   of Labour Gazette', 19 November 1931.
8. Details were given of the number and percentages of the total of men and
   women 21–64, young men and women 18–20, boys and girls 16–17, who had
   been on the registers for periods of (a) not more than one week, (b) more
   than one week and not more than two weeks, (c) more than two weeks and
   not more than three, (d) more than three weeks and not more than four,
   (e) more than four weeks.

date in each month, who were applicants for benefit or assistance, and who had been continuously on the registers for a varying number of months rather than weeks.[9] As such the classification excluded those who had discontinued registration, even though their unemployment books remained lodged at an Employment Exchange, and those who were unable to satisfy the conditions for making an application for benefit or assistance. From April 1937 applicants for assistance were no longer required to have a minimum number of stamps to their credit. The duration data, therefore, included a larger proportion of the long-term unemployed than hitherto. But some adults were still excluded from benefit or assistance and excluded also from the duration data. To this extent the statistics continued to understate the degree of long-period unemployment.[10]

These duration returns related only to the last spell of unemployment. In determining the length of spell short periods of employment lasting not more than three days were ignored. Since they were based

9. The number and percentages for men (aged 18 to 64), women (from 18–64), for boys, and for girls were divided among those who had been on the register (a) less than 3 months, (b) 3 months but less than 6, (c) 6 months but less than 12, (d) 12 months or more. Although the duration statistics for the 1930s are comparable for each classification only from 1932 the figures of those unemployed for 12 months or more are directly comparable from the date of the September 1929 sample onwards. The figures of those recorded as unemployed up to 12 weeks in September 1929 are also comparable with those unemployed less than 3 months in the post-1932 data since broken weeks of unemployment were disregarded in the 1929 sample. The information regularly published from 1932 did not distinguish duration of unemployment by industry or Ministry of Labour Division. The data included the temporarily stopped and casual workers, but excluded those aged 65 and over.

10. For information on long-term unemployment between the wars see W.H. Beveridge, 'An Analysis of Unemployment II', *Economica*, IV, 1937; *Men Without Work. A Report Made to the Pilgrim Trust*, Cambridge 1938; E.W. Bakke, *The Unemployed Man*, London 1933; H.L. Beales and R.S. Lambert, *Memoirs of the Unemployed*, London 1934; *Gazette*, October 1935 (analysis made on 29 July 1935 of those unemployed applicants for benefit who had been on the registers for over a year).

From 1930 the *Gazette* also published details of how many persons drawing unemployment benefit had paid fewer than 30 contributions in the preceding two years. Data on the duration of unemployment for earlier and later dates are also available from the contributions and benefit records of those individuals involved in various Ministry of Labour sample surveys. See above pp. 139–44.

on counts made on particular days the statistics could not adequately reflect the full cycle of employment and unemployment experienced by registrants. Those who on a given day appeared to have been unemployed for 12 months or more would have appeared at an earlier date among the count of those unemployed for less than three months and would have progressed through the subsequent classifications. On the other hand, some of those who at any given date appeared as having been unemployed for less than three months may within the preceding year have had far more unemployment than employment. Moreover, since the statistics were predominantly of persons registered as unemployed it is possible that actual unemployment was greater than that indicated in the returns. Failure after repeated calls to obtain work through an Employment Exchange could result in a high proportion of lapsed registrations without a corresponding proportion of cases of employment found by other means. The duration statistics, therefore, must be taken as only a rough indication of the distribution of unemployment among individuals and of the proportion of long- and short-term unemployment at any given time.

Statistics corresponding to the post-1932 classification were available by Ministry of Labour Division only on selected dates until 1939.[11] An analysis of the duration of unemployment by Divisions every three months and back to 1937 appeared in the *Gazette* in April 1939 but the duration analysis as a whole was suspended with the outbreak of war. An earlier study of duration of unemployment in particular industries[12] proved to be the only official survey of its kind for the remainder of the interwar period.

The duration of unemployment series throw some light on the extent to which changes occurred in the personnel of the unemployed during the 1930s. By examining the figures for various dates from 1932 one can determine, for example, the proportion of the total number of

11. Details by Ministry of Labour Divisions of the number of men applying for benefit who had been continuously on the register for less than 3 months in June, December 1932, June, December 1936 and for 12 months or more in June, December 1933 are in the *Gazette,* January 1937. Similar data for particular towns, though not Ministry Divisions, during 1932–4 are in the Pilgrim Trust Report, op. cit., and Beveridge, loc. cit.

12. The *Gazette,* January 1937, published details of the number of male and female applicants for benefit or assistance aged 18–64 who on 8 June 1936 had been on the registers (a) less than 3 months, (b) 3 but less than 12 months, and (c) 12 months or more in those industries where the total number of applicants was 10,000 or more.

applicants on the registers at any given date who had found employment within the ensuing 3, 6, 9, and 12 months. Equally, for any given
year it is possible to compare the average number of claims current at
any given date with the estimated number of separate individuals with
claims during the year. The data shows, for example, that in a year of
poor employment such as 1929 the average number of persons with
claims current on any one date represented only about 27 per cent of
the total number of separate individuals who had been claimants
during the year. In a time of depression such as 1933 this percentage
rose to 42. By 1936 the proportion had fallen to 36. By that time it
appeared that persons who were applicants for benefit or assistance
were unemployed on the average for approximately one-third of the
year. This figure represented the average amount of unemployment
experienced in aggregate during a period of 12 months by persons who
had claimed benefit or assistance during that period, some of whom
were unemployed for a single day only while others were unemployed
for the whole year. In a large proportion of the cases, of course, the
aggregate amount of unemployment experienced during the year
consisted of a number of distinct spells of unemployment separated
by periods of employment.

It was this process rather than the state of unemployment which
was so inadequately reflected in the official statistics. The considerable
'turn-over' within the unemployment register, and the varying prospects which individual unemployed men had of leaving the register in
relation to how long they had already been on it, defied precise
statistical analysis in this period. Indeed such issues were not seriously
analysed until the late 1960s.[13] A rare though somewhat limited contemporary approach to a more realistic assessment of unemployment
duration was provided by Singer in the late 1930s. He analysed the
dynamics of the labour market by separating the net movement of the
total of the register into absorptions from the ranks of the unemployed
men with varying durations of unemployment and new additions to
the register. Thus persons who in any September had been unemployed
for periods ranging from 3-6 months were regarded as the residue of
those who in June had been unemployed for up to 3 months; by
subtracting one figure from the other it was possible to obtain the
percentage who were employed during the quarter. Such 're-
employment rates' were calculated for each duration category, con-
firming the marked difference between the re-employment rates of

13. See below pp. 192-6.

those unemployed for less than three months and those unemployed for longer periods. Because of the deficiencies within the official duration data his results for 1935–8 were based on annual information of the 'wholly unemployed' men in the Special Areas only. The extension of official duration statistics in 1939, providing three-monthly analyses nationally and by Divisions back to 1937, enabled a similar analysis to be conducted for the country as a whole.[14]

Duration Statistics Since the Second World War

Statistics of the duration of unemployment, suspended following the outbreak of the Second World War, were only regularly compiled again from October 1945. A number of special analyses were made during the war which, though limited in scope, at least indicated the changing importance of long-term unemployment.[15]

The 'duration' categories in which the published data were presented from October 1945 differed from those of pre-war returns and were subject to change over time. The position is summarized in Table 18.

From 1946 to July 1948 the duration analyses had a coverage similar to those of the pre-war period, excluding persons insured under special schemes for the banking and insurance industries, persons classified as unsuitable for ordinary employment, and persons aged 65 and over. The duration data covering the years 1932–9 included the temporarily stopped and casual workers. Until April 1972 the latter group was excluded from the analyses of duration. The current series include school leavers whose numbers affect the duration analysis

14. H.W. Singer, 'The Process of Unemployment in the Depressed Areas (1935–1938)', *Review of Economic Studies*, VI, 1938–9; 'Regional Labour Markets and the Process of Unemployment', *Review of Economic Studies*, VII, 1939–40.

15. The Ministry of Labour conducted a special analysis of workers on the registers of Employment Exchanges on 1 January 1940, paying particular attention to male registrants (aged 18–64) unemployed for a year or more. *Gazette*, February 1940. A general review of all unemployed men who had been on the registers for a month or more was made in July 1940, the results of which are in the *Gazette*, August, October, and December 1940. In March 1941, a return was made of all the wholly unemployed adult women on the registers (excluding the temporarily stopped and casuals) which included details of unemployment duration. *Gazette*, May 1941. For further details see 'The Impact of War on Long-Term Unemployment in Great Britain', *International Labour Review*, XLV, 1942 and Reubens, loc. cit.

particularly in the summer months. Up to July 1975 the series also included adult students registered for temporary employment during vacations. The quarterly analyses for the period 1946-62 were published for the March, June, September, and December counts. Since July 1962, they have been published for the January, April, July, and October counts.[16]

TABLE 18
CLASSIFICATION OF THE UNEMPLOYED BY 'DURATION' CATEGORIES

From October 1945:
Figures obtained every month showing the number who had been continuously unemployed for not more than two weeks and for more than two weeks.

From June 1946:
Further sub-divisions were introduced to the monthly returns to show the number who had been unemployed for two to eight weeks and more than eight weeks. Separate figures were obtained for males and females under and over 18 years of age. A series of half-yearly returns began analysing the wholly unemployed by age and by duration for June and December. Separate figures for males and females distinguished duration of unemployment in the following categories and age groups: 4 weeks or less; over 4 and up to 6; over 6 and up to 8; over 8 and up to 13; over 13 and up to 26; over 26 and up to 39; over 39 and up to 52; over 52. Age groups 14 and 15; 16 and 17; 18 and under 21; 21 and under 41; 41 and under 56; 56 and under 60 (females); 65 (males). The figures excluded casuals, the temporarily stopped, persons insured under special schemes and those classified as unavailable for ordinary employment.

From September 1946:
A series of quarterly returns was begun analysing the number of registered wholly unemployed by duration of unemployment according to the following categories: 4 weeks or less; over 4 and up to 6 weeks; over 6 and up to 8; over 8 and up to 13; over 13 and up to 26; over 26 and up to 39; over 39 and up to 52; over 52 weeks. (From July 1962 the month of the duration analysis was changed from the last to the

---

16. Quarterly data from September 1948 to October 1968 can be found in table 175 of the *Historical Abstract* and more recent information in the subsequent *Year Books*. The current quarterly series relate to Great Britain and include figures of the percentage of unemployed in each duration category. A condensed version of the statistics is provided for Standard Regions.

first month in the quarter). There was a further sub-division in the bi-annual returns showing the number who had been unemployed for more than 104 weeks.

From June 1953:
The more detailed figures published bi-annually were further sub-divided to show the number who had been unemployed for one week or less, over one week and up to two weeks, and over two and up to four weeks. The bi-annual returns were combined with an age and regional analysis. The two months chosen for this were later changed to January and July.

The detailed age/duration analyses provide national data for males and females separately for the following groups: ages: under 18; 18–19; 20–24; 25–29; 30–34; 35–39; 40–44; 45–49; 50–54; 55–59; 60–64; 65 and over; duration of unemployment in weeks: one or less; over 1 and up to 2; over 2 and up to 3; over 3 and up to 4; over 4 and up to 5; over 5 and up to 6; over 6 and up to 7; over 7 and up to 8; over 8 and up to 9; over 9 and up to 13; over 13 and up to 26; over 26 and up to 39; over 39 and up to 52; over 52.

The bi-annual analysis by region is more restricted applying to age groups under 20; 20–39; 40 and over for durations in weeks of 2 or less; over 2 and up to 4; over 4 and up to 8; over 8 and up to 13; over 13 and up to 26; over 26 and up to 52; over 52. They are subject too to the changes in the statistical definition of Standard Regions. For the intervening months a regional analysis by duration for those unemployed for less than 8 weeks was published up to and including June 1978.

From July 1978:
The age duration analysis of the unemployed, hitherto made only in January and July, was thereafter made also in April and October. The age groups were revised to provide more detailed information about youth employment. Those aged 18 and 19 were shown separately. The number aged 35–39 and 40–44, formerly given separately, were now included as a single group.

For regions, the age groups were revised to show those under 25, 25–44 and 45 and over. The monthly regional analysis by duration gives numbers unemployed for less than 4 weeks.

From April 1979:
The duration categories in weeks were changed to: one or less; over 1 and up to 2; over 2 and up to 4; over 4 and up to 6; over 6 and up to 8; over 8 and up to 13; over 13 and up to 26; over 26 and up to 39; over 39 and up to 52; over 52 and up to 65; over 65 and up to 78; over 78 and up to 104; over 104 and up to 156; over 156. The published duration categories for regions were extended so that the over 52 week category was split into over 52 and up to 104; over 104 and up to 156; over 156.

A continuing feature of the statistics is that they refer only to the current spell of registration. Persons are counted as leaving the register if they are sick and their recorded duration of unemployment is measured only from the date on which they return to the register. (Breaks of 2 or 3 days are not counted.) It appears that on average about 5 per cent of each duration group leave the register each quarter through sickness and that a total of up to 10 per cent would leave the register from the longer duration groups even if none of those registered became re-employed.[17]

What is particularly noticeable about the official duration series is that by focusing on current spells of unemployment they tell us little more about frequent and long-term unemployment than did pre-1939 data. Long-term unemployment is under-estimated to some extent by the practice of classifying any period of work lasting three days or more as a break in continuous unemployment. Any person unemployed, say, for over two years who then obtained a temporary job during a busy season would re-enter the statistics as just beginning a period of unemployment. There are no regular analyses of the distribution of the long-term unemployed by industry or broad occupational group though such information has been included in recent surveys of the characteristics of the unemployed.[18] Quarterly returns allow us to follow the progress of groups coming on to the unemployment register and to discern how many remain unemployed in the subsequent quarter. However, until April 1979 these more detailed returns provided data only of those males and females unemployed up to 26 weeks, over 26 weeks and up to 52 weeks, and over 52 weeks. There were therefore no regularly published statistical series relating to the long-term unemployed in between quarters or over longer time periods.[19] Since

---

17. T.F. Cripps and R.J. Tarling, 'An Analysis of the Duration of Male Unemployment in Great Britain 1932–73', *Economic Journal*, 84, June 1974, p. 292.
18. See pp. 145–51.
19. Information is also available from other sources. The Department of Employment itself has begun to chart the record of recurrent unemployment among samples of the registered unemployed. See above pp. 145–51. See also 'Statistics on long-term unemployment', *Gazette*, June 1978, (covering the period March 1951–January 1978). In addition, the Manpower Services Commission conducted a detailed investigation of a sample of the long-term unemployed in 1979 (defined as those persons unemployed for more than one year) to determine their educational, training, and employment background and the social, physical and psychological factors affecting

April 1979 quarterly analyses are available splitting the over 52 weeks category into five groups.[20]

The official statistics provide a good deal of useful information on which an analysis of the number of people who have been on the registers for various periods of time on the day of the count can be based. Calculations of seasonally adjusted median and quartile values of duration at quarterly count dates between 1948 and 1978 indicate, for example, that duration rises and falls with the level of unemployment but tends to lag behind the unemployment curve as it changes direction. Median unemployment duration is greater among males than females. It also increases rapidly with age and is generally higher in regions with higher unemployment rates.[21]

Such data do not, however, tell us directly the length of completed spells of unemployment nor do they indicate for an individual or group coming on to the register the length of time to be expected before they leave the register. The accepted practice was to count together those who began their unemployment at different times, and possibly under different economic circumstances, and not to assess in any way the duration prospects of persons registering at a particular time. But this method ignored the basic differences in the characteristics of the stock of unemployed people from those becoming unemployed at any given time. The result was that the unemployed registered in the monthly count data did not provide a representative sample of all cases of unemployment. Those suffering longer durations were proportionately

---

their ability to take up work. See *A Study of the Long-Term Unemployed*, Manpower Intelligence and Planning Division, Manpower Services Commission, 1979.

For other details of frequent and long-term unemployment (variously defined) among sample groups of the unemployed see A. Sinfield, *The Long-Term Unemployed*, ECD, Paris 1968; A. Sinfield, 'Poor and Out of Work in Shields', in P. Townsend (ed.), *The Concept of Poverty*, London 1970; J.L. Baxter, 'Long-Term Unemployment in Great Britain, 1953–71', *Bulletin of the Oxford University Institute of Economics and Statistics*, 34, 1972; Hill, *et. al., Men Out of Work*, op. cit., Cambridge 1973; W. Daniel, *A National Survey of the Unemployed*, op. cit.; M. Hill and O. Stevenson, *From the General to the Specific*, Oxford 1976; A. Sinfield, 'Unemployment and the Social Structure', in Worswick op. cit., 1976; W. Daniel and E. Stilgoe, *Where are they now?* PEP, op. cit.

20. See above, p. 190.

21. *Gazette,* February 1973; September 1978.

over-represented and those of shorter durations under-represented—those joining and leaving the register within one month might never appear in the official count. The flows through the unemployment register, in other words, were much larger than was the stock of the unemployed.

What was lacking until the late 1960s was a direct measure of how long those newly registering for employment or those who had already been on the register for some time could expect to remain unemployed. As R. Fowler, Director of Statistical Research, explained in 1968:

For purposes of economic policy we need to know by how much an increase in the general level of unemployment raises the expectation of remaining on the register for those who have already been on the register for x weeks; and whether this expectation is raised more for those who have been on the register for a long time than for those who have been on the register for a short time. Does an increase in the general level of unemployment lead to an increased turnover of the register or to an increase in the time spent on the register and by how much?[22]

The ingenious method which Fowler adopted in 1968 to answer such questions was to construct a stationary unemployed register,[23] similar to an actuarial life table. Unlike actuarial calculations, however, it was not possible as a first step to compute a series of the number of persons who had been on the register for x weeks exactly from which could be produced a column of figures giving for a group of persons coming on to the register at the same time estimates of how many would still be on the register at the end of 2, 3, 4 . . . weeks.[24] The difficulty was that there were no figures available analysing by duration on the register those who had left the register in a given period. A first approximation to a stationary register was therefore obtained by

22. R.F. Fowler, *Duration of Unemployment on the Register of Wholly Unemployed,* Studies in Official Statistics, Research Series No. 1, HMSO 1968, p. 1.
23. Defined as: 'a situation in which the total stock and the numbers in each duration group are not changing because the flows of people leaving the register are exactly balanced by the flow of new registrations and by the lengthening duration of unemployment of those who remain on the register'. Cripps and Tarling, loc. cit., p. 294.
24. Based on the rather extreme assumption that conditions determining the rate of withdrawal from the register remained constant.

averaging over a period of years (1961-5) the frequency distributions of a series of wholly unemployed registers (for Great Britain, males and females separately). From these were calculated specific withdrawal rates and the probabilities that a person who had been on the register for x weeks exactly would either still be on the register at the end of the following week or would have left the register during the following week.[25]

What is striking from Fowler's study is its confirmation of the importance of short-period turnover among the wholly out of work. Out of any group joining the register on a given day, it appeared that nearly half would leave it within two weeks and that about two-thirds would leave it within a month.[26] The considerable short-term fluctuations in the monthly flows on and off the register arose partly as a result of variations in the lengths of time to which they related and partly because of seasonal factors. Fowler estimated that at the observed level of unemployment during 1961-5 (1.7 per cent) the average flows on to the register were about 39,000 males and 16,000 females per week with similar numbers flowing off. Thus large numbers of people both joined and left the register in between successive monthly counts and were therefore excluded in the monthly unemployment totals. Put another way, it was recognized that the changes in the monthly recorded unemployment figures arose from relatively small differences between the large flows each month on to and off the unemployment register—the same being true for vacancy figures. Relatively small changes in registration and leaving rates could result, therefore, in substantial changes in the stock of unemployment.

Statistics of the number of people joining and leaving the unemployment register became available in 1966. The current data are derived from a count in employment offices and Jobcentres of the number of unemployed persons registering each month (between the monthly counts of the level of unemployment). This figure represents inflow. From the inflow and the counts of the unemployed at the beginning and end of the month, the unemployment outflow—the number

25. For the mathematical basis upon which the calculations were based see Fowler, op. cit., appendices II, III and IV.
26. This pattern was found to persist during 1971-72, the period of highest post-war unemployment until 1975. Fowler's calculations were subsequently updated for 1967 to 1970 and the results published in the *Gazette*, February 1973. The calculations were not continued for subsequent years because the register was not regarded as sufficiently stable.

leaving the register—is calculated. The procedure is similar for vacancies, except that it is the outflow which is measured directly (through placings in employment and cancellations of vacancies by employers) and it is the inflow which is calculated.

The flow figures include a number of people who are excluded from the unemployment count, namely those looking for part-time employment who are not claiming unemployment benefit (mainly affecting the figures for females) and certain people using the 'self-service' system. A count is made of the number of 'self-service submissions' to employers by local offices made on behalf of those people who apply for vacancies displayed at employment offices and Jobcentres. Any application considered suitable is included in the flow statistics as an inflow and an outflow if the person is unemployed but not previously registered as unemployed. Such people are not included in the count of the unemployed.

The flow figures exclude persons on the special Professional and Executive Register; adult students seeking vacation employment (from June 1976); young people seeking jobs through careers officers of local education authorities (though since April 1974 in England and Wales and May 1975 in Scotland, school leavers and others under 18 years of age have been free to register at employment offices and the flow figures have been increased to the extent to which young people have exercised this option); vacancies which are not notified to the employment service and unemployed people who choose not to register at an employment office. The differences in coverage are numerically small. The total of the unemployed (flow statistics coverage) in June 1976 was about 3½ per cent less than the published total.[27]

---

27. Regular publication of unemployment and vacancy flow statistics began in the *Gazette* in September 1966. Details of the data for 1970–July 1974 are in the *British Labour Statistics Year Book 1974* and the trend figures for earlier years in the *Gazette,* September 1972. The flow figures normally collected for 4 or 5 week periods between unemployment and vacancy counts, are converted to a standard 4-1/3 week month and are seasonally adjusted. While the coverage of the flow statistics is different from the published totals of wholly unemployed excluding school leavers and of vacancies notified, the movements in the respective series are closely related. Cripps and Tarling, loc. cit., identified sixteen approximately stationary registers, using a variation of Fowler's approach, and used them to estimate changes in the inflow of people on to the register and the average expected duration of unemployment at selected dates over the period 1932–73.

Inquiries presenting hitherto unpublished data of monthly unemployment and vacancy flow statistics since 1967 have shown that the flows on and off the register are even higher in relation to the total on the register than those indicated by actuarial estimates[28] and that the turnover is proportionately greater for notified vacancies. Over the period August 1975 to July 1976 4,395,000 people registered as unemployed while 4,088,000 left the register. The average stock of unemployment was 1,088,250.[29]

Duration of Unemployment and the Probability of Re-Employment

It has been determined so far that the size of the unemployment register fluctuates according to the net outflow or inflow of people newly unemployed and that the duration of unemployment as far as individuals are concerned varies enormously, and is by no means fairly reflected in the official statistics. Detailed information on duration of unemployment is an even more critical aid to policy formulation now that recent research suggests that it is changes in duration rather than in flows into unemployment that are the principal cause of aggregate unemployment fluctuations. The shift in emphasis in recent empirical studies towards measuring the decline in average probability of leaving the register with the length of time people have been on the register has naturally directed attention to the direct effects of the duration of unemployment on the probability of re-employment. It is worth examining this issue in some detail because it serves to illustrate the limitations of the official duration data as an interpretative guide to the dynamics of the labour market.

28. The existence of flow data has given rise to cruder estimates of the expected duration of unemployment than are obtained by actuarial-type calculations. Thus the Department of Employment has calculated the expected duration of completed spells of unemployment on joining the register (employment offices, 1971–8) by dividing the average level of unemployment in a quarter by the average of the weekly flows on and off the register. See 'The Duration of Unemployment', *Gazette*, September 1978.

29. Registrations include males plus females, but exclude registrants at Careers Offices and Professional and Executive Recruitment and exclude adult students registered for vacation employment. The 4 million registrations do not, of course, necessarily refer to 4 million separate individuals. *Gazette*, September 1976.

Studies of the impact of unemployment between the wars[30] have helped to substantiate a *prima facie* case that there is a causal link between duration of unemployment and the probability of re-employment. Thus prolonged unemployment may demoralize a man in his willingness to search for work and lead to physical and mental deterioration. It might also prejudice employers against him in so far as a record of lengthy unemployment is regarded as an indication of a man's general unfitness for work. A ready explanation of why leaving rates from the register would fall with increased duration of unemployment would be that the latter determined the former.

Fowler's pioneering study of duration of unemployment on the register confirmed the proposition that the longer a person was unemployed the longer he or she was likely to continue to be out of work. Females on average were expected to spend less time on the register than males. The difference was not very marked during the early weeks, but the gap widened thereafter to the point where, after 52 weeks on the register, males could expect to stay on it half as long again as females before obtaining employment. More generally, in the chosen period 1961-5 the average number of weeks per person that would be spent on the register by a group of new entrants was 7.0 weeks. But those who had been on the register for 52 weeks could expect to spend on the average a further 59 weeks per person on the register. For someone who had been on the register for not more than 2 weeks the chances of going off the register within a week were 27 out of 100. But for the person who had been on the register for 26 weeks the chances of going off it within a week were only 5 out of 100 and for the person who had been on the register for 52 weeks the chances were only 3 out of 100.[31] These characteristics were found to apply in general to the unemployed in each of the Standard Regions of Great Britain.[32]

Although this exercise provided estimates which were free of seasonal and cyclical variations it had obvious limitations. Apart from the inherent assumption that the conditions affecting the nature of the

30. For example Bakke, op. cit. and Pilgrim Trust, *Men Out of Work,* op. cit.
31. Fowler, op. cit. Corresponding estimates were made later using data for the period 1967-70. See *Gazette,* February 1973.
32. The stationary registers compiled for the Standard Regions did not distinguish between males and females separately. The regional variations in the expressed duration of unemployment were not directly associated with regional differences in employment conditions.

stationary register remained constant it was based on data about the duration of the current spell of unemployment among the registered wholly unemployed. This was not necessarily equivalent to the time people actually spent out of work because some people leave the register without obtaining other employment. The extent to which the frequency or duration of past unemployment affects the prospects of future employment for particular groups of workers will continue to be problematical in the absence of regular statistics of the unemployment history of the workforce. The surveys of the characteristics of the unemployed conducted by the Department of Employment have proved a valuable source of extra information in this respect but the results are by no means conclusive. The 1973 survey, for example, found that for a given duration group enthusiasm and prospects both decline with length of unemployment. But, as was point out, 'whether this . . . connection is because long durations of unemployment sap enthusiasm, or because those who are somewhat unenthusiastic tend to have long periods of unemployment cannot be decided from the survey'.[33]

The proposition that the longer a man is unemployed the less likely he is to leave the unemployment register may, however, have no causal significance. An alternative hypothesis is to accept that the inflow to the register is heterogeneous, consisting of workers with personal characteristics which have a direct bearing on their chances of re-employment, independent of the time spent on the register. The rate of unemployment is, accordingly, the product of workers becoming unemployed either for involuntary reasons (of being laid off or fired) or for voluntary reasons (by quitting) and of the average duration of unemployment (dependent on being offered and being prepared to accept another job).

Thus the different rates at which people enter or leave the unemployment register are thought to be affected by personal characteristics such as age, skill, sex, and race. It has long been recognized that the mean duration of unemployment rises with age.[34] Fowler showed that both

33. *Gazette,* March 1974, p. 213.
34. See above pp. 39, 192. This is confirmed by the half-yearly counts of the unemployed classified by duration and by age, available from the early 1950s. Beveridge emphasized the important point, namely that older people were not necessarily more likely to lose their jobs as to remain unemployed once they fell out of work. See also A.G. Rose, *The Older Unemployed Man in Hull,* University College of Hull, 1953.

males and females over 55 could expect to spend four or five times longer on the register than those members of their sex under 25.[35] More recently it has been demonstrated that rising unemployment during the decade 1963-73 had its greatest impact on the duration of unemployment of older workers.[36] Age accounted for half the explained variations in unemployment durations among the sample of 431 males reported in the 1972 General Household Survey as unemployed and seeking work.[37]

Other personal characteristics, namely marital status, health, race, and degree of employability, especially in terms of skill, can have a direct bearing on employment prospects. It appears from recent empirical evidence that unmarried men have longer uncompleted duration spells than do married men and that the expected unemployment duration of married men increases with the number of their dependant children.[38] Moreover the unskilled tend to suffer longer periods of unemployment. Few of those who are readily re-employed by virtue of their particular skills stay on the unemployment register for long. Skilled unemployed men tend to have a greater incentive to seek new employment, prove relatively more adaptable than unskilled workers to the varying requirements of employers, suffer a lower ratio of benefit to wage income than the unskilled, and are able to compete for lower skilled job vacancies.[39] Detailed local studies of a variety of English towns and boroughs have shown that their relative unemployment rates are directly influenced by the composition of their local labour markets—those areas having a disproportionate number of

35. Fowler, op. cit.
36. J.K. Bowers and D. Harkness, 'Duration of Unemployment by Age and Sex', *Economica*, 46, August 1979. See also D.I. MacKay, 'After the Shake-Out', *Oxford Economic Papers*, 24, 1972; D.I. MacKay and G.L. Reid, 'Redundancy, Unemployment and Manpower Policy', *Economic Journal*, 82, December 1972.
37. D. Metcalf and S. Nickell, 'The Plain Man's Guide to the Out-of-Work: the Nature and Composition of Male Unemployment in Britain', London School of Economics, Discussion Paper No. 6, January 1977, pp. 10–11.
38. Information on the number of dependants per unemployed man is available for those receiving National Insurance Benefits and Supplementary Benefits. See pp. 145-51. There are no comparable data on the family characteristics of the unemployed not receiving benefits.
39. MacKay, *Oxford Economic Papers*, loc. cit.; *Economic Journal*, loc. cit., 'Redundancy and Re-Employment: A Study of Car Workers', *Manchester School*, 40, 1972; Metcalf and Nickell, op. cit., pp. 13–16.

unskilled, old, or single people suffering most.[40] There is little evidence
that industrial affiliation bears directly on unemployment duration.

One suggested means of estimating the pattern of completed spells
of unemployment from the pattern of uncompleted spells is to use
'maximum likelihood' techniques, comparing the average duration of
a selected representative worker with that of someone who differed
from the representative type in one particular characteristic. The
results of such an exercise for 1972 are given in Table 19.

TABLE 19
AVERAGE COMPLETED DURATION (WEEKS); PERCENTAGE
UNEMPLOYED; AND PERCENTAGE BECOMING UNEMPLOYED
EACH WEEK (1972)*

The table shows the averages for the 'representative man' and for men
who differ from the representative man in specified ways. The representative man is in a manual job, aged 40, married with 1 child, healthy
and has a manual father.

Characteristics of representative man	Variation from representative man	Average completed spell (weeks) (1)	Percentage unemployed (2)	Percentage becoming unemployed each week (3)
	No variation	12.5	6.8	0.54
Manual	Non-manual	10.7	0.7	0.07
Aged 40	Aged 20	10.0	8.8	0.88
	Aged 60	16.9	9.4	0.56
Married	Single	15.6	10.5	0.67
1 child	3 children	13.8	9.4	0.68
healthy	long-standing illness	18.3	15.1	0.83
Father, manual	Father, non-manual	11.3	6.3	0.56

* Cited in Layard, *et al., Causes of Poverty,* op. cit., p. 76.

40. D. Metcalf, 'Urban Unemployment in England', *Economic Journal,* 85,
September 1975; D. Metcalf and R. Richardson, 'Unemployment in London',
in Worswick (ed.), op. cit., chapter 11. Hill, *et. al., Men Out of Work,* op. cit.

Thus in 1972, the average completed spell of a worker in a non-manual job was shorter than that of the representative worker but longer if the man was old or had a long-standing illness.

The implication of recent research is that 'the main reason why the chance of leaving the register is much lower for those who have been unemployed for longer durations is simply that few of those who are easily re-employed will stay on the register for more than a few days or weeks'.[41] What is not clear, however, is the precise relative importance of duration of unemployment and other individual characteristics in explaining the probability of re-employment and how far such influences are mutually exclusive. Details of the job-search behaviour of the registered unemployed, as witnessed for example by the conditions under which and the reasons why unemployed workers prefer to remain unemployed until a suitable job appears or prefer to take the first available opportunity of employment[42] (the 'stickers' and 'snatchers'),[43] can tell us something of the nature of long-term and short-term unemployment and help us to judge the sensitivity of the structure of unemployment[44] to changing labour market conditions. But the notion that 'job-search intensity' thus explains variations in unemployment duration ignores the extent to which those persons suffering longer unemployment durations lower their search intensity, discouraged by their lack of success in obtaining fresh employment.[45]

Clearly it would be useful to know, at a time when the overall duration of unemployment is rising, whether this is because the leaving rates for all unemployed have fallen or whether the inflow is composed more of the 'long-term unemployed' than of the 'short-term unemployed'. However to the extent that duration data continue to be analysed in terms of inflows to and outflows from the register, together with the probabilities of various groups of workers finding another job,

---

41. Cripps and Tarling, loc. cit., p. 290.
42. The extent to which social security payments may influence the incentive to work is considered above. See pp. 102–9. On both counts see also Hill, *et al.*, *Men Out of Work*, op. cit.
43. MacKay, *Oxford Economic Papers*, loc. cit.; MacKay and Reid, *Economic Journal*, December 1972, loc. cit.
44. Defined as the distribution of the registered unemployed categorized by the duration of their unemployment.
45. Cf. MacKay and Reid, 'The speed and intensity with which men looked for work and the particular job-search strategy they adopted had a considerable effect on the length of transitional unemployment they experienced', *Economic Journal*, December 1972, loc. cit., p. 1266.

it will provide an indirect but useful means of assessing the magnitude of frictional unemployment (defined loosely to include those workers who are involved in job-search) and thereby help to fill a gap in the current statistical coverage.[46]

The thesis that when workers are classified by personal characteristics their probability of employment is independent of their current duration of unemployment may itself be true only at certain levels of unemployment. Analysis of a model of flows on to and off the unemployment register during 1967–73 seen in terms of the probability of there being a job available at the completion of the search suggests that at least between successive quarters of a year the changing demands for labour have a significant effect on the duration–specific leaving rates of the unemployed.[47] Other evidence that actual duration of unemployment appears to be positively related to the level of unemployment[48] raises the whole question of the extent to which a valid distinction can be made between 'voluntary' and 'involuntary' unemployment and whether the *post hoc* duration data so readily available disguise the extent to which individuals have any control over their pattern and frequency of employment. It is quite conceivable, for example, that duration of unemployment is affected by an unemployed person's expectation of regaining his lost job; the number and types of job-search methods used, including the intensity of job-search and the speed with which it is conducted, and his expectations as to the type of job he is likely to obtain and be willing to accept.[49]

46. Institute of Manpower Studies, 'Research Notes: Short-term and Long-term Unemployment', *IMS Monitor,* 2, April 1973.
47. C. Leicester, 'The Duration of Unemployment and Job Search', in Worswick, op. cit. McAnley, on the other hand, has suggested that the structure and duration of unemployment during 1962–73 was influenced more by changes in capacity utilization and relative factor prices than by changing demand. See A. McAnley, 'An Analysis of the Structure and Duration of Male Unemployment in Great Britain 1962–73', University of Essex, Department of Economics, Discussion Paper No. 66, June 1975.
48. R. Weedon, 'Duration of Unemployment and Labour Turnover', University of Reading, *Mimeo,* May 1974; C.S. Leicester, 'The Structure of Unemployment Under Changing Labour Market Conditions', Social Science Research Council, Final Report (HR 3777).
49. For a detailed analysis of the factors influencing job-search on and off the unemployment register see, C.A. Pissarides, *Labour Market Adjustment,* Cambridge 1976 and W. Daniel, op. cit., chapters 3, 7, and 8.

It is often difficult to discern the extent to which those personal characteristics thought to have a bearing on duration of unemployment interact with one another, e.g. the affect of age on the intensity of job-search, or whether, for example, older workers becoming unemployed 'bump down' the skill ladder in order to secure a job.[50] The official tendency to be somewhat cautious in the occupational classification of the unemployed may itself push men further down the occupational ladder than is warranted. Low grading of particular groups such as the disabled may actually increase the difficulties they face in obtaining jobs.

Undue emphasis on personal factors can, moreover, lead to an unwarranted devaluation of macro-economic and structural forces as determinants of unemployment and as explanatory variables of the duration of unemployment among various groups.[51] Not that the two are entirely unrelated. Personal characteristics such as skill and health may be the direct result of participation in particular industries in particular labour markets. To this extent the significant explanatory variable of unemployment will not necessarily be that set of personal characteristics associated with long-term uninterrupted single periods of unemployment but rather the total amount of unemployment experienced over a given period.[52] Thus low skill, one of the important 'personal characteristics', could be the result rather than the cause of unemployment. A recent empirical analysis of one local labour market in Paisley, though accepting a link between the personal characteristics of the unemployed and the speed of re-employment, has demonstrated that, after correcting for these characteristics, 'the speed and likelihood

---

50. Metcalf and Richardson, in Worswick, op. cit., p. 211. There is little published work available in this respect. A notable exception is Hill, *et. al.*, *Men Out of Work*, op. cit., which is based on sample surveys of wholly unemployed adult males registered at the Employment Exchanges in Newcastle, Coventry, and Hammersmith on 1 October 1971. Its aim essentially was 'to show how certain key variables are associated with a gradation of unemployment lengths', p. 39. See also M.J. Hill, 'Can we Distinguish Voluntary from Involuntary Unemployment?', in Worswick, op. cit., chapter 9: M. Hill and Olive Stevenson, *From the General to the Specific*, op. cit.—an analysis of 42 interviews with unemployed men, drawn from the main sample described in *Men Out of Work*.

51. To this extent the emphasis can shift easily towards the view that the long-term unemployed and the 'unemployables', however defined, ought not to figure in the official classification of the unemployed. See above pp. 76–80.

52. See G.M. Norris, 'Unemployment, Subemployment and Personal Characteristics', *Sociological Review*, 26, February, May 1978.

of re-employment are significantly related to the total time spent out of work'. Moreover this disadvantage of unemployment duration appears to manifest itself at an early stage relative to the conventional definition of long-term unemployment, i.e. six months and beyond.[53]

It is precisely the experience of recurrent unemployment that is so sadly lacking in the regular statistical appraisals of those out of work.[54] The emphasis in recent studies of the duration of unemployment has been on the process of moving from unemployment to employment, i.e. on the distribution of the number of spells of unemployment by length of spell. But investigation of the experience of unemployed claimants during 1971–3 has demonstrated the extent to which unemployment was concentrated among a minority of people who suffered repeated spells out of work.[55] Clearly there is scope for more detailed investigation of the determinants of individual duration of unemployment, defined not in terms of the average length of interrupted spells but in terms of the average completed duration of all spells of unemployment over a given period of time.

Despite the advance of sophisticated econometric techniques, it is still extremely difficult to be very precise as to the variation over time in the probability of an unemployed person returning to work.[56] More disaggregated data of the demographic, occupational, and industrial

53. A. McGregor, 'Unemployment Duration and Re-employment Probability', *Economic Journal*, 88, December 1978.

54. The Department of Employment's surveys of characteristics of the unemployed have emphasized this aspect more and more in recent years but the official duration data are still based on strict classification of single completed spells of unemployment. Cf. Sinfield's comment in 1968: 'Additional measurements of long-term unemployment are needed, not simply the duration of unemployment since registration or the end of the last spell of work, but over a period of a year or more . . . Governments need to know the amount of unemployment experienced by the whole labour force over a period of time and the degree of concentration among certain groups', Sinfield, op. cit., p. 82.

55. J. Smee and J. Stern, *The Unemployed in a Period of High Unemployment: Some Notes on Characteristics and Benefit Status*, Government Economic Service Working Paper no. 11, November 1978; R. Disney, 'Recurrent Spells and the Concentration of Unemployment in Great Britain', *Economic Journal*, 89, March 1979.

56. T. Lancaster, 'Econometric Methods for the Duration of Unemployment', *Econometrica*, 47, July 1979; S. Nickell, 'Estimating the Probability of Leaving Unemployment', *Econometrica*, 47, September 1979.

characteristics of those persons flowing onto the unemployment register would be welcome; but perhaps more important is the need to expand our knowledge of the work experience of a cohort of individuals from week to week, not least because of its potential value in charting both the duration and the frequency of spells of unemployment. Current information of spell recurrence relies largely on sample surveys of the unemployed at a particular date which take no account of the varying characteristics of those on the register in terms of their probability both of leaving unemployment and of employment.

7

Seasonal Fluctuations in Unemployment

Movements over time in the unadjusted unemployment series can be attributed to a number of influences, namely, the trend of the underlying level of unemployment, seasonal variations, which occur at the same period in each year because of the effects of normal seasonal influences, and irregular variations such as those arising from abnormally bad weather conditions.[1] The aim in producing a seasonally adjusted monthly series is to remove from the series that part of the variation which can be attributed to the effect of normal seasonal influences. In the case of unemployment the actual figures rise (or fall less rapidly) in winter months because there are fewer jobs available, especially in industries such as construction which are affected by adverse weather conditions, or industries which depend to some extent on summer trade, such as the hotel and catering industries. Conversely, actual unemployment falls (or rises less rapidly) in summer months when these industries recruit seasonal workers.

These seasonal movements complicate comparisons between the figures at different times of the year. In the seasonally adjusted series the normal seasonal movements are removed, and a clearer picture is provided of the underlying trend in unemployment, though the effects of irregular variations mentioned above are still present. These variations can affect the seasonally adjusted series for any one month so that attention ought to be paid to movements in the series over several months rather than to changes between successive months.

1. This chapter is concerned principally with movements in aggregate data. Details of the seasonal adjustment of other unemployment series can be found in previous chapters.

Although it was possible to discern in both the pre-1914 trade union returns on unemployment and in the general percentages of unemployment between the wars the tendency of upward and downward turns in the trade cycle to occur at particular times of the year, there was no systematic attempt to construct an official unemployment series free of normal seasonal fluctuations. The data on this and related points stem, in the main, from the work of particular investigators and it was only in 1960 that significant efforts were officially made to determine the extent to which changes in unemployment during a particular period were attributable to prevailing seasonal influences.

Estimates of Seasonal Fluctuations in Unemployment Before 1948

The trade union figures of the number and proportion of members unemployed at the end of each month provide the most important means of testing, over a long series of years, the seasonal fluctuations in unemployment before 1914, since the period for which unemployment insurance figures were available is too short to afford a satisfactory basis for such calculations. The trade union returns from 1887–1925 revealed that unemployment had a marked tendency to increase in December, to fall during the first four months of the year, and to increase in August and fall in November. During the remaining months the positive and negative tendencies more or less balanced one another.[2] But the season of maximum or minimum unemployment differed among trades. Every month of the year except July was the busiest season for some trade and every month except April and May the

---

2. The first serious attempt at using trade union and employers' returns to indicate the irregularity of employment was made by H. Llewellyn Smith of the Board of Trade. In evidence to the *Third Report of the House of Commons Committee on Distress from Want of Employment* (H.C. (365) IX 1895) he provided estimates of the magnitude of seasonal and cyclical unemployment during the years 1887 to 1894, distinguishing the stable from the comparatively unstable industries. Similar data for later years can be found in 'Seasonal Fluctuations in Employment', *International Labour Review*, XVII, March 1928; Board of Trade, 'Statistics of Seasonal Industries and Industries Carried On by Casual Labour', *Royal Commission on Poor Laws and Relief of Distress, Volume IX*, Cd. 5068, 1910, Appendix XXI (D). This memorandum indicates from trade union returns the seasonal fluctuations in employment in fifteen separate industries or groups of industries over the period 1897 to 1906.

slackest for some trade. The returns did show, however, that the relative importance of seasonal unemployment was reduced in years of general depression. Though the trade union returns are useful it is worth remembering that it was the trades which suffered most from seasonal fluctuations which were the least able to pay unemployment benefit and therefore the least likely to be included in the returns. Nor was there any way of indicating precisely on the basis of such data the distribution of unemployment among the members included in the returns.

Reports by employers of the average number of days or of shifts worked per week in each month in coal and iron mines and iron and steel works, and of the actual number of persons employed or paid wages by them daily provide two other sources of information on seasonal fluctuations in employment. Statistics of the former type are available for a considerable number of years, but, except for dock labour, pre-war data on actual numbers employed are very selective and only marginally useful as an indication of seasonal fluctuations.[3]

The comparative neglect of the problems of seasonal fluctuations in employment was equally apparent within official sources of labour statistics between the wars. This was due in part to the fact that the contemporary monthly aggregate returns of insured persons unemployed in the country as a whole showed only slight seasonal variation compared with, say, Germany or Sweden and hence it was easy to assume that seasonal variations contributed only an insignificant element to the general problem of unemployment.

3. The returns of days or shifts worked per week for the period 1897 to 1906 are in Cd. 5068, Appendix XXI (D), op. cit. Information is also included of the percentage proportion of the number employed at the end of each month in the trades during October 1906 of September 1907. A more detailed analysis is provided of fluctuations in the average number employed daily in each month in London Docks and Wharves during 1897–1906.

A number of studies are available of pre-1914 seasonality of employment, though they are all based on the data referred to above and do not offer any fresh statistical evidence. See, for example, Dearle, op. cit.; A. Webb, 'Statistics of Unemployment, with special reference to Seasonal Unemployment', in *National Conference on the Prevention of Destitution*, London 1911; S. Webb and A. Freeman (eds.), 'Seasonal Fluctuations in Employment in the Gas Industry', *Journal of the Royal Statistical Society*, LXXIV, 1911; London and Cambridge Economic Service, *Special Memorandum No. 7. Seasonal Variations in Finance, Prices and Industry by A.L. Bowley and K.C. Smith*, London 1924.

Seasonal fluctuations in inter-war employment were a much more prominent feature of overall unemployment than is generally recognized. The slight amplitude of seasonal variation in total employment was due, not so much to the absence of markedly seasonal industries, as to the fact that seasonal patterns so coincided that seasonal industries almost compensated, statistically speaking, for each other; there was not a month in the year in which there were not some industries enjoying their busy season, and others undergoing slack periods.[4] This statistical compensation did not correspond to anything that actually took place in industry. The range of fluctuation shown in the unemployment figures for an entire industry or branch of an industry was almost invariably less than that actually occurring in the various separate occupations to which the workers covered by the statistics belonged. This was particularly true in industries such as clothing and in others where the unemployment data for the 'industry' covered in reality several distinct trades or branches.[5]

The pattern and amplitude of the seasonal variation in a time series are not necessarily stable and permanent characteristics of that series. Changes in markets, technique, the general level of unemployment, or labour supply can directly affect the seasonal curve. To what extent was the seasonal element becoming more or less significant during the inter-war period? Was there a relation between seasonal and cyclical fluctuation?

Saunder's study of the seasonal movement of post-war unemployment insurance statistics showed that in no industry was there any significant change in the amplitude of seasonal variation from 1924 to 1929 though the changing balance of importance between seasonal industries within the economic structure tended indirectly to diminish the importance of seasonal fluctuation. Comparisons of the range of seasonal variation, i.e. the average difference between seasonal peaks and lows in the 26 principal seasonal industries during 1930-2 with the average for the whole period 1924-32 showed a marked tendency in

---

4. The determination of just how many industries covered by unemployment insurance between the wars were subject to seasonal variation owes much to the work of C.T. Saunders. See his *Seasonal Variations in Employment*, London 1936 and 'The Importance of Seasonal Variations in Employment in the United Kingdom', *Economic Journal*, XLV, 1935.
5. 'Seasonal Unemployment in the Clothing Industries', *International Labour Review*, XVIII, July 1928.

most, though not all, industries for seasonal fluctuations to increase in years of high general unemployment.[6]

Although there were no official attempts between the wars to provide an unemployment series free of seasonal fluctuations, Beveridge provided such a general unemployment percentage for males during the period 1927-38. Seasonal elements were eliminated from the unemployment insurance data 'by writing out the changes (plus or minus) of the male unemployment percentage . . . striking out for each month the four extremes (two largest positives and largest negatives), averaging the remaining seven figures for each month, eliminating by cumulation secular trend and error in the starting point, and adding or subtracting the final seasonal variation thus obtained'.[7]

Recent Practices in the Seasonal Adjustment of Unemployment Statistics

By the time of the introduction of a comprehensive national insurance scheme in July 1948 there had clearly been little progress in the systematic determination of the extent to which changes in unemployment during a particular period were attributable to prevailing seasonal

6. An opposite effect had been discovered for the pre-1914 period. See above p. 208. Saunders also provided detailed case studies of seasonality of employment in the motor and associated industries, clothing, building, wholly seasonal occupations, and agriculture. The London and Cambridge Economic Service investigated post-war seasonal variation in employment in total and by industry for the 1923-29 period using insurance data. Their results, however, did not indicate the changes in seasonality from year to year. *Special Memorandum No. 36, Post-War Seasonal Variations* by K.C. Smith & G.F. Horne, London 1932.

Seasonal fluctuations of employment in the building industry and among occupational groups within the industry, calculated on the basis of unemployment insurance returns for 1913-27, are examined by L. Hersch, 'Seasonal Unemployment in the Building Industry in Certain European Countries', *International Labour Review*, XIX, February 1929. The extent of fluctuations in employment were found to be greater in certain occupations than in the industry as a whole. A similar study for the building industry as a whole and a smaller number of occupational groups during the period 1915-35 can be found in H. Menderhausen, 'The Elimination of Seasonal Fluctuations in the Building Industry', *International Labour Review*, XXXVI, August 1937.

7. W.H. Beveridge, 'Unemployment in the Trade Cycle', *Economic Journal*, 49, March 1939.

influences. It was not until 1960 that the then Ministry of Labour published estimates of the extent to which movements in unemployment could be attributed to average or normal influences. For five years the Ministry published estimates of these seasonal movements in the form of normal monthly seasonal deviations and changes.

The method adopted was to calculate for each individual month in a period of years a centred moving average of the figures in the relevant series over a twelve-month period;[8] to measure the absolute deviations of the actual figures in the series from the corresponding moving averages; to average the deviations for corresponding calendar months over a period of years; and finally to obtain the difference between the average deviations for successive months. The difference between the normal deviations for successive months was regarded as the normal seasonal change between two months. Months or periods of time which were clearly exceptional were ignored.[9] The method was applied to the series of registered wholly unemployed (excluding school leavers) from 1949 and to vacancies notified and remaining unfilled from July 1958.[10]

Estimates of normal seasonal movements were, by their very nature, only of limited interpretative value. Their indiscriminate use implicitly assumed that the experience of the recent past provided a reasonably satisfactory indication of the seasonal fluctuations to be expected

8. This involved taking the arithmetic mean of the monthly averages for two overlapping periods of twelve months. Thus for January 1949 the centred moving average was calculated by taking the mean of the monthly averages for the two periods July 1948–June 1949 and August 1948–July 1949.

9. The details are in Department of Employment, *Historical Abstract*, tables 165-7 and 179. More detailed data were published in the *Gazette* from 1960 onwards. The latter provided two sets of information for each series: estimated normal seasonal deviations (i.e. the average amount by which the actual figure for the month of the year was greater (+) or less (–) than the corresponding centred twelve-month moving average) and estimated normal seasonal changes (i.e. the normal seasonal change between successive months being the difference between the two normal seasonal deviations). This gave an estimate of the average change from the first to the second month due to seasonal factors. Each of the series was classified by sex and excluded temporarily unemployed. They also provided the relevant data for the Administrative Regions of the Ministry of Labour in England, Scotland, and Wales. The seasonally adjusted wholly unemployed figures were further classified by industry to May 1969 on the basis of the 1958 Standard Industrial Classification. The vacancy data were estimated for the entire field of industrial employment alone. For further details see pp. 223-7.

10. See chapter 3, pp. 67-8.

under prevailing conditions. Deciding the appropriate relationship between observed deviations from the trend and the predicted seasonal effects presupposes that we have some knowledge of the underlying trend. Clearly there are problems here as the trend and the seasonal effects are calculated from the same data, estimating the seasonal requires knowledge of the trend, and estimating the trend involves eliminating the seasonal. In practice, rough estimates of the trend are often made from moving averages and used to give a preliminary estimate of the seasonal component. Successive approximation then permits a final estimate of the seasonal effect to be obtained and applied to the original unmodified series. Nevertheless there is the additional problem of variations both in time and extent in the influence of seasonal factors, such as weather conditions, from year to year, and it is unlikely that such estimated seasonal movements will coincide exactly with the actual movements in a particular year. The pattern of seasonal fluctuations can be directly influenced, moreover, by current economic conditions arising from changes in the structure of industry,[11] in the level of economic activity or from random fluctuations in the demand for and supply of labour which are themselves unconnected with seasonal fluctuations. In any particular January, for example, when the number of wholly unemployed is comparatively low, there may be insufficient scope for the estimated normal seasonal reduction in unemployment in the first half of the year to occur, because the register at any date tends to include a large number of persons who are moving from job to job. Similarly, substantial numbers of unfilled vacancies may represent continuous demands for labour to replace workers moving from job to job and for those whose particular

11. Seasonal fluctuations in unemployment generally arise from variations in weather conditions or from movements in demand. The latter may be affected by changes in production practices, with noticeably long-term effects. A comparison of the seasonal pattern of unemployment in Coventry during the period 1927–69 has revealed almost directly opposite trends. In the pre-war period, the seasonal 'peak' tended to come from June to August as car manufacturers spent their summer months in research and development, at the expense of production, prior to the autumn Motor Show. The increased scale of post-war activity has allowed both research and production to occur simultaneously and the timing of the Motor Show has become far less an influence on the supply of and demand for new models, helping to remove the traditional summer peak of unemployment. P. Smith, 'Seasonal Fluctuations in the Motor Vehicle Industry: A Comment', *Journal of Industrial Economics*, 2, April 1973.

skills are in short supply. Consequently in periods of low demand for labour normal seasonal reductions in the number of unfilled vacancies are unlikely to occur. Because, therefore, the estimates of normal seasonal changes are themselves subject to margins of error and because there can often be substantial abnormal short-term influences at work it does not necessarily follow that a seasonally adjusted series will reveal the underlying trend of unemployment. It was in recognition of this fact that the Ministry of Labour adopted a new method of calculating the seasonal adjustment in 1965.

The *additive* method of estimating normal seasonal movements described above assumed that the size of the seasonal movements did not vary according to the general level of unemployment. The actual number unemployed was taken as the sum of the three components (i.e. the trend component, the normal seasonal component, and the residual component resulting from abnormal seasonal influences and other short-term irregularities) and that, for each of the 12 calendar months, the normal seasonal component was constant from year to year. For example, if the figures for past years showed that the number unemployed in January was, on average, 53,000 higher than the estimated underlying trend, and the number unemployed in August was, on average 44,000 lower than the trend, the numbers +53,000 and –44,000 were regarded as normal seasonal deviations for January and August respectively and –97,000 as the normal seasonal change between January and August. Despite the limitations of this method already referred to, it proved to be a reasonably satisfactory method of estimating normal seasonal movements, except during short periods of abnormally high unemployment such as occurred at the beginning of 1963. Then the seasonal estimates were least reliable as the actual seasonal movements proved greater than the normal movements.

In an effort to obtain improved estimates, the Ministry of Labour adopted a new approach from 1965. Normal seasonal movements in employment were acknowledged to depend in part on the current level of unemployment, i.e. that in periods when unemployment was relatively high the seasonal movements would be correspondingly greater than when unemployment was lower. On this basis, the actual number unemployed in a particular month was assumed to be the sum of a constant which did not vary with the level of unemployment in that month, a variable amount equal to the trend value for that month multiplied by a factor appropriate to the month, and a residual component representing abnormal or irregular influences. The additive constant and the multiplicative factor were estimated for each calendar month from the data of past years. If it were found, for example, that on average unemployment in January was 16.7 per cent higher than the estimated trend, the number 1.167 would be regarded as the normal seasonal factor for January.

From the actual figures in the monthly unemployment series were removed the movements in the series which could be attributed to normal seasonal influences to provide a seasonally adjusted series. Thus, to use the figures of the example given above, the seasonally adjusted figure for January would be obtained by deducting the constant 53,000 from the actual number unemployed in January, and that for August by adding 44,000 to the actual number in August. Similarly, in the example of the multiplicative method, the seasonally adjusted figure for January would be obtained by dividing the actual number of the factor 1.167. In the new method the corresponding calculation would be as follows:-

$$\text{Seasonally adjusted number} = \frac{\text{(actual number) minus (constant for the month)}}{\text{(factor for the month)}}$$

With the normal seasonal constants and factors for each month known to the Ministry (but not published) it was thus possible to calculate the difference between the actual and adjusted figures for a month as an estimate of the effect of normal seasonal influences. The additive method had previously allowed this component to be estimated from past data and published in advance as the normal seasonal deviation. The change in the deviation from one month to the next was also published to show the extent to which the actual change in unemployment during the month could be attributed to normal seasonal influences. Such deviations and changes could not, however, be published in advance under the new method since they could be calculated only when the actual unemployment figures became available.

The revised method adopted in 1965 for seasonally adjusting the data of the wholly unemployed (excluding school leavers) was based on the observed variations of the actual figures during the period January 1950 to August 1965. The results of the application of the new method to the unemployment statistics for Great Britain and for each Standard Region were given in the *Gazette* in September 1965. They replaced those previously published which had been based on the estimates of normal seasonal movements obtained from analysis of data for an earlier base period using the additive method of seasonal adjustment. They included the results for the wholly unemployed (excluding school leavers) January 1950–August 1965 (annually, males and females together) distinguishing (a) actual numbers—unadjusted for seasonal variations and (b) numbers adjusted for seasonal variations. The latter were obtained by using a specially prepared computer programme which included tests to show whether, for a particular series, the data were consistent with purely additive or multiplicative assumptions and whether the pattern of the normal seasonal movements had changed.

Early in 1968 it became clear that the seasonally adjusted series was tending to move in the opposite direction to the actual series. As the *Gazette* pointed out:

From mid-1967 onwards the seasonally adjusted unemployment series has regularly fallen in winter and risen in summer, so that the method of seasonal adjustment appeared to be over-correcting for seasonal movement, and so introducing a spurious variation into the seasonally adjusted series.[12]

Further study showed that the amplitude of seasonal fluctuations had suddenly become smaller during 1966–7 than they used to be. In periods when unemployment had been relatively high, as in 1958–9 and 1962–3, the differences due to seasonal variation between the winter peak and summer trough of unemployment amounted to nearly 150,000. Between 1966 and 1970, with unemployment at about the same level, the difference was only about 100,000, a figure normally reached at much lower levels of unemployment. There was no apparent change in the seasonal pattern, i.e. the way in which the seasonal variation was distributed between the various months of the year.

With these changes in mind, the seasonal pattern in the unemployment series has been estimated since April 1970 from the most recent ten-year base period, and the seasonal amplitude calculated on the observed changes of the last two or three years.[13] Because the results obtained by the two official methods of seasonal adjustment had proved reasonably acceptable for the purposes for which they had been

12. *Gazette*, April 1970, p. 285.
13. For a full discussion of the statistical technique involved see R.L. Brown, A.H. Cowley and J. Durbin, *Seasonal Adjustment of Unemployment Series*, Studied in Official Statistics, Research Series No. 4, HMSO 1971.

used up to July 1966, this further revision was applied retrospectively only from that date. Adjustments thereafter were related to the most recent ten-year period in order to accommodate any change in both the amplitude and pattern of seasonal fluctuations.[14]

This revised method, like the one it superseded, assumed that the normal seasonal variations were partly (but not entirely) dependent on the level of unemployment. The extra technical improvement it introduced was to identify those monthly unemployment figures within the base period which had been abnormally affected by extreme weather conditions and other factors. Although the new statistical technique adopted in April 1970 was initially applied to all the component series (unemployment classified by sex, by industry, and by region) and to the vacancy series, the further refinements subsequently introduced down to 1972 made it extremely complicated to apply in the time available to anything other than the series of total national unemployment. Accordingly, seasonal adjustments for the remaining series were obtained retrospectively from April 1968 from a standard seasonal adjustment computer programme (Census Method 11 Variant X-11) which gave results comparable to those obtained by the method adopted for the national total.[15] By mid-1972, however, it was clear that the magnitude of recent seasonal variations had been largely unaffected by quite substantial changes in the level of unemployment, i.e. the variations exhibited an additive pattern. The Census Method of adjustment was therefore also applied to the national total of wholly unemployed (excluding school leavers and adult students).

---

14. Periodic up-dating is a normal feature of the seasonal adjustment procedure. The latest revisions (introduced with the May 1979 figures) apply new adjustment factors to the seasonally adjusted data for January 1976 onwards. Details of the Census Method can be found in P.B. Kenny, 'Problems of Seasonal Adjustment', *Statistical News,* 29, May 1975. The current unemployment series to which this method is applied to produce seasonally adjusted data include: unemployment flow statistics; the rate of unemployment; the number of unemployed persons (excluding school leavers and adult students), nationally, by region, and by broad industrial group, and adult vacancies notified and remaining unfilled. Because the proportions of males and females within the unemployment total change, the seasonally adjusted series is separately calculated for males and females. The seasonally adjusted vacancy figures are now based on an analysis of data for the period July 1958–June 1967, the margins of error in the adjusted figures being somewhat wider than if it had been practicable to use a longer base period for analysis.

15. *Gazette,* August 1972.

This procedure was further amended in 1979. In a special effort to measure the changes in seasonality attributable to the flow of unemployed adult students on to the register in the summer months, the Department of Employment now separately adjusts this group, using the multiplicative version of the X-11 programme. The results are then re-combined with the remainder of the unemployed, seasonally adjusted in the normal way, to achieve an improved adjustment. This new method is currently applied only to the figures for Great Britain.[16]

Statistical refinements cannot eliminate entirely the problems associated with seasonally adjusted data. When the seasonally adjusted series continues to show evidence of seasonal variation in either the same or opposite direction as the original it can become under- or over-adjusted, as the case may be. Sir Harold Wilson has recounted the difficulties caused by over-adjustment of the unemployment series during the late sixties:

After rising seasonally adjusted figures, in late 1966 and the first half of 1967, I was glad to receive through the Downing Street teleprinter while on holiday August figures showing virtually no change. The remaining months of the year showed a significant fall on a seasonally adjusted basis. This was comforting, especially as for seasonal returns the crude figures were bound to rise. . . . The following February, the adjusted trend was reversed, and continued to act in a contumacious manner until August proclaimed a stop, and the autumn trend was favourable. When this was again reversed the following February, and we were embarked on a fourth perverse 6-month period, I felt enough was enough. It had been vastly comforting . . . to point to the improved underlying trend in the wholly unemployed. But there is diminishing comfort in reliance on a series in which you increasingly disbelieve.[17]

The variety of statistical improvements adopted during the late sixties and early seventies sought to overcome both the extent to which the seasonal component of the unemployment series varied in proportion to the absolute magnitude of the series and the influence of short-term changes in the amplitude and pattern of seasonal fluctuations. But despite the improvements, there are doubts as to whether conventional techniques of estimating seasonal components are

16. ibid., May 1979.
17. Wilson, loc. cit., p. 12.

appropriate in the case of unemployment statistics. Surrey has pointed out that:

Since in reality the seasonal elements in supply and demand are in some measure multiplicative, then the seasonal component of any unemployment level depends not only on the level of unemployment—i.e. on the *relative* levels of supply and demand—but also in their *absolute* levels. The problem arises with the seasonal adjustments of a series which is itself the difference between two series which are in some sense independently determined economically.[18]

Although further refined calculations of the seasonal component in the British data for 1950-70 have failed to reveal any major discrepancy compared with the official series, the search for a more sophisticated measure must be encouraged[19] not least because of the attention paid to the seasonally-corrected series in monitoring the state of the economy and because of the importance of the seasonal component in producing acceptable estimates of the overall trend of unemployment.

18. M.S.C. Surrey, 'The Seasonal Adjustment of Unemployment Statistics—A Note', *Bulletin of the Oxford University Institute of Economics and Statistics*, 34, 1972.
19. For background details of the work on seasonal adjustments currently being undertaken by statisticians in the Department of Employment and the Central Statistical Office, see A.E. Radford and G.I. Webb, 'Some Problems in Assessing Unemployment Trends', *Economic Trends*, 298, August 1978.

8

The Industrial and Occupational Classification of the Unemployed

Unemployment By Industry

(a) Sources of Statistics before 1940

By their very nature the unemployment returns supplied by certain trade unions and groups of employers before 1912 related to conditions in particular industries. The extent to which such industrial coverage was both complete and an adequate basis from which to derive a meaningful unemployment series has been discussed in detail in Chapter 1.

Apart from the trade union series, the other source of information on industrial employment and unemployment bridging the Edwardian and inter-war periods was that published monthly in the *Gazette* as 'Detailed Repots on Employment in the Principal Industries in the United Kingdom'. However, because of the need for economy in government expenditure it was decided in 1922 to discontinue separate returns for a number of industries and trades and the series thereafter provided even more selective data than it had before the First World War.[1]

1. The origins and content of the original series are discussed above pp. 26–7. The industries and trades excluded from July 1922 were iron, shale and other mining and quarrying; miscellaneous metal trades; linen; jute; hosiery; silk, lace; carpet bleaching, printing, dyeing and finishing; felt hat trade; tailoring; shirt and collar trade; leather trades; woodworking and furnishing trades; paper, printing and bookbinding trades; glass trades; food preparation trades; brick and cement trades; fishing and agriculture.

A more systematic if not entirely comprehensive or totally reliable industrial classification became available on the introduction of unemployment insurance in 1911. The unemployment books from which a new count of those out of work was obtained from September 1912 were given an industry code letter at the time of their annual exchange. The figures of the number unemployed in each industry could therefore be expressed as a percentage of the estimated total number of insured persons in the industry in the preceding July. Percentage rates of unemployment were calculated for each of the industries covered by the insurance scheme during the period 1913-18.[2]

The industrial classification of the unemployed was determined before 1923 by stamping each lodged book with a code symbol taken from a list supplied to every local office by the Employment Department of the Ministry of Labour. This was a relatively simple matter when the total insured population under the 1911 and 1916 Insurance Acts was less than 4 million. With the extension of insurance in 1920 nearly 8 million additional workers were brought within the scope of the scheme. The issue of books and the industrial coding for these extra persons were done at great speed by a staff in large part newly recruited and untrained, with the result that errors arose.

Although in the main the pre-1923 classification was carried out on an industrial basis, it was not followed strictly to the exclusion of all occupational groupings. Accordingly in 1923 a new industrial classification was adopted under which an unemployment book was classified not by the occupation of the insured person but by the nature of the employer's business or, in the case of the unemployed person, of his last employer's business. Thus a bricklayer employed by a firm of builders was classified under the building trade whereas a bricklayer in an iron and steel works was classified in that industrial group.[3] The appropriate code letters were retained on the unemployment book throughout the entire twelve-month period. The effect was that even though a person moved from one industry to another during an insur-

---

2. Details of the average annual percentage of unemployment in each insured trade during the years 1913–18 are in *Report on National Unemployment Insurance, July 1923*, 1923, Appendix XIII. Monthly percentage figures for the same industries in that period are in the *Eighteenth Abstract of Labour Statistics of the United Kingdom 1910 to 1925*, Cmd. 2740, 1926.

3. The books of persons employed in government or local authority industrial undertakings were classified according to the industry or service in which they were employed, and not under national or local government service.

ance year he remained throughout that year coded to the industry in which he worked at the time of the last exchange of books or, if then unemployed, to the industry of his previous employer. It was possible therefore for the ranks of those unemployed in any industry to be swollen by the inclusion of a number of workers who had been in that industry even though they had not been in it for the greatest occupied period of their lives, though such bias was unlikely to have been of any great magnitude. Hilton, Assistant Secretary to the Ministry of Labour, claimed in 1931 that the system 'though arbitrary in principle' gave results which did not differ greatly 'from those which would be obtained from a theoretically more perfect procedure'.[4]

There was thus a complete break in June 1923[5] in the comparability of the unemployment statistics relating to industry. The number of insured persons[6] was thereafter analysed in a hundred separate industry groups compared with 63 in the early post-war series, the increase arising mainly from the adoption of an industrial classification similar to that used for the Census of population. Thus in the general engineering group sub-divisions were later adopted for electrical engineering, for marine engineering, and for constructional engineering. The basis for the motor industry was enlarged and new sub-divisions were employed for the explosives and chemicals group; bricks, tiles and artificial building materials; mining; clothing; food and drink; and other groups. In some cases industrial groups were separated entirely

---

4. *Royal Commission on Unemployment Insurance, Minutes of Evidence,* 3 July 1931, p. 1163.
5. Details of the number of persons in each of the principal industries insured under the Unemployment Insurance Acts during the period 1920 to 1923 and the percentages unemployed in each industry in July 1923 on the basis of the new classification were first given in the *Gazette,* November 1923 and continued monthly thereafter. Separate figures were given for males and females. Since it was not possible to compute the annual estimates of the total number of persons insured against unemployment until the end of October in any year it was necessary to revise regularly the percentages of insured persons recorded as unemployed in any July, August, and September since these results were based on the estimated number of insured workpeople in July of the previous year. Revised estimates of the percentage of unemployment by industry in each of these months, calculated on the basis of the estimated number of insured persons in the year to which they related, were subsequently published in the *Gazette.*
6. The Live Register, recording unemployment among the insured and uninsured alike, was not classified on an industrial basis. See above pp. 40–45.

from their previous classification; pig-iron manufacture and iron and steel tube manufacture were separated from iron and steel manufacture, glass bottle manufacture was separated from the other glass trades. The new classification continued with only minor modifications until 1948.[7]

The extended range of industrial classification adopted after 1923 did nothing to reduce the difficulty of using gross figures of unemployment in all insured trades as an adequate reflection of the general condition within British industry. Such data could not adequately disclose the unduly varying courses which the main industries took. The unemployment figures shown industry by industry in each monthly *Gazette* required considerable special analysis before they could be made to reveal the sectional movements which, in combination, caused the movement of the figures as a whole. The influence of changing prosperity within certain seasonal industries and the downturn in others such as coalmining, for example, could well act independently, or in conjunction with one another, to affect the nature and timing of employment fluctuations in other sectors. Substantial changes in the number of insured workers attached to an industry between each July count would, moreover, rule out strict comparisons of the monthly unemployment rate by industry. Although the Ministry of Labour published revised figures for the June to September period when the new total of insured workers became available, only monthly revisions throughout the year could have entirely eliminated the distortion.

A notable deficiency in the industrial series was the lack of any systematic regional analysis. The only kind readily available for the inter-war period on fluctuations in industrial unemployment among insured workers by Ministry of Labour Division was that provided for the coal, engineering, shipbuilding, and paper and building industries in the special reports on industrial employment produced monthly in the *Gazette* between the years 1922 and 1939. The reports also

7. Details of the numbers of insured persons unemployed at each mid-year by industry during the periods 1923–1939 and 1945–1947 (UK only) and of the percentage of insured workers unemployed by industry during the years 1923 to 1939 (UK) are in *Historical Abstract*, tables 163, 164. Estimates of the rate of unemployment among insured persons wholly unemployed in manufacturing, construction and mining as a separate group (UK 1927–39) are in Galenson, loc. cit., pp. 578–9. For extra details of unemployment in the engineering industry see *Unemployment. Its Realities and Problems*, Engineering and Allied Employers' National Federation, July 1933.

included details of the number of persons registered as unemployed in the principal cotton, woollen, and boot and shoe producing regions.[8] More surprising is the fact that it was not until 1969 that regular statistics became available of the number of persons registered as wholly unemployed by industry Order by region and then only on a quarterly basis.

(b) The Industrial Classification of the Unemployed after the Second World War

The publication of statistics of the industrial distribution of the insured unemployed was suspended for security reasons in September 1940 and resumed in July 1945. Relevant analyses for the wartime period were published separately at a later date.[9] The post-1945 industrial

8. This information can be supplemented with data from other primary and secondary sources. For the cotton industry see G.W. Daniels and J. Jewkes, 'The Post-War Depression in the Lancashire Cotton Industry', *Journal of the Royal Statistical Society,* XCI, 1928 (on the adequacy of employers' returns to the Ministry of changes in monthly employment); J.H. Richardson, *Industrial Employment and Unemployment in West Yorkshire,* London 1936 (insured unemployment in woollen and worsted textiles, dyeing and finishing, tailoring, coalmining, printing, building, and distribution in selected West Yorkshire towns 1924 and 1928-36); PRO, Lab. 2/1378, Unemployment in the Cotton Industry, 16 May 1930 (analysis of the insured and Live Register population nationally and in each principal cotton trade centre); PRO, Lab. 2/1577, Report on an Investigation into Conditions of Employment in the Cotton Industry (Manufacturing Section), 1933 (unemployment in nine Lancashire cotton districts January–July 1933); PRO, Lab. 2/1577, Stats 588/1927 (details not normally available of the number of men and women on the 'wholly unemployed and temporarily stopped' files and live file of non-claimants at 33 Employment Exchanges in cotton areas for November, December 1927 and January 1928). See also PRO, Lab. 2/1477, Unemployment in the Coal Trade, 1927 (and see the evidence of a sample inquiry 1929, above p. 140). D.C. Jones, *Merseyside, Trade and Employment,* Liverpool 1935 (analysis of official returns on industrial unemployment classified to distinguish normal and abnormal unemployment).

9. Analyses of the figures of the total number of persons insured against unemployment by industry (1939-45) were published in the *Gazette* in November, December 1946 and November, December 1947. Analyses by regions and industries combined were published separately in 'Tables Relating to Employment and Unemployment in respect of the years 1939, 1945, 1946, 1947 and 1948'. Details of the total number of insured workpeople registered as unemployed by industry during the period 1935 to 1946 (July of each year) are in Central Statistical Office, *Annual Abstract of Statistics, No. 84, 1935-1946,* HMSO 1948.

unemployment data were substantially altered in 1948 with the adoption of a new Standard Industrial Classification. In the intervening period a number of minor alterations occurred in the classification of particular groups of persons. From 1945, persons classified as unsuitable for ordinary employment and insured ex-members of the Forces on demobilization leave were not included in the industrial analysis of unemployed insured persons. The number of these persons was shown separately against the entry 'other insured persons' for 1945 and later years. The totals for 'all industries and services' for 1945, 1946, and 1947 included a number of insured ex-members of the Forces who had not taken up employment since release or discharge but who had registered for employment and, for 1947 only, a number of ex-colliery workers who were no longer fit for employment in coalmining; these persons were not included in the unemployed for individual industry groups or against the entry 'other insured persons'.

The estimates for agriculture in 1945, 1946, and 1947 relate to the agricultural industry. They are not comparable with those for 1937, 1938, and 1939 which relate to unemployed persons insured under the agricultural scheme then operative. The agricultural scheme covered persons in 'private gardening' and 'other (gardening) employments' who in 1947 were included in 'miscellaneous services'. Conversely, the agricultural scheme did not cover those persons in the General Scheme in 'farming, forestry, etc.' and in 'market gardening, horticulture, etc.' who were included in the industry 'agriculture' in 1945, 1946, and 1947. In the period 1923 to 1939 these categories were included in 'miscellaneous services'. In addition unemployed insured persons classified to 'other manufactures' and included in 'other manufacturing industries' in 1945, 1946, and 1947 were not separately classified in earlier years but were included in 'miscellaneous services' during the years 1923 to 1939.

The new industrial classification introduced in 1948, apart from providing more detailed sub-divisions, also transferred in some cases certain types of establishment from one category to another, thus making it difficult to draw strict comparisons between the old and new series. The 1948 classification, which aimed at the presentation industrial statistics produced by different government departments on a consistent basis, was revised in 1958 in the light of subsequent experience and as a result of changes in the organization of industry. Further amendments were incorporated in 1963 and further changes in the industrial structure led to a second revision in 1968. The general form of the classification remained unchanged though changes in definition and in the number and content of Orders and Minimum List Headings were adopted. The figures of the industrial distribution of the unemployed between 1960 and May 1969 were compiled using the 1958 edition of the Standard Industrial Classification. The figures from June 1969 onwards were compiled using the 1968 edition. This change slightly affected the number unemployed in some industries so that the figures since June 1969 may not be strictly comparable with those for earlier periods.[10]

From 1948 to June 1976 the industrial analysis of the unemployed was carried out monthly and thereafter in February, May, August, and November. The industry to which a wholly unemployed person was assigned was that in which he was most recently employed for more than three days.[11] This at least was an improvement on the pre-war industrial classification of the unemployed. The industrial coding

10. It is notoriously difficult to provide a system of industrial classification which adequately spans the different versions of the SIC available since 1948. The best survey of all major changes in industrial classification during the period 1923–75 is in Buxton and MacKay, op. cit., chapter 5.

11. For details of the number of persons registered as wholly unemployed by industry Order and by broad industrial groups, quarterly during the period 1948 to 1968 (UK only) and excluding school leavers (Great Britain) see *Historical Abstract,* tables 171, 172, 173. More detailed information became available from 1969 in subsequent *Year Books* including: Number of persons registered as wholly unemployed by industry Order and by region quarterly, total males and females, and males separately; number of persons registered as wholly unemployed, excluding school leavers, by broad industrial groups. Great Britain; number of persons registered as wholly unemployed and as temporarily stopped, by industry (Minimum List Heading) and sex, quarterly. The current series of industrial unemployment is seasonally adjusted according to the revised method introduced in 1965, except that a quarterly rather than a monthly programme from the Census Method is used. See above pp. 216–17. Seasonally adjusted data of monthly statistics of the wholly unemployed in Great Britain in a number of selected industries during the period January 1950–September 1965 are in the *Gazette,* October 1965.

Until May 1959, the 1948 edition of the Standard Industrial Classification was used for the registered unemployed; from June 1959 to May 1969, the 1958 edition was used. The current series is applied to the 1968 Standard Industrial Classification. Consequently, precise data of seasonal adjustment by industry are not available for the whole of the period from January 1950 on a completely uniform basis. To estimate the normal seasonal constants and factors for industrial unemployment, a series was constructed which was, so far as possible, on a comparable basis from June 1949 to May 1965, on which the constants and factors had been estimated. The adjustments to the original

of industrial insurance books during any year in the inter-war period was that indicated at the date when the book was last exchanged; it was not altered if the worker changed his industry before the next annual exchange.[12]

This is not to say, however, that the current practice of determining a person's position in the industrial disaggregation by his job immediately prior to a current spell of unemployment could not itself be misleading. The extent to which the official series of the distribution of unemployed workers by industry adequately reflects the industrial composition of the unemployed at a given time depends in part on the strength of attachment of the worker to his industry. If the attachment is well established and lasting it provides some means of judging his past employment activity and his present and future labour market actions. If it is not strong then the industrial distribution of the unemployed may merely reflect past events, telling us little of the reasons for any differences in the unemployed worker's previous job compared with the industry in which he obtained his next job.[13] Nor is the unemployment rate by industry[14] necessarily a satisfactory measure of the relative

---

data were made by transferring the number unemployed in wholesale bottling from manufacturing industries to the distributive trades and the number in motor vehicle repairing and garages, book and shoe repairing, and the production and printing of cinematograph films from manufacturing industries to the residual group of all other industries and services. In order to pick up more quickly any changing seasonal pattern during the summer months a shorter run of years has been used since 1978 to estimate the seasonal factors for July, August, and September.

12. See above, pp. 33-4.
13. The volume of the registered wholly unemployed in the cotton industry in the 1950s, for example, was often reduced by the readiness of operatives to take jobs in other trades only to lose them again as recession spread or because the work obtained was seasonal. Such people, if registered as unemployed, were counted under the trade in which they last worked, and not under that to which they considered themselves to belong. See H. Turner and R. Smith, 'The Slump in the Cotton Industry, 1952', *Bulletin of the Oxford University Institute of Statistics*, 15, April 1953; H. Turner, 'Unemployment in Textiles: A Note and Some Conclusions', ibid., August 1953 and Turner, 'Measuring Unemployment', *Journal of the Royal Statistical Society*, loc. cit.
14. Before the Second World War the Ministry of Labour published a monthly unemployment percentage for each industry, showing males and females separately. The practice was not resumed after the war although the data on which industrial unemployment rates could be calculated were readily available.

economic status of an industry at any particular time. The number of unemployed men attached to an industry may be only partially affected by its economic status. The rapidity with which the economy can absorb an industry's separated workers, who together encompass a variety of skills belonging to many different occupations, could make short term inter-industry comparisons of the unemployment rate a very suspect indicator of the economic conditions of the industry in human terms.[15] An improved unemployment percentage could result, also, either from a decrease in the numbers estimated to be insured in an industry, with the total actually employed remaining the same, or from an improvement in the industry which brings more workpeople back into employment, or to a combination of both influences.

Unemployment By Occupation

The statistical treatment of occupational unemployment has been sadly neglected in official published series. The industrial classification of the insured unemployed before 1923 did include some statistics on separate occupations but the information is limited and selective, and in any event is virtually useless for time series analysis because of the change in the basis of the series from 1923. Analyses by occupation of the wholly unemployed portion of the adult Live Register (excluding the temporarily stopped) were made monthly by the Ministry of Labour for administrative purposes between the wars but the results were not published.[16] The only regularly published unemployment

15. The unemployment rate may, however, prove a more satisfactory measure of an industry's fortune over time in as much as the occupational composition of an industry and the relative vulnerability to unemployment of the various occupational groups within it are less subject to frequent change. See C.L. Kaplan, 'Unemployment by Industry—Some Comments on its Measurement and Behavior' in *Measurement and Behavior of Unemployment,* op. cit., pp. 281–324.

16. *Royal Commission on Unemployment Insurance, Minutes of Evidence,* J. Hilton, 3 July 1931, p. 1163. The exceptions are the special analysis of unemployed adults registered at Employment Exchanges in Great Britain on 9 April 1934 as applicants for work as bricklayers, plasterers, slaters, and tilers. (*Gazette,* June 1934) and the details by occupation of those unemployed persons included in the Ministry's sample surveys. See Chapter 4 pp. 139–44. It was natural for the Live Register to be analysed according to occupations rather than industries since the object of the Employment

percentages by occupation between the wars referred to the building industry. The data were included in the *Gazette's* monthly survey of unemployment in the principal industries and provided details of the estimated number insured and unemployed aged 16 to 64 and of the rate of unemployment nationally and by Ministry of Labour Division for the following occupational groups: carpenters, bricklayers, masons, slaters, tilers, plasterers, painters, plumbers, builder's labourers, general labourers, and all other building occupations. Although direct evidence of occupational unemployment during a specified reference period became available from Census returns from 1931[17] regular data relating to wholly unemployed adults in general only became available in 1954.

From September of that year a quarterly analysis began of men and women according to the occupation for which they were registered as out of work and not that in which they last worked. Casual workers and severely disabled persons classified as unlikely to obtain employment other than under special conditions were excluded from the beginning. Later unemployed registrants at, and vacancies notified to, careers offices were excluded from the statistics, and adult students were similarly excluded from December 1975.[18]

The most significant revision of the series occurred at the end of 1961 when an effort was made to present an occupational analysis closely related to the International Standard Classification of Occupations. Information was gathered for a greater number of individual occupations than had previously been the case, with, for men, 26

Exchange operation was to offer applicants jobs they could do, irrespective of the industry in which an employer offering a job was engaged.

Allen obtained some unpublished occupational data of the regional distribution of wholly unemployed men and non-claimants, excluding the temporarily stopped, aged 18 and over on the registers of Employment Exchanges in certain engineering occupations, Great Britain, during the period 1935–39. See 'The Unemployment Situation at the Outbreak of War', *Journal of the Royal Statistical Society,* loc. cit.

17. See pp. 130–38, 152–61.

18. Details of the registered wholly unemployed men and women by occupation at September each year during the period 1954–68 are in *Historical Abstract,* table 174; subsequent years (analysed for each quarter and by region) are in the relevant *Year Books.* Tables summarizing the occupational spread of registered unemployed adults and of unfilled adult vacancies appeared at quarterly intervals in the *Gazette* from May 1958. The occupational classification of notified unfilled vacancies is dealt with separately in Chapter 5.

groups embracing 105 occupations (compared with a former total of only 62) and for women 25 groups covering 66 occupations (compared with 29). The basis of the revised grouping was that all occupations in a group should be related to each other by general similarity of the characteristics of the work which they entailed. Where particular occupations were of such a nature that there was more than one group in which they could be included they were analysed according to the International Standard Classification.

This revised scheme was itself replaced in December 1972 by the new list of Key Occupations for Statistical Purposes (KOS). This was based on the Classification of Occupations and Directory of Occupational Titles (CODOT) which described and coded some 3,500 occupations. In response to a growing need to standardize the collection of occupational statistics in the country, the Department of Employment prepared a selective list of key occupations for which it was agreed that figures ought to be collected at national level. To ensure compatability between the CODOT and the key list, all key occupations were identified and defined in CODOT and grouped in the same broad structure of 18 major groups.

Although these revisions added greater detail to the series the subject of occupational unemployment still remains a neglected field of statistical enquiry. The current data have still to be interpreted with caution. Some of the unemployed can frequently fill vacancies in an occupational group different from that under which they are registered. Vacancies are usually notified for particular jobs but, nevertheless, all unemployed registrants who could do such jobs are considered for them. The policy of the Manpower Services Commission is to classify registrants on the basis of what they are known to be capable of according to their experience and training.

What is especially striking is the paucity of regular disaggregated data and of information of the extent of unemployment by virtue of skill. Detailed knowledge of the structure of employment at a local level could tell us a great deal more about the effective unemployment rate facing workers at a particular occupational and skill level in a given travel-to-work area[19] than is currently available in the published statistics; and to the extent that higher levels of unemployment appear to have greater effects in absolute terms on the unskilled than on other unemployed groups we are clearly in need of more detailed analyses of

19. For an explanation see below, p. 238.

the incidence of unemployment between skill levels and of the variations which exist locally and nationally in the state of the labour
market for particular occupations.[20]

Although the current series of the occupational classification of the
registered unemployed appears quarterly it is not possible from the
information collected to make regular cross-classifications with other
published information such as age, or duration of unemployment. The
extra effort devoted to sample surveys of the characteristics of the
unemployed, following the recommendations of the Government White
Paper (Cmnd. 5157) has, however, produced detailed analyses by
occupational group. The value of such information as a means of
drawing general conclusions about occupational unemployment is
subject to the reservations common to survey material in general but
its importance should not be under-estimated.[21]

20. The growing shortage of craftsmen in the construction industry prompted the
    Ministry of Labour to carry out an enquiry in June 1964 into the character-
    istics of unemployed skilled construction workers. It covered 5,749 men
    registered as wholly unemployed on 15 June and set out to establish the
    standard of skill of the unemployed, the duration of their current spell of
    unemployment, what proportion of them were difficult to place and why,
    and their suitability for retraining. See *Gazette,* November 1965, pp. 483–6.
21. For further details see above pp. 122–6.

9

Unemployment by Area and Region

Regional Statistics

Official regional unemployment figures became regularly available from the returns of the Employment Exchanges from 1912 onwards. From January 1923 (except for the war years), a table was published monthly in the *Gazette* showing the total number on the registers of Employment Exchanges in each Division and in each of a number of large towns. Percentage rates of unemployment by Division became available from October 1926.[1]

These regular Divisional and local unemployment statistics were supplemented in 1927 by a separate Local Unemployment Index issued by the Ministry of Labour. The idea of issuing such an index was first raised in a letter to the Stationery Office on 25 February 1926. The Ministry had had a number of inquiries from manufacturers and distributors requesting regular monthly returns on the state of employment in their particular locality to assist them in adjusting sales activities.

---

1. The comparability of the data over time was obviously affected by changes in the boundaries of the Ministry's Administrative Divisions. For details of such changes between 1923 and 1968 see *Historical Abstract,* appendix E. In August 1941 Divisions became known as Regions. The original Employment Exchange returns are available for all years from 1938 from the Statistics Division of the Department of Employment. For years up to 1937 the detailed returns are no longer available, but the monthly totals of unemployment for each Exchange have been recorded. From July 1946 to March 1949 the unemployed percentages by region were available only in the *Monthly Digest of Statistics.*

Rowntrees of York, in particular, had pressed for such information and had offered to pay a substantial sum for the supply of the data.[2] The monthly table which had already appeared in the *Gazette* since January 1923, though the only regular source of local unemployment data, was regarded as inadequate for the purposes required.

Having once canvassed a representative sample of employers for their views on the proposal for a new local unemployment index, the Ministry was able to persuade the Treasury to support the venture from January 1927 'as an experiment'.[3] The scheme proved profitable within its first year of operation, with a varying number of subscribers initially paying £5 for the service,[4] and the Treasury agreed to continue its support. The Local Unemployment Index was published each month from 1927 to 1939 as a four-page foolscap document giving for 637 towns and for county areas in Great Britain the number of insured persons in each area, and the percentage rates of unemployment for men, women, and juveniles on the Monday nearest the 14th of each month, together with comparisons for a month before and a year before.

The figures supplied in the index were only rough approximations and were unsuitable for general statistical purposes. Until 1937 the ratios of unemployment were calculated by expressing the total number of persons insured and uninsured of all ages on the registers as a percentage of the estimated number insured aged 16-64 (excluding agricultural workers). Such calculations could never provide a precise indication of the actual rate of unemployment in the areas concerned since they related the Live Register figures to the number of insured persons. The figures of insured persons in each area, based on books exchanged, were in many cases seriously defective as an indication of the number of insured persons resident in the area in which the Exchange was situated. Moreover the fact that agricultural workers were included in the register totals but excluded from the number insured invalidated particularly the percentage rates of unemployment

2. PRO, Lab. 2/2172, Local Unemployment Index n.d.
3. ibid., p. 2.
4. Cf. the comments of the *New Statesman,* 22 January 1927: 'We are grateful to the Ministry for making the information public, but we are not grateful to the idiot, whoever he may be, who proposes, by an exorbitant charge to make it impossible for us to use it.... When will the authorities learn that the general diffusion of reliable and detailed information about industrial conditions is an essential part of any enlightened economic policy?' The subscription rate was reduced in subsequent years.

in districts which were largely agricultural. The percentage figures given for juveniles, computed by relating the number aged 14 and under 18 on the registers to the number insured aged 16 and 17 gave an exaggerated notion of the actual extent of unemployment among the younger element in the workforce.[5]

The deficiencies in the index, especially as an adequate reflection of variations in local unemployment at a time of mounting concern over the plight of depressed industrial areas, prompted the Ministry in 1937 to change the basis on which the figures were calculated. Thereafter the number unemployed used for calculating the percentages excluded all uninsured persons and also insured juveniles aged 14 and 15.[6] Furthermore, in making the calculations the number of unemployed insured persons aged 16 to 64 (exclusive of those then insured under the agricultural scheme) was related to the corresponding total number of insured persons (also exclusive of agriculture) in the same group. For areas within a radius of ten miles from the centre of London the figures relating to the number insured represented estimates of the number of such persons resident in the areas. For all other places the figures represented approximately the number of insured persons aged 16 to 64 whose unemployment books were exchanged at Employment Exchanges serving the respective areas. The number unemployed used in calculating the percentages was the number of insured persons recorded as unemployed at those Exchanges. The figures for the earlier years were thus somewhat higher than if they had been prepared on the 1937 basis. A comparison of figures compiled on both bases for January 1936 shows a difference of 0.6 in England (15.2 on the old and 14.6 on the new basis), of 1.9 in Scotland (between 24.6 and 22.7), of 2.3 in Wales (between 33.7 and 31.4), and of 1.1 in Britain as a whole (between 17.1 and 16.0).[7]

This classification did not entirely remedy the deficiencies inherent in the index. While the unemployed usually registered at the Employment Exchange nearest their place of residence, those in employment at the date of the exchange of books in July had their unemployment

5. PRO, Lab. 17/120. Proposed Revision in the 'Local Unemployment Index', January 1937.
6. Shortly before the revisions in the index substantial increases had occurred in the number of juveniles becoming available for employment at the end of the school-leaving periods. This resulted in variations in the percentage figures for such groups which bore little relation to variations in economic prosperity.
7. Beveridge, *Full Employment*, op. cit., pp. 323–8.

books exchanged at the Exchange serving the area in which their place of employment was situated. In some industrial areas it was possible for considerable numbers of persons to register during periods of unemployment at Exchanges other than those at which their unemployment books were subsequently exchanged. The percentages shown in the index did not, therefore, necessarily reflect the rates of unemployment among persons resident in particular localities.[8]

The official unemployment and vacancy series developed from 1948 continued on the whole to provide equivalent regional data, details of which have already been given in the text. The introduction of Standard Regions for official statistical purposes, as a co-ordinating measure to facilitate post-war economic planning, did not affect the validity of the unemployment series since their boundaries were generally co-terminous with those used by the Ministry of Labour, despite changes in the latter in the post-Second-World-War period. Even when the

---

8. See below pp. 238–9. Further details of unemployment data by region or area not normally available from official sources can be found in Astor *et al.,* op. cit. (districts in Great Britain where the number and percentages of unemployed exceeded 10 per cent, or over 1,000 men in the autumn of 1922, together with reports of the local unemployment situation in Birmingham, Burnley, Sheffield, Stoke-on-Trent and Woolwich); Richardson, op. cit., (number and percentage of unemployed in the 12 largest towns of West Yorkshire, May, November, each year between 1924 and 1936); details of the rate of unemployment among insured workers in Hull 1923–30 are in Social Survey Committee, Hull Community Council, *Unemployment in Hull,* Hull 1933; equivalent data for Merseyside in 1924, 1929, and 1932 to 1934 are in D.C. Jones, op. cit.; for an analysis of Live Register returns for Oxford during 1927–37 see A.F.C. Bourdillon, *A Survey of the Social Services in the Oxford District 1: Economics and Government of a Changing Area,* Oxford 1938. A classification of unemployment by districts is in W.H. Beveridge, 'An Analysis of Unemployment', *Economica,* 111, 1936.

Details of the number of persons on the Live Register in Employment Exchange Divisions in 1920 and 1921 are in PRO, Cab. 27/116 and Cab. 27/118. Similar analyses of areas with populations exceeding 40,000, distinguishing their relative rates of insured unemployment and number on the Live Register, can be found in PRO, Lab. 900/10, Unemployment in Great Britain 15 October 1925; Unemployment in Great Britain. Particulars of Areas in Which Unemployment was Heavy on 23rd February 1925, 31 March 1925; Unemployment in Great Britain. Particulars of the Areas in Which Unemployment was Heavy as shown by the Live Registers . . . on 3rd March 1924, 31 March 1924; Unemployment in Great Britain, Statement showing the extent of Unemployment in certain industrial areas, 1924. A detailed analysis of unemployment within Durham and Tyneside at selected dates between May 1926 and June 1939 can be found in PRO, Lab. 23/170.

Central Statistical Office introduced revised Standard Regions for Statistical Purposes in 1966 they coincided broadly with the administrative regions of what was then the Department of Employment and Productivity. Statistics of unemployment and vacancies were consequently presented thereafter by Standard Region. Some minor difficulties arose, however, because unemployment figures were compiled from local employment offices. The areas thus covered sometimes extended across the boundaries of Standard Regions leading to slight differences in the aggregated regional figures. The composition of the Standard Regions was again revised in 1974.[9]

9. For details see *British Labour Statistics Year Book 1974,* appendix D. To meet a growing demand for information on regional matters the Central Statistical Office launched a new publication in 1965 entitled *Abstract of Regional Statistics* (currently *Regional Statistics*) providing time series by Standard Region of unemployment among males and females separately and of unemployment rates for males and females together. More detailed information of unemployment within sub-divisions of particular Standard Regions can be found in *Scottish Abstract of Statistics* (1971-) and *Digest of Welsh Statistics* (1954-). For a full discussion of the differences between Standard Regions for Statistical Purposes and Ministry of Labour Administrative Regions see *Gazette,* February 1966, and D.B. Kent-Smith and A. Pritchard, 'Development of Statistical Regions in the United Kingdom', *Statistical News,* 22, November 1974. Summaries of pre-1966 regional unemployment data are in E. Hammond, *Analysis of Regional Economic and Social Statistics,* London 1968; Ministry of Labour and National Service, *Employment and Unemployment in Great Britain 1939, 1945 and 1946. Tables relating to Regional and Industrial Analysis of Persons Insured against Unemployment, 1947; Employment and Unemployment in Great Britain 1947, Tables relating . . . etc., 1948; Employment and Unemployment, Tables relating to Employment and Unemployment in Great Britain 1948. Regional and Industrial Analysis,* 1949; Ministry of Labour, *Tables relating to Employment and Unemployment in Great Britain, 1948, 1949 and 1950,* 1951.

For a general if now somewhat dated discussion of the adequacy of regional unemployment data see K.S. Lomax, 'Regional Economic Statistics', *Journal of the Royal Statistical Society,* 117, 1954; C.W. Peare and H. Thomas, 'Regional Economic Statistics', *Journal of the Royal Statistical Society,* 30, 1968. The course of unemployment in the various regions between 1920-58, analysed from official sources, is in D.A. Shinton, 'Post-War Regional Unemployment and Development', M.A. thesis, University of Exeter 1965.

Seasonal adjustments to regional unemployment data for the period January 1950–December 1965 were obtained from 1965 from data of wholly unemployed males and females (excluding school leavers) in the Standard Regions as then defined. Suitably amended data were published regularly in the *Gazette* thereafter. Regional data are also available as part of the Department of Employment's surveys of the characteristics of the unemployed. See above pp. 145–51.

New regional unemployment series have arisen directly as a result of government economic policy, especially that aimed at steering new and expanding industries to areas of heavy unemployment. The Industrial Development Act (1966), for example, designated particular areas according to their actual and expected level of unemployment as 'development areas' requiring special assistance to encourage growth and a 'proper' distribution of industry. They covered most of Scotland, most of Wales, the Northern Region of England, the Furness Peninsula, Merseyside, most of Cornwall, and North Devon. Special government assistance was offered later to more narrowly defined localities within and outside the development areas which, among other things, were suffering from high and persistent unemployment; first in 1967 to 'special development areas' in central Scotland, South Wales, the north-east of England, and West Cumberland where colliery closures were expected to aggravate the unemployment situation; second in 1969, following the Hunt Committee Report,[10] to the intermediate areas of the Yorkshire coalfield, North Humberside, North East Lancashire, the Nottingham/Derbyshire coalfield, Plymouth, part of South East Wales, and Leith in Scotland where there were problems of maldistribution of industry and rising unemployment but on a scale relatively less than that of the development areas.[11] Retrospective information on the volume and rate of unemployment is available for Development Areas for June of each year from 1956 to 1966 and thereafter monthly from August 1966; for Intermediate Areas for June of each year from 1956 to 1969 and thereafter monthly; and for Special Development Areas monthly from October 1974.[12]

Area Statistics

Because most of the statistics of unemployment in Great Britain are based on returns rendered from the network of employment and careers offices covering the whole of the country there is no shortage of available data for individual localities. The only regularly published

10. *The Intermediate Areas,* Cmnd. 3998, April 1969.
11. The areas granted intermediate, development and special development area status have changed during the 1970s. For a summary of the coverage of assisted areas after 1966 see *Year Book 1974,* appendix E and *Gazette,* June 1977.
12. See *Historical Abstract,* table 170 and appropriate *Year Books* and 'Area Statistics of Unemployment' in *Gazette,* September 1970 and November 1974.

statistics before 1960 referred to the total number of men, boys, women, and girls registered as unemployed in a number of principal towns[13] although more detailed unemployment data for assisted areas became available on a retrospective basis in later years.[14]

Percentage rates of unemployment for local areas were not published before 1960. An overriding difficulty was that the employment data for any local area related principally to those people who worked in the area. As the Ministry of Labour explained in 1960:

The returns prepared by Local Offices . . . relate to National Insurance cards exchanged in that particular area and the number of Insurance cards held by employers in that area. In the case of a large firm with a number of establishments in different parts of the country, the cards may be held at a central office of the firm; if they are, they will be exchanged at a single place and included in the figures for that place, although some of the associated establishments are situated elsewhere. Employers are asked to supply full particulars about all known cases of this kind, and appropriate adjustments are made to the figures for the Local Offices concerned, a figure being reduced if it includes cards for employees who work elsewhere and increased if it excludes employees who work in the area but whose cards have been exchanged elsewhere. The result is that the figure for any area relates more closely to the number of persons working in the area than it otherwise would. It is not possible to say that the figures represent precisely the number working in the area as employers are not compelled to exchange insurance cards at any particular Local Office. The great majority of employers, however, exchange their cards at the Local Office nearest to their establishments, and when it is known that they have not done so, an adjustment is made; it can, therefore, be assumed that generally the figure for any area is a fair reflection of the number of employees working in the area.[15]

13. See above pp. 231–4. The published tables of the number on the register in the principal towns of Great Britain were suspended from August 1940 and resumed in May 1945. The number of towns included in the series fluctuated over time from 96 before 1939 to 114 in 1960.
14. See above p. 236.
15. *Gazette,* April 1960, p. 134. The principal qualification is that the local figures were based on counts of National Insurance Cards and therefore excluded certain civil servants and merchant seamen on long voyages whose contributions were recorded on separate documents. Adjustments for these categories were made to national and regional figures, but not to local figures. Their omission has little effect, however, on the value of the series for the purpose of calculating unemployment rates.

The difficulty in arriving at a local rate of unemployment stems from the fact that the unemployed often register at an employment or career office nearest to their homes, even though they work in the area of a different office. For practical purposes therefore Employment Exchanges have been grouped together since 1953 to constitute a single 'travel-to-work' area for which a percentage rate of unemployment can be calculated.

The previous designation of principal towns was amended for this purpose. Those localities subsequently designated as Development Areas and, later, Intermediate Areas appeared in the relevant series; all others continued to appear as principal towns. Those localities whose area of coverage was altered to permit a percentage rate of unemployment to be calculated were separately identified. (It was not possible to analyse Greater London into smaller areas.) The current percentage rate of unemployment for certain local areas relates to the total number registered as unemployed, expressed as a percentage of the estimated number of employees (employed and unemployed) based on the Census of Employment at the latest available date.

As the number of workers living in one area and working in another and the distances over which they travelled to work increased during the late sixties and early seventies, the designated 'travel-to-work' areas became out of date, and their published percentage rate of unemployment an inadequate reflection of the real level of unemployment in the wider labour market area of which they had become a part. Revised groupings were therefore compiled in 1968, 1970, and 1978. As a result, percentage rates relating to areas which proved different from those for which rates had previously been calculated and published are no longer strictly comparable. Despite such problems the local area unemployment rates remain the only frequent source of data by which to monitor regional policies on unemployment and to identify areas particularly in need of government assistance.[16]

The Department of Employment does not calculate unemployment rates for areas smaller than 'travel-to-work' areas. It is possible, however, to combine statistics from local Jobcentres or Employment Office Areas with those contained in the Department of the Environment's

---

16. Details of the number of unemployed persons and unemployment rates in certain local areas are available on a quarterly basis in the current *British Labour Statistics Year Books*. Equivalent monthly data have been available in the *Gazette* since 1960.

National Dwelling and Housing Survey to provide disaggregated data on employment and unemployment in English inner cities. The results of an *ad hoc* survey of conditions in five inner city areas during 1973-9 were published in the *Gazette* in August 1979.

Interpreting Inter-Regional Differences in Unemployment Rates

One of the most notable features of unemployment in Great Britain is that despite the post-war commitment to full employment there has been little real tendency for spatial unemployment rate differences to disappear; indeed, unemployment differences between regions have remained remarkably stable over time.[17] Only recently have the possible causes of these differences in the level of unemployment come under close scrutiny. The results are important here because they help to identify which factors most influence the reliability of registered unemployment as an indicator of involuntary worklessness in the various regions.

The question arises as to whether inter-regional differences in the percentage level of unemployment are caused primarily by differences in demand pressure or by differences in the level of structural and frictional unemployment.[18] Differences in the sensitivity of regions to unemployment, an important source of inter-regional variations in unemployment, could arise from the fact that fluctuations in the rate of unemployment vary between industries so that regional differences in industrial structure are an important determinant of sensitivity to unemployment, or from the fact that fluctuations in unemployment in a given industry may differ between regions. Dixon and Thirlwall found from the evidence of regional unemployment between 1951 and 1972 that the major source of difference lay not in dissimilar industrial structures but in the tendency of industries to fluctuate more in some regions than in others. Cheshire, too, has emphasized the point that unemployment rates are not industry-specific. The pattern of regional unemployment differentials is not attributable in the main to the fact

17. Cheshire, *Regional Unemployment Differences in Great Britain*, op. cit.; D. Metcalf and R. Richardson, 'Unemployment in London', in Worswick (ed.), op. cit.
18. The following analysis is based largely on R.I. Dixon and A.P. Thirlwall, *Regional Growth and Unemployment in the United Kingdom*, London 1975.

that some regions suffer from a disproportionate share of declining industries but rather that all industries in high-unemployment areas tend to have unemployment rates above the average for those industries.[19] Changes in industrial structure have been found to exert only a limited effect on regional unemployment. Moreover, inter-regional differences in the cyclical component of unemployment do not appear to be a major source of differences in regional unemployment rates.[20]

The analysis of regional unemployment differences has been carried further by using the U/V method already described to divide registered unemployment in each region into that due to demand-deficiency and that attributed to frictional and structural factors (i.e. non demand-deficient unemployment).[21] There appears to be very little difference between regions in the extent of non demand-deficient unemployment. The major source of inter-regional differences in the level of unemployment appears to be demand-deficient unemployment.[22] The examination by the National Institute of Economic and Social Research of data of unemployed adult males has shown that the estimates of non

---

19. Dixon and Thirlwall, op. cit., chapter 4. Cheshire, op. cit., chapter 1; Brown, op. cit., pp. 218–19. A similar point was made by D. Champernowne in 1937. See 'The Uneven Distribution of Unemployment in the United Kingdom, 1929–36', *Review of Economic Studies*, V, 1937–8.

20. A.P. Thirlwall, 'Regional Unemployment as a Cyclical Phenomenon', *Scottish Journal of Political Economy*, 13, June 1966; C.P. Harris and A.P. Thirlwall, 'Inter-regional Variations in Cyclical Sensitivity to Unemployment', *Bulletin of the Oxford Institute of Statistics*, 30, February 1968. See also F. Brechling, 'Trends and Cycles in British Regional Unemployment', *Oxford Economic Papers*, 19, 1967.

21. i.e. by defining demand-deficient unemployment as the excess of unemployment over vacancies minus the maximum sum of frictional and structural unemployment that the region is capable of showing—as indicated by the level of unemployment at which U=V. This level represents zero demand-deficient unemployment. Any level of actual unemployment below it is classified as entirely structural and frictional and any excess above it as due to deficiency of demand. One cannot rely implicitly, however, on conclusions derived from the U/V analysis. The presumption that deficient demand unemployment is zero when U=V is itself open to some doubt (see M.W. Reder, 'The Theory of Frictional Unemployment', *Economica*, XXXVI, 1969). Moreover, as long as there are fundamental inaccuracies in the recording of both unemployment and vacancies and in so far as the U/V relationship is itself unstable, the equality of the two variables can only represent a very imperfect division between different types of unemployment.

22. Dixon and Thirlwall, op. cit., chapter 5.

demand-deficient unemployment rose in all regions before and after the shift in the U/V relationship in 1966 but still remained a fraction of the corresponding range of actual unemployment rates.[23] Inter-regional variations in the imperfection of labour markets (as measured by frictional, structural, and personal-deficiency unemployment) appear only of secondary importance in explaining inter-regional unemployment differences to 1968.[24] Such analyses suggest that regional imbalances arise mainly from the way in which a given level of aggregate demand impinges on demand in the various regions.[25] The importance of this as far as registered unemployment statistics are concerned has been clearly indicated by A.J. Brown:

Where there is high pressure of labour demand there is never much registered unemployment because those actively offering themselves for work are snapped up. In relatively slack times workers already employed tend to be 'hoarded'; a boom—a push to get more labour—tends to draw largely on those who are only marginal members of the labour force, and who tend to drop out of it spontaneously in a slump, so that their numbers in employment decline without adding to registered unemployment. In the regions of lower demand pressure these conditions do not apply: redundant labour is laid off more freely—since labour is not expected to be scarce, there is less reason to incur the costs of hoarding it—and those laid off will normally register for benefit. . . . The unregistered unemployed vary very little as a proportion of the labour force from one region to another; in regions of slack demand they are a small proportion of the actual reserve of labour, in regions of high demand a large one. . . . At all events it is clear that, in general, the fluctuations of registered unemployment give very much fuller indications of the true variations in involuntary worklessness in some regions than in others; they are more inefficient indicators of it where demand is high, so that they tend to overstate the

23. Bowers, Cheshire and Webb, *National Institute Economic Review,* November 1970, loc. cit.; Bowers, Cheshire, Webb and Weedon, *NIER,* November 1972, loc. cit.
24. Cheshire, op. cit., chapters 3, 4, and 5. For details of the importance of personal-deficiency unemployment nationally and within regions see the section above 'Characteristics of the Unemployed', pp. 145–51. For a measure of the magnitude of the different types of unemployment in Great Britain and the various regions see A.P. Thirlwall, 'Types of Unemployment in the Regions of Great Britain', *Manchester School,* 4, 1974.
25. See D. Elias, 'Regional Unemployment Elasticities: Further Evidence', *Scottish Journal of Political Economy,* 25, February 1978.

relative (though perhaps not the absolute) differences in regional incidence of cyclical unemployment.[26]

This is borne out further by the evidence of marked regional differences in registering habits across the country, the depressed areas having higher registration propensities than the more prosperous regions.

The studies of spatial unemployment referred to so far make little or no reference to conditions in local labour markets or to the personal characteristics, the flow into unemployment, or the duration of unemployment of the persons found in them. Although regional unemployment differences appear positively related to spatial differences in excess demand, the effect of the latter, according to some observers, seems less significant in explaining inter- and intra-urban unemployment than do socio-demographic characteristics of the workforce (age, skill, marital status, race, and number of dependants), urban size, and industrial structure and patterns of residential location.[27] There is no reason to believe, however, that such analyses are mutually exclusive. As far as personal characteristics are concerned it is clear from the available data that relatively disadvantaged persons (by virtue of, say, age and/or skill) suffer disproportionately as aggregate unemployment increases. But observed differences in the personal characteristics of one group of workers suffering a higher rate of unemployment than another in any one spatial labour market tells us nothing about the causes of unemployment. The concurrence of lack of skill and relatively higher unemployment could be perfectly consistent with a general decline in the demand for labour and a shortage of jobs.[28] In this context there is clearly a need for more detailed unemployment data. One of the difficulties in determining precisely the nature of such regional or local unemployment problems is the lack of disaggregated data between Census years, especially of unemploy-

26. Brown, op. cit., p. 221.
27. D. Metcalf, 'Urban Unemployment in England', *Economic Journal*, 85, 1975; J. Vipond, 'City Size and Unemployment', *Urban Studies*, 11, 1974; C.F. Sirmans, 'City Size and Unemployment: Some New Estimates', *Urban Studies*, 14, 1977; A. McGregor, 'Intra-Urban Variations in Unemployment Duration: A Case Study', *Urban Studies*, 14, 1977; S. Holtermann, 'Unemployment in Urban Areas', *Urban Studies*, 15, 1978; P. Cheshire, 'Inner Areas as Spatial Labour Markets: A Critique of the Inner Areas Studies', *Urban Studies*, 16, 1979.
28. Cheshire, loc. cit., 1979, pp. 33–4.

ment in standard conurbations outside of the Greater London Council and Birmingham[29] and of urban/rural aggregates of the number out of work.[30]

29. See in this respect the *Annual Abstract of Greater London Statistics* (1968–); D. Metcalfe, 'Unemployment in London', in Worswick (ed.), op. cit.; V. Earl, 'Some Data on London's Unemployment', *Greater London Intelligence Journal*, 41, 1978; and *Birmingham Statistics* (formerly City of Birmingham *Annual Abstract of Statistics*) (1951–)–the first issue of which provided data for the period 1931–49.

30. Although unemployment data for separate exchanges could be used for urban and various sub-regional aggregates there have been few analyses of local unemployment registers from which a clearer perception of the content of national aggregate percentages can be obtained. Some interesting exceptions are R.L. Smyth, 'Male Unemployment Problems in Large Ports and Urban Areas, with special reference to Kingston-upon-Hull', *Yorkshire Bulletin of Economic and Social Research*, 2, August 1953; E.W. Evans and K. Hartley, *Employment and Unemployment in the Hull Region*, University of Hull, 1964; J. Craig, E.W. Evans and B. Showler, 'Humberside: Employment, Unemployment and Migration. The Evolution of Industrial Structure', *Yorkshire Bulletin of Economic and Social Research*, 22, November 1970; B. Showler, 'An Analysis of Adult Unemployment in the Sub-Region of Humberside since 1951', M.Sc.(Econ) thesis, Hull 1969; D.I. MacKay, *et al.*, *Labour Markets Under Different Employment Conditions*, London 1971, (analyses unemployment in Birmingham and in parts of Scotland 1959–66).

Epilogue

Regular sources of unemployment statistics can be traced back to 1851 for the engineering, shipbuilding, and metal trades and are more generally available for numerous benefit-paying trade unions from 1888 to 1926. This trade union material is the primary source of unemployment data until 1913 when the Labour Department of the Board of Trade (and subsequently the Ministry of Labour) began to collect statistics as part of their duties under the National Insurance Act, 1911. From the time when the Ministry of Labour and its successors assumed full responsibility for the administration of unemployment insurance the manner and scope of the official count of the unemployed became increasingly dictated by administrative practice and convenience.

It was not until 1923 that the first really reliable returns became available from the operation of the unemployment insurance scheme. The trade union returns are therefore of special value in providing some indication of conditions in the late Victorian and Edwardian periods. They also provide an alternative source of data during the thirteen years in which they overlapped with the official government series and are a particularly important source of information for the First World War period. The trade union unemployment percentages are not and were never intended to be an absolute measure of the total amount of unemployment among the labour force as a whole; they are a valuable guide to the fluctuations in but not the volume of unemployment.

The caution with which informed observers of the Edwardian period viewed the available unemployment statistics as representative of general conditions was not matched by the readiness with which the more voluminous unemployment insurance statistics of the 1920s were regarded as key indices of economic progress. There is no doubt that by 1939 the country was far better served in terms of unemployment

244

statistics than it had been previously and more adequately than was the case in some other European countries. The fact that authoritative monthly statements of the number unemployed were being regularly published added greatly to the public consciousness of the unemployment problem. The available series were, after all, reasonably comparable within if not between the periods 1900–21 and 1922–47.

To some extent, however, the sheer magnitude of the volume of recorded unemployment and the existence of an official source of statistics apparently free of the most serious shortcomings of the trade union returns reduced questions as to the reliability and the internal consistency of the inter-war data to almost academic proportions. The count of the insured unemployed undoubtedly excluded some people whose incidence of unemployment tended to be below the average and to that extent the recorded results exaggerated unemployment among wage- and salary-earners as a whole. Moreover, the prime source of this particular series was the volume of registered unemployment. To the extent that the jobless failed to register the insured statistics underestimated the true situation. They were based furthermore on data of 'Books Lodged' and the 'Two Months file', each compiled in accordance with regulations and definitions of unemployment which had no strict parallels in the pre-1923 period. It is true that the Live Register series contained details of the uninsured unemployed who chose to register as such but there is no way of knowing precisely what proportion the registered uninsured represented of the total uninsured workforce without jobs. None of the efforts recently made to recalculate inter-war unemployment by making due allowance for the groups excluded from the insurance series has produced revised estimates sufficiently trustworthy to apply to the entire period.

Inter-war unemployment statistics cannot be fully understood unless close attention is paid to the many changes in administrative and legislative practice which directly influenced an individual's incentive to register as unemployed. Changes that made it more worth while for unemployment benefit claimants to register, for example, may have produced results which reflected not so much an increase in unemployment as a more efficient recording of the existing level of unemployment. But it is difficult to distinguish either the initial impact or the ultimate duration of such effects from all other possible influences. The problem is further complicated by the fact that changes in administration and the law did not affect the pattern and timing of registration in the insured and Live Register series in the same way.

Despite the fact that the Ministry of Labour was one of the few government departments between the wars to have its own Statistical Branch little work was done by way of analysis and interpretation of the existing material. What is particularly striking is the almost total absence of any attempt to distinguish the different types of unemployment in existence, to indicate its distribution by age and skill, to assess adequately the duration and seasonality of unemployment and its industrial incidence by region, or to investigate fully the changing characteristics and personnel of the unemployed. The sample surveys conducted by the Ministry of Labour at varying intervals between the wars were not sufficiently broad in scope nor varied enough in the type of information obtained to support generalizations about the unemployed population as a whole.

Nor were such weaknesses readily acknowledged or speedily corrected. Regular details of the duration of unemployment only became available in the early 1930s and were restricted to registered benefit claimants. The emphasis put on recording only the most recent spell of unemployment disguised the severity of frequent and long-term unemployment. Although the development of flow statistics has enabled recent observers to monitor fluctuations in the stock of the unemployed between monthly counts there is still today no systematic analysis of the employment and unemployment cycle of a cohort of individuals over time.

Official attempts to indicate the relative importance of seasonal influences in determining the overall course of unemployment were only developed to any degree of sophistication after 1960, though the methodology was applied retrospectively to the unemployment figures from 1949 and to the vacancy figures from 1958. The unemployed have been classified by industry from 1913 but the available data are subject to breaks in continuity. The industrial classification adopted in 1923 coded individuals to the industry in which they last worked during the preceding insurance year. This classification was itself amended in 1948, 1958, and again in 1968 by which time persons were classified according to the job they had held immediately prior to their current spell of unemployment. It is very difficult therefore to judge precisely how far the statistics of industrial unemployment fairly reflect on any consistent basis the changing fortunes of British industry since the end of the First World War. The statistics of occupational unemployment are even more wanting. Regularly published figures date only from 1954 and though determined efforts have been made since

1961 to provide standardized occupational classifications for statistical purposes the entire subject of unemployment by skill at both national and local level remains sorely neglected.

The introduction of a new national insurance scheme in 1948 brought most of the uninsured work force of the pre-1939 period into the official count of the unemployed. This makes comparisons of pre- and post-war unemployment rates somewhat difficult because the previously excluded groups tended to be less prone to unemployment. The effect was to add proportionately more to the number insured than to the number unemployed, thus exaggerating the pre-1939 unemployment rates relative to those for the post-1948 period.

Although the numerous modifications made to the unemployment data since 1948 have given them a high degree of internal consistency the figures still do not represent an exact measure of unemployment. Some of the deficiencies of disaggregation noticeable in the pre-1939 period have persisted. Age-specific unemployment rates, for example, only became available in 1975 and there are still no comparable figures for vacancies. The entire question of the validity of the post-war unemployment figures as a true measure of the volume of unused labour reserves has, however, become the subject of intense debate and inquiry during the past decade.

From 1966 it became increasingly clear that long-established relationships between unemployment, vacancies, employment, output, and earnings, which had fostered the belief that the unemployment statistics were the most important single indicator of the state of the labour market, had broken down. The results of the numerous empirical investigations to which this phenomenon gave rise have been outlined in previous chapters. Evidence of unregistered unemployment and of the under-utilization of labour indicated strongly that the published registered statistics, though still important in reflecting changes in the number of persons seeking work, were an imperfect measure of the extent of involuntary unemployment in the economy and by themselves an inadequate indicator of changes in labour market pressures.

What has become clear during the 1960s and 1970s is the degree to which the conventional wisdom about unemployment, hitherto drawn largely from the contrasting experience of the inter-war and post-1945 periods, is an insufficient and often misleading guide to the dynamics of the present day labour market. Assumptions held during the 1950s about the characteristics, attitudes, and behaviour patterns of the unemployed had never been sufficiently tested. Once unemployment emerged again as a serious economic, social, and political problem, the field of investigation was widened to encompass survey and other sampling techniques. The evidence which gradually emerged, for example, of the determinants of unemployment duration, of the scale of hidden unemployment, of variations in registration habits, and of alleged benefit-induced unemployment further encouraged econometricians and statisticians to test the reliability of the official sources as measures of unsatisfied labour supply.

This continuing preoccupation with the nature of British unemployment statistics has important implications for the future. Improvements will undoubtedly be made to methods of computation as the search for a more generally acceptable measure of joblessness continues. The labour market is now formally recognized to be more dynamic and diversified than was previously thought, providing a market for work even in times of sluggish demand for labour. This explains in part why the pressure to examine unemployment in micro- rather than macro-economic terms has increased over recent years and is likely to increase further, because it is at that level that the more significant deficiencies in the official data have been found to exist.

What is particularly interesting is the potential impact that such a developing concern will have on the content and direction of public policy. If future research suggests, for example, that fluctuations in unemployment arise primarily from demand- side explanations (no jobs) then government corrective policy may well concentrate on fiscal and monetary weapons. Supply-based explanations (e.g. lack of incentive among the unemployed, increased duration of job search) may, on the other hand, encourage the belief that registered unemployment is to remain permanently high, the solution of which lies in improving information on job opportunities, reorganizing the public employment service and, possibly, amending social security legislation. But recent and detailed investigations into the determinants of unemployment duration demonstrate the dangers of supposing that such policy options are either practically available or mutually exclusive. The probability of returning to work appears to fall progressively for most workers the longer they remain on the unemployment register and more so in the case of the older and, especially, the unskilled person. It seems too that changes in unemployment compensation have little or no effect on the duration of unemployment of those people who have already been out of work for over six months. It is questionable, therefore, whether the long-term unemployed can ever be adequately helped by improving job search methods, unless employers are specifically encouraged to take them on or unless more active and direct steps are taken to expand the number of real job opportunities available.

Perhaps the most rewarding areas for future research lie in determining the distribution of unemployment between individuals and in investigating whether the distribution is associated with any clearly identifiable set of influences or personal characteristics. If subsequent inquiries confirm, for example, that recurrent unemployment among a particular set of individuals is more widespread and more involuntary than was formerly believed then the current emphasis in social security legislation on defining benefit eligibility in terms of one's previous record of uninterrupted employment may need careful reconsideration.

There is now sufficient evidence to suggest that policy-makers should not take the unemployment figures at their face value as a guide to the state of the labour market. High unemployment by historical standards can co-exist with acute shortages of labour and ought not necessarily to be viewed as an indicator of slack in the market. Decisions of how best to tackle a generally higher level of unemployment can no longer rely on the operation of market forces alone. A realistic labour market policy must aim to achieve a better match geographically, occupationally, and by skill, between vacancies and the unemployed on the basis of a more informed analysis of the nature and the relative importance of the different types of unemployment in existence and of the varying characteristics of the unemployed themselves.

If registered unemployment remains comparatively high during the next few years it would be instructive to know, for example, how much of the increase compared with previous years was a response, not to reduced demand for labour, but to more generous unemployment and social security benefits, or to demographic factors, or to a change in the propensity of those on the periphery of the labour force to register as unemployed. It might be necessary, moreover, to concentrate man-power policy in the future towards assisting certain groups of people in all labour markets (unemployed unskilled manual workers in particular) rather than reacting to excess demand in specific labour markets if 'structural' unemployment is, in reality, found to have less to do with an increase in dispersion between local and occupational markets than with a general and long-term shift in aggregate demand against a broadly defined group within the labour market as a whole.[1]

1. See N. Bosanquet, 'Structuralism' and 'Structural Unemployment', *British Journal of Industrial Relations*, 17, November 1979.

Ideally some measure is needed of the actual volume of unused labour resources that could confidently be drawn into employment via government action. To this end more sophisticated methods of estimating hidden and unregistered unemployment (among the under 18s as well as adults) must be sought, especially if fluctuations in demand in the future reflect themselves in changes in the number of secondary workers in the labour market and in variations in the utilization of labour more than they do in the number of unemployed as generally understood. Furthermore, to the extent that advances in technology require changing and even greater skills or necessitate a different distribution of the labour force between the manufacturing and service sectors than now prevails it will be necessary to distinguish clearly between frictional and other types of unemployment and to monitor more carefully than at present the incidence of unemployment among differing occupational, skill, and, perhaps, educational[2] groups. This is particularly important in view of the over-supply of unskilled and of the relative shortage of skilled workers within the labour market in recent years.

Few will deny either that existing methods of measuring unemployment are especially inadequate in reflecting the social or psychic distress arising from loss of work. The range of personal and ideological influences that produce an acceptance of unemployment are difficult enough to identify let alone to 'measure'. But if, as seems likely, unemployment is to remain a persistent and serious feature of modern industrial capitalism over the next few decades, than the fears to which it gives rise, the speed by and the direction in which it spreads, and the characteristics it assumes must remain issues of prime economic, moral, and statistical concern.

2. The quantitative relationship between education and the incidence of unemployment has received little attention in this country. A recent exception is S. Nickell, 'Education and Lifetime Patterns of Unemployment', *Journal of Political Economy*, 87, October 1979.

Bibliography

I Parliamentary Papers and Other Official Publications

Hand-Loom Weavers. Report of the Commissioners, 1841.

Memorandum explaining arrangements made by the Board of Trade for collecting and publishing statistics of Labour, 1886.

Tabulation of the Statements made by Men Living in Certain Districts March 1887, 1887.

Memorandum explaining progress made in carrying out arrangements, 1888.

Board of Trade, *Report on Agencies and Methods for Dealing with the Unemployed,* 1893.

Royal Commission on Labour, 1892–4.

Report on Work of Department Since its formation; with Supplement of Labour Statistics, 1894.

Select Committee on Distress from Want of Employment, 1895.

British and Foreign Trade and Industrial Conditions (Second Series), 1905.

Royal Commission on the Poor Laws and Relief of Distress, 1905-9.

Return as to the Proceedings of Distress Committees under the Unemployed Workmen Act, 1905 in England and Wales, up to 31 March 1906, 1906.

Report by the Local Government Board for Scotland as to the Proceedings of Distress Committees in Scotland from the Date of their Appointment to 15 May 1906, 1907.

Return as to the Proceedings of Distress Committees in England and Wales and of the Central (Unemployed) Body of London during the year ended 31 March 1910, 1910.

First Report on the Proceedings of the Board of Trade under Part II of the National Insurance Act, with Appendices, 1913.

Memorandum on the steps taken for the Prevention and Relief of Distress due to the War, 1914.

Report of the Board of Trade on the State of Employment in the United Kingdom in October, 1914, 1914.

Report of the Board of Trade on the State of Employment in the United Kingdom in December, 1914, 1915.

Report of the Board of Trade on the State of Employment in the United Kingdom in February, 1915, 1916.

Report of Committee on Re-Employment of Ex-Servicemen, 1920.

Report of the Committee on Unemployment Insurance in Agriculture, 1921.

Ministry of Labour, *Report on an Investigation into the Personal Circumstances and Industrial History of 10,000 Claimants to Unemployment Benefit, November 5th to 10th, 1923*, 1924.

Report on National Unemployment Insurance to July 1923, 1924.

Ministry of Labour, *Report on an Investigation into the Personal Circumstances and Industrial History of 10,903 Claimants to Unemployment Benefit, November 24th to 29th, 1924*, 1925.

Committee on Industry and Trade, *Survey of Industrial Relations*, London 1926.

Memorandum on the Influence of Legislative and Administrative Changes on the Official Unemployment Statistics, 1926.

Ministry of Labour, *Report on an Enquiry into the Personal Circumstances and Industrial History of 3331 Boys and 2701 Girls Registered for Employment at Employment Exchanges and Juvenile Employment Bureaux, June and July 1925*, 1926.

Memorandum on Certain Points Concerning the Statistics of Unemployment and of Poor Law Relief, 1927.

Ministry of Labour, *Report of an Investigation into the Employment and Insurance History of a Sample of Persons Insured Against Unemployment*, 1927.

Unemployed Persons in receipt of domiciliary Poor Law Relief in England and Wales during the week ended 18th June, 1927, 1927.

Ministry of Labour, *Report on an Investigation into the Personal Circumstances and Industrial History of 9748 Claimants to Unemployment Benefit, April 4th to 9th, 1927*, 1928.

Royal Commission on Unemployment Insurance, 1930–31.

Report of the Proceedings under the Agricultural Wages (Regulations) Act 1924, 1931.

Board of Trade, *An Industrial Survey of the Lancashire Area (excluding Merseyside),* London 1932.

Report of the Statutory Committee on the Financial Condition of the Unemployment Fund on 31 December 1934, 1934–35.

Unemployment Assistance Board, *Report for the period ended 31st December, 1935,* 1935–36.

Unemployment Assistance Board, *Return of the number of Payments made at Local Offices of the Ministry of Labour in the week ended Friday, 26th June 1936, by way of Unemployment Benefit . . . and of Unemployment Allowances,* 1935–36.

Ministry of Labour and National Service, *Employment and Unemployment in Great Britain 1939, 1945 and 1946. Tables relating to Regional and Industrial Analysis of Persons Insured Against Unemployment,* January 1947.

Central Statistical Office, *Annual Abstract of Statistics, No. 84, 1934–1946,* 1948.

Ministry of Labour and National Service, *Employment and Unemployment in Great Britain 1947,* 1948.

Ministry of Labour and National Service, *Employment and Unemployment. Tables relating to Employment and Unemployment in Great Britain 1948. Regional and Industrial Analysis,* 1949.

Ministry of Labour, *Tables relating to Employment and Unemployment in Great Britain 1948, 1949 and 1950,* 1951.

Interdepartmental Committee on Social and Economic Research, *Guide to Official Sources: No. 1. Labour Statistics,* 1958.

Interdepartmental Committee on Social and Economic Research, *Guides to Official Sources. No. 5. Social Security Statistics,* 1961.

Report from the Select Committee on Race Relations and Immigration. The Problems of Coloured School-Leavers, 1969.

The Intermediate Areas, April 1969.

Office of Population Censuses and Surveys, *Effects of the Redundancy Payments Act,* 1971.

Department of Employment, *British Labour Statistics: Historical Abstract, 1886–1968,* 1971.

Unemployment Statistics. Report of an Inter-Departmental Working Party, 1972.

National Economic Development Office, *Labour Statistics: Report of a Conference held under the General Auspices of the Standing Committee of Statistics Users,* 1973.

Report of the Committee on Abuse of the Social Security Benefits, 1973.

Home Office, *Unemployment and Homelessness: A Report,* 1974.

Ninth Report of the Committee of Public Accounts, 1976-7.

Commission for Racial Equality, *Looking for Work: Black and White School-Leavers in Lewisham,* 1978.

Department of Health and Social Security, *Social Security Statistics 1976,* 1978.

Manpower Services Commission, *Jobcentres: an evaluation,* 1978.

Department of the Environment, *National Dwelling and Household Survey,* 1979.

Statistical Office of the European Communities, *Labour Force Sample Survey 1975,* 1976; . . . *1977,* 1979.

Manpower Services Commission, *A Study of the Long-Term Unemployed,* 1979.

Manpower Services Commission, *The Employment Service in the 1980s,* 1979.

Annual Abstract of Greater London Statistics.

Annual Reports on Trade Unions from 1892.

Birmingham Statistics (formerly City of Birmingham, *Annual Abstract of Statistics).*

Census of Population, 1921-1971.

Department of Employment, *Gazette,* 1893-1979.

Digest of Welsh Statistics.

Eighteenth, Nineteenth and Twentieth Abstracts of Labour Statistics.

Ministry of Labour, *Annual Reports.*

Parliamentary Debates, Third Series.

Public Record Office, Departmental Papers Series, Cab. 2, 27, 37, 58; Lab. 2, 17, 23, 900.

Regional Statistics (formerly *Abstract of Regional Statistics).*

Scottish Abstract of Statistics.

Year Book of Labour Statistics.

II Secondary Authorities

(a) Books, Articles and Other Sources

Ainsworth, R.B., 'The Sources and Nature of Statistical Information in Special Fields of Statistics. United Kingdom Labour Statistics', *Journal of the Royal Statistical Society,* CXIII, 1950.

Alington, C.W., 'Aspects of Unemployment in West Ham', *Economic Review*, XVI, 1906.

Allen, R.G.D., 'The Unemployment Situation at the Outbreak of War', *Journal of the Royal Statistical Society*, CIII, 1940.

Allen, R.G.D., and Thomas, B., 'The London Building Industry and Labour Recruitment through Employment Exchanges', *Economic Journal*, XLVII, 1937.

Astor, J., *et al.*, *The Third Winter of Unemployment*, London 1923.

Atkinson, A., and Flemming, J., 'Unemployment, Social Security and Incentives', *Midland Bank Review*, Autumn 1978.

Bailey, D., 'Notes on British Unemployment Statistics', *Applied Statistics*, 1, 1960.

Bakke, E.W., *The Unemployed Man*, London 1933.

Barnes, R., 'Estimating the Characteristics of non-respondents in the General Household Survey', *Statistical News*, 30, August 1975.

Baxter, J.L., 'Long-Term Unemployment in Great Britain, 1953–71', *Bulletin of the Oxford University Institute of Economics and Statistics*, 34, 1972.

Beales, H.L., and Lambert, R.S., *Memoirs of the Unemployed*, London 1934.

Beaumont, P.B., 'The Means of Finding Jobs beyond Local Labour Market Conditions', *Industrial Relations Journal*, 8, Spring 1977.

Beaumont, P.B., 'The Duration of Registered Vacancies: An Exploratory Exercise', *Scottish Journal of Political Economy*, 25, February 1978.

Beaumont, P.B., 'Some Evidence of the Speed of Filling Registered Job Vacancies', *Bulletin of Economic Research*, 31, 1979.

Benjamin, B., *The Population Census*, London 1970.

Benjamin, D.K., and Kochin, L.A., 'Searching for an Explanation of Unemployment in Interwar Britain', *Journal of Political Economy*, 87, 1979.

Benjamin, D.K., and Kochin, L.A., 'What Went Right with Juvenile Unemployment Policy between the Wars: A Comment', *Economic History Review*, XXXII, November 1979.

Berg, S.V., and Dalton, J.R., 'United Kingdom Labour Force Activity Rates: Unemployment and Real Wages', *Applied Economics*, 9, 1977.

Berridge, W.A., 'Employment and the Business Cycle', *Review of Economic Statistics*, January 1922.

Beveridge, W.H., 'The Pulse of the Nation', *Albany Review*, 2, 1907.

Beveridge, W.H., 'Unemployment in the Trade Cycle', *Economic Journal*, 49, March 1939.

Beveridge, W.H., 'Unemployment in the Trade Cycle', *Economic Journal*, 49, March 1939.

Beveridge, W.H., *Full Employment in a Free Society*, London 1944.

Bewley, R.A., 'The Dynamic Behaviour of Unemployment and Unfilled Vacancies in Great Britain: 1958-1971', *Applied Economics*, 11, 1979.

Booth, A.E., and Glynn, S., 'Unemployment in the Interwar Period: A Multiple Problem', *Journal of Contemporary History*, October 1975.

Booth, C., *Life and Labour of the People of London*, London 2 vols., 1889 and 17 vols., 1903.

Bosanquet, N., and Standing, G., 'Government and Unemployment 1966-1970: A Study of Policy and Evidence', *British Journal of Industrial Relations*, X, 1972.

Bosanquet, N., ' "Structuralism" and "Structural Unemployment" ', *British Journal of Industrial Relations*, 17, November 1979.

Bourdillon, A.F.C. (ed.)., *A Survey of the Social Services in the Oxford District. 1: Economics and Government of a Changing Area*, Oxford 1938.

Bourlet, J., and Bell, A., *Unemployment and Inflation. The Need for a Trustworthy Unemployment Indicator*, Economic Research Council, October 1973.

Bowers, J.K., *The Anatomy of Regional Activity Rates*, Cambridge 1970.

Bowers, J.K., 'Unemployment Statistics, 1966-70: A note', *British Journal of Industrial Relations*, XI, July 1973.

Bowers, J.K., 'Some Notes on Current Unemployment', in Worswick (ed)., op. cit.

Bowers, J.K., Cheshire, P.C., and Webb, A.E., 'The Change in the Relationship between Unemployment and Earnings Increases: A Review of Some Possible Explanations', *National Institute Economic Review*, 54, November 1970.

Bowers, J.K., Cheshire, P.C., Webb, A.E., and Weedon, R., 'Some Aspects of Unemployment and the Labour Market, 1966-71', *National Institute Economic Review*, 62, November 1972.

Bowers, J.K., and Harkness, D., 'Duration of Unemployment by Age and Sex', *Economica*, 46, August 1979.

Bowley, A.L., 'The Abstract of Labour Statistics, 1894-5', *Economic Journal*, September 1896.

Bowley, A.L., 'The Problem of the Unemployed', *Sociological Papers,* III, 1907.

Bowley, A.L., 'The Measurement of Employment: an Experiment', *Journal of the Royal Statistical Society,* LXXV, 1912.

Bowley, A.L., *The War and Employment,* Oxford Pamphlets 1914-15.

Brechling, F., 'Trends and Cycles in British Regional Unemployment', *Oxford Economic Papers,* 19, 1967.

Brew, E., 'The "Out of Work" Enquiry of 1931', *Manchester School,* X, 1939.

Brichall, E.V., 'The Conditions of Distress', *Economic Review,* XX, 1910.

Brittan, S., 'Some Ways to Improve the Unemployment Figures', *Financial Times,* 22 November 1972.

Brittan, S., *Second Thoughts on Full Employment Policy,* London 1975.

Brittan, S., 'Full Employment Policy: A Reappraisal' in Worswick (ed.), op. cit.

Brown, A.J., *A Framework of Regional Economics,* Cambridge 1972.

Brown, A.J., 'UV analysis' in Worswick (ed.), op. cit.

Brown, R.L., Cowley, A.H., and Durbin, J., *Seasonal Adjustment of Unemployment Series,* HMSO 1971.

Buckle, Judith, *Work and Housing of Impaired Persons in Great Britain,* HMSO 1971.

Burns, E.M., *British Unemployment Programs, 1920-1938,* Washington 1941.

Buxton, N., and MacKay, D., *British Employment Statistics,* Oxford 1977.

Cameron, C., Lush, A., and Meara, G., *Disinherited Youth,* Edinburgh 1943.

Casson, M., *Youth Unemployment,* London 1979.

Chapernowne, D., 'The Uneven Distribution of Unemployment in the United Kingdom, 1929-36', *Review of Economic Studies,* V, 1937-38.

Chapman, A.L., and Knight, R., *Wages and Salaries in the United Kingdom, 1920-1938,* Cambridge 1952.

Chapman, S.J., and Hallsworth, H.M., *Unemployment: The Result of an Investigation made in Lancashire,* Manchester 1909.

Cheshire, P.C., 'Regional Unemployment Differences in Great Britain' in NIESR, *Regional Papers II,* Cambridge 1973.

Cheshire, P.C., 'Inner Areas as Spatial Labour Markets: A Critique of the Inner Areas Studies', *Urban Studies,* 16, 1979.

Chiozza-Money, L., 'The Extent of British Unemployment', *The International*, 2, 1908.

Clark, C., *National Income and Outlay*, London 1937.

Clark, C., *The Conditions of Economic Progress*, London 1951.

Clark, G.G., 'A Graphical Analysis of the Unemployment Position, 1920-1928', *Journal of the Royal Statistical Society*, XCII, 1929.

Cleary, E., 'The Placing Service of the Ministry of Labour', *Sociological Review*, 4, 1956.

Coleman, B., and Roberts, J.A., 'Activity Rates and Unemployment: The Experience of the United Kingdom, 1951-66', *Applied Economics*, 2, 1970.

Corry, B., and Roberts, J.A., 'Activity Rates and Unemployment. The U.K. Experience: Some Further Results', *Applied Economics*, 6, 1974.

Craig, J., Evans, E.W., and Showler, B., 'Humberside: Employment, Unemployment and Migration. The Evolution of Industrial Structure', *Yorkshire Bulletin of Economic and Social Research*, 22, November 1970.

Cripps, T.F., and Tarling, R.J., 'An Analysis of the Duration of Male Unemployment in Great Britain, 1932-73', *Economic Journal*, 84, June 1974.

Cubbin, J.S., and Foley, K., 'The Extent of Benefit-Induced Unemployment in Great Britain: Some New Evidence', *Oxford Economic Papers*, 29, March, 1977.

Cutler, R., and Rowles, K.J., 'The Unemployment Statistics and Government Policy', *Journal of Industrial Affairs*, 4, 1977.

Dale, J., 'The Interpretation of the Statistics of Unemployment', *Journal of the Royal Statistical Society*, XCVII, 1934.

Daniel, W.W., *Whatever Happened to the Workers in Woolwich? A Survey of Redundancy in S.E. London*, Political and Economic Planning 1972.

Daniel, W.W., *A National Survey of the Unemployed*, Political and Economic Planning 1974.

Daniel, W.W., and Stilgoe, Elizabeth, *Where Are They Now?* Political and Economic Planning 1977.

Daniels, E.W., and Jewkes, J., 'The Post-War Depression in the Lancashire Cotton Industry', *Journal of the Royal Statistical Society*, XCI, 1928.

Davies, G., 'Regional Unemployment, Labour Availability and Redeployment', *Oxford Economic Papers*, 19, 1967.

Davison, R.B., 'Immigration and Unemployment in the United Kingdom, 1955-62', *British Journal of Industrial Relations*, 1, 1963.

Deacon, A., *In Search of the Scrounger. The Administration of Unemployment Insurance in Britain, 1920-1931*, 1976.

Deacon, A., 'The Scrounging Controversy: Public Attitudes Towards the Unemployed in Contemporary Britain', *Social and Economic Administration*, 12, Summer 1978.

Dean, A.J.H., 'Unemployment Among School-Leavers: An Analysis of the Problem', *National Institute Economic Review*, 78, November 1976.

Dearle, N.B., *Problems of Unemployment in London Building Trades*, London 1908.

Dearle, N.B., 'English Statistics of Unemployment', *International Conference on Unemployment, Paris, September 1910*, Paris 1911.

Dessauer, Marie, 'Monthly Unemployment Records, 1845-1892', *Economica*, 17, August 1940.

Dessauer, Marie, 'Unemployment Records, 1848-59', *Economic History Review*, X, 1940.

Devons, E., *An Introduction to British Economic Statistics*, Cambridge 1961.

Dex, Shirley, 'Measuring Women's Unemployment', *Social and Economic Administration*, 12, Summer 1978.

Dex, Shirley, 'Job Search Methods and Ethnic Discrimination', *New Community*, VII, 1978/9.

Disney, R., 'Recurrent Spells and the Concentration of Unemployment in Great Britain', *Economic Journal*, 89, March 1979.

Dixon, R.I., and Thirlwall, A.P., *Regional Growth and Unemployment in the United Kingdom*, London 1975.

Donaldson, Alison, *United Kingdom Unemployment Statistics*, Berlin 1978.

Dow, J.C.R., *The Management of the British Economy 1945-60*, Cambridge 1968.

Dow, J.C.R., and Dicks-Mireaux, L.A., 'The Excess Demand for Labour: A Study of Conditions in Great Britain, 1946-1956', *Oxford Economic Papers*, 10, 1958.

Earl, V., 'Some Data on London's Unemployment', *Greater London Intelligence Journal*, 41, 1978.

Elias, D., 'Regional Unemployment Elasticities: Further Evidence', *Scottish Journal of Political Economy*, 25, February 1978.

Engineering and Allied Employers' National Federation, *Unemployment. Its Realities and Problems*, July 1933.

Evans, A., 'Notes on the Changing Relationship between Registered Unemployment and Notified Vacancies: 1961-66 and 1966-71', *Economica*, 44, May 1977.

Evans, E.W., and Hartley, K., *Employment and Unemployment in the Hull Region*, Hull 1964.

Evans, G., 'The Labour Market Mechanism and the Hoarding of Manpower', in Wabe, J.S., (ed.), *Problems in Manpower Forecasting*, Saxon House 1974.

Evans, G., 'A Note on Trends in the Relationship between Unemployment and Unfilled Vacancies', *Economic Journal*, 85, 1975.

Feinstein, C., *National Income, Expenditure and Output of the United Kingdom, 1855-1965*, Cambridge 1972.

Field, F., (ed.)., *The Conscript Army*, London 1977.

Field, F., *et al.*, *To Him Who Hath*, Harmondsworth 1977.

Foster, J., 'The relationship between Unemployment and Vacancies in Great Britain (1958-72): Some further evidence', in Laidler and Purdy, (eds.), *Inflation and Labour Markets*.

Fowler, R.F., *Duration of Unemployment on the Register of Wholly Unemployed*, HMSO 1968.

Galambos, P., 'The Activity Rates of the Population of Great Britain, 1951-64', *Scottish Journal of Political Economy*, February 1967.

Galenson, W., and Zellner, A., 'International Comparison of Unemployment Rates', in Universities—National Bureau Committee for Economic Research, *The Measurement and Behavior of Unemployment*, Princeton 1957.

Garraty, J.A., *Unemployment in History. Economic Thought and Public Policy*, New York 1978.

Garside, W.R., 'Juvenile Unemployment Statistics Between the Wars: A Commentary and Guide to Sources', *Bulletin of the Society for the Study of Labour History*, XXXIII, 1976.

Garside, W.R., 'Juvenile Unemployment and Public Policy Between the Wars', *Economic History Review*, XXX, May 1977.

Garside, W.R., 'Juvenile Unemployment Between the Wars: A Rejoinder', *Economic History Review*, XXXII, November 1979.

Gash, N., 'Rural unemployment', *Economic History Review*, VI, 1935.

Gayer, A.D., Rostow, W.W., and Schwartz, A.J., *The Growth and Fluctuation of the British Economy, 1798-1850*, 2 vols., Oxford 1953.

Gilson, Mary, *Unemployment Insurance in Great Britain*, New York 1931.

Glynn, S., and Oxborrow, J., *Interwar Britain: A Social and Economic History,* London 1976.

Gordon, I.E., 'Activity Rates: Regional and Sub-Regional Differentials', *Regional Studies,* 4, 1970.

Gray, E.M., 'Under-Employment in Cotton-Weaving: A Recent Wage Census', *Manchester School,* X, 1939.

Gray, P., and Gee, F.A., *A Quality Check on the 1966 Ten Per Cent Sample Census of England and Wales,* London 1972.

Greenhalgh, Christine, 'A Labour Supply Function for Married Women in Great Britain', *Economica,* 44, 1977.

Greenhalgh, Christine, 'Male Labour Force Participation in Great Britain', *Scottish Journal of Political Economy,* 26, November 1979.

Greenwood, A., and Kettlewell, J.E., 'Some Statistics of Juvenile Employment and Unemployment', *Journal of the Royal Statistical Society,* LXXV, 1911-12.

Grubel, H.G., and Walker, M.A., *Unemployment Insurance. Global Evidence of its Effects on Unemployment,* The Fraser Institute 1978.

Gujarati, D., 'The Behaviour of Unemployment and Unfilled Vacancies: Great Britain, 1958-1971', *Economic Journal,* 82, March 1972.

Hammermesh, D.S., 'A Note on Income and Substitution Effects in Search Unemployment', *Economic Journal,* 87, June 1977.

Hammond, E., *Analysis of Regional Economic and Social Statistics,* London 1968.

Hanham, F.G., *Report of Enquiry into Casual Labour in the Merseyside Area,* Liverpool 1930.

Harris, C.P., and Thirlwall, A.P., 'Inter-regional Variations in Cyclical Sensitivity to Unemployment', *Bulletin of the Oxford Institute of Statistics,* 30, February 1968.

Harris, Jose, *Unemployment and Politics. A Study in English Social Policy, 1886-1914,* Oxford 1972.

Hartley, E.L., 'Trade Union Expenditure on Unemployment Benefit', *Journal of the Royal Statistical Society,* LXVII, 1904.

Herron, F., *Labour Market in Crisis,* London 1975.

Hersch, L., 'Seasonal Unemployment in the Building Industry in Certain European Countries', *International Labour Review,* XIX, February 1929.

Hill, M.J., 'Can we Distinguish Voluntary from Involuntary Unemployment?' in Worswick (ed.), op. cit.

Hill, M., and Stevenson, Olive, *From the General to the Specific,* Oxford 1976.

Hilton, J., 'Statistics of Unemployment Derived from the Working of the Unemployment Insurance Acts', *Journal of the Royal Statistical Society*, LXXXVI, March 1923.

Hilton, J., 'Enquiry by Sample: An Experiment and its Results', *Journal of the Royal Statistical Society*, LXXXVII, 1928.

Hilton, J., 'Some Further Enquiry by Sample', *Journal of the Royal Statistical Society*, XII, 1928.

Hobsbawm, E.J., 'The Tramping Artisan', *Economic History Review*, III, 1951.

Hobsbawm, E.J., 'The British Standard of Living, 1790-1850', *Economic History Review*, X, 1957.

Hobson, J.A., 'The Meaning and Measure of "Unemployment",' *Contemporary Review*, LXVII, March 1895.

Hobson, J.A., *The Problem of the Unemployed*, London 1896.

Holden, K., and Peel, D.A., 'The Determinants of Unemployment and the "UV" Relationship', *Applied Economics*, 7, 1975.

Holden, K., and Peel, D.A., 'The 'Shake-Out' Hypothesis: A Note', *Oxford Bulletin of Economics and Statistics*, 38, 1976.

Holterman, S., 'Unemployment in the Urban Areas', *Urban Studies*, 15, 1978.

Hughes, J.J., 'The Use of Vacancy Statistics in Classifying and Measuring Structural and Frictional Unemployment in Great Britain, 1958-72', *Bulletin of Economic Research*, 26, May 1974.

Hughes, J.J., 'How Should We Measure Unemployment?', *British Journal of Industrial Relations*, 13, November 1975.

Hughes, J.J., 'The Measurement of Unemployment: An exercise in Political Economy?', *Industrial Relations Journal*, 7, 1976-7.

Hughes, J.R.T., *Fluctuations in Trade, Industry and Finance. A Study of British Economic Development, 1850-1860*, Oxford 1960.

Hull Community Council, *Unemployment in Hull*, Hull 1933.

Hunter, N., 'Who are the Unemployed?', *New Society*, 23 July 1970.

Hunter, L.C., 'Cyclical Variations in the Labour Supply: British Experience 1951-60', *Oxford Economic Papers*, 15, 1963.

Hunter, L.C., 'Unemployment in a Full Employment Society', *Scottish Journal of Political Economy*, X, 1963.

Hutchison, T.W., *A Review of Economic Doctrines, 1870-1929*, Oxford 1953.

Institute of Manpower Studies, 'Research Notes: Short-Term and Long-Term Unemployment', *IMS Monitor*, 2, April 1973.

International Labour Office, *Unemployment: Some International Aspects, 1920-28*, Geneva 1929.

Jay, P., 'Where have all the Workers gone?', *The Times*, 9 October 1971.

Jones, D.C., *Merseyside: Trade and Employment*, Liverpool 1935.

Kahn, H.R., *Repercussions of Redundancy*, London 1964.

Kaplan, C.L., 'Unemployment by Industry—Some Comments on its Measurement and Behavior', in Universities—National Bureau Committee, *The Measurement and Behavior of Unemployment*.

Kenny, P.B., 'Problems of Seasonal Adjustment', *Statistical News*, 29, May 1975.

Kent-Smith, D.B., and Pritchard, A., 'Development of Statistical Regions in the United Kingdom', *Statistical News*, 22, November 1974.

Kotsching, W.M., *Unemployment in the Learned Professions*, Oxford 1937.

Knight, K.G., and Wilson, R.A., 'Labour Hoarding, Employment and Unemployment in British Manufacturing Industry', *Applied Economics*, 6, 1974.

Laidler, D., and Purdy, D., (eds.)., *Inflation and Labour Markets*, Manchester 1974.

Lancaster, T., 'Econometric Methods for the Duration of Unemployment', *Econometrica*, 47, July 1979.

Layard, R., *et al.*, *The Causes of Poverty*, HMSO 1978.

Layard, R., 'Have the Jobcentres increased unemployment?', *The Guardian*, 5 November 1979.

Layard, R. *et al.*, 'Married Women's Participation and Hours', *Economica*, 47, February 1980.

Leicester, C., 'The Duration of Unemployment and Job Search', in Worswick (ed.), op. cit.

Leicester, C., 'The Structure of Unemployment Under Changing Labour Market Conditions', Social Science Research Council, Final Report, (HR 3777).

Leslie, D., and Laing, C., 'The Theory and Measurement of Labour Hoarding', *Scottish Journal of Political Economy*, 25, 1978.

Llewellyn, D.T., and Newbold, P., 'The Behaviour of Unemployment and Unfilled Vacancies', *Industrial Relations Journal*, 4, 1973.

Lomax, K.S., 'Regional Economic Statistics', *Journal of the Royal Statistical Society*, 117, 1954.

London and Cambridge Economic Service, *Special Memorandum No. 7. Seasonal Variations in Finance, Prices and Industry by A.L. Bowley and K.C. Smith*, London 1924.

London and Cambridge Economic Service, *Special Memorandum No. 36, Post-War Seasonal Variations by K.C. Smith and G.F. Horne*, London 1932.

McAnley, A., 'An Analysis of the Structure and Duration of Male Unemployment in Great Britain, 1962-73', University of Essex, Discussion Paper No. 66, June 1975.

MacKay, D.I., 'Redundancy and Re-employment: A Study of Car Workers', *Manchester School*, 40, 1972.

MacKay, D.I., 'After the Shake-Out', *Oxford Economic Papers*, 24, 1972.

MacKay, D.I., 'Labour reserves: some problems of measurement', in National Economic Development Office, *Labour Statistics*, NEDO, May 1973.

MacKay, D.I., and Reid, G.L., 'Redundancy, Unemployment and Manpower Policy', *Economic Journal*, 82, December 1972.

MacKay, D.I. *et al.*, *Labour Markets Under Different Employment Conditions*, London 1971.

McGregor, A., 'Intra-Urban Variations in Unemployment Duration: A Case Study', *Urban Studies*, 14, 1977.

McGregor, A., 'The Placement Activity of the Employment Service Agency', *British Journal of Industrial Relations*, XVI, 1978.

McGregor, A., 'Unemployment Duration and Re-employment Probability', *Economic Journal*, 88, December 1978.

McKendrick, S., 'An Inter-Industry Analysis of Labour Hoarding in Britain, 1953-72', *Applied Economics*, 7, 1975.

McNabb, R., 'The Labour Force Participation of Married Women', *Manchester School*, 3, 1977.

Maki, D., and Spindler, Z.A., 'The Effect of Unemployment Compensation on the Rate of Unemployment in Great Britain', *Oxford Economic Papers*, 27, 1975.

Matthews, R.C.O., *A Study in Trade Cycle History, 1833-1842*, Cambridge 1954.

Menderhausen, H., 'The Elimination of Seasonal Fluctuations in the Building Industry', *International Labour Review*, XXXVI, August 1937.

Mercer, A., 'Unemployment', *Economic Review*, XVII, 1907.

Metcalf, D., 'Urban Unemployment in England', *Economic Journal*, 85, September 1975.

Metcalf, D., and Nickell, S., 'The Plain Man's Guide to the Out-of-Work: the Nature and Composition of Male Unemployment in Britain', London 1977.

Metcalf, D., and Richardson, R., 'The Nature and Measurement of Unemployment in the U.K.', *Three Banks Review*, 93, March 1972.

Metcalf, D., and Richardson, R., 'Unemployment in London' in Worswick, op. cit.

Morely, F., 'The Incidence of Unemployment by Age and Sex', *Economic Journal*, XXXII, 1922.

Morrison, G.B., 'Age and Unemployment', *Journal of the Royal Statistical Society*, LXXIV, 1911.

Nickell, S., 'The Effect of Unemployment and Related Benefits on the Duration of Unemployment', *Economic Journal*, 89, March 1979.

Nickell, S., 'Estimating the Probability of Leaving Unemployment', *Econometrica*, 47, September 1979.

Nickell, S., 'Education and Lifetime Patterns of Unemployment', *Journal of Political Economy*, 87, October 1979.

Norris, G.M., 'Unemployment, Subemployment and Personal Characteristics', *Sociological Review*, 26, February, May 1978.

'Notes on Statistics of Manpower Costs and Unemployment in Major Industrial Countries', *National Institute Economic Review*, May 1971.

O'Dea, D.J., *Cyclical Indicators for the Post-war British Economy*, Cambridge 1975.

Organisation for Economic Co-operation and Development, *Economic Surveys, United Kingdom*, January 1973.

Organisation for Economic Co-operation and Development, *Economic Surveys, United Kingdom*, February 1973.

Organisation for Economic Co-operation and Development, *Measuring Employment and Unemployment*, Paris 1979.

Paish, F.W., *Policy for Incomes*, Institute of Economic Affairs, 1968.

Parikh, A., 'The Relationship between Unemployment and Vacancies: a Comment', *Applied Economics*, 9, 1977.

Parkin, M., and Sumner, M.T., *Incomes Policy and Inflation*, Manchester 1972.

Pearce, C.W., and Thomas, H., 'Regional Economic Statistics', *Journal of the Royal Statistical Society*, 30, 1968.

Peston, M., 'Unemployment: Why We Need a New Measurement', *Lloyds Bank Review*, 104, April 1972.

Phelps-Brown, E.H., and Browne, M.H., 'Carroll D. Wright and the Development of British Labour Statistics', *Economica*, 30, 1963.

Pilgrim Trust, *Men Without Work*, Cambridge 1938.

Pissarides, C.A., *Labour Market Adjustment*, Cambridge 1976.

Pissarides, C.A., 'Job Matchings with State Employment Agencies and Random Search', *Economic Journal,* 89, December 1979.

Popplewell, F., 'Seasonal Fluctuations in Employment in the Gas Industry', *Journal of the Royal Statistical Society,* LXXIV, 1911.

Radford, A.E., and Webb, G.I., 'Some Problems in Assessing Unemployment Trends', *Economic Trends,* 298, August 1978.

Reder, M.W., 'The Theory of Frictional Unemployment', *Economica,* XXXVI, 1969.

Reid, G.L., 'The Role of the Employment Service in Redeployment', *British Journal of Industrial Relations,* IX, 1971.

Reid, G.L., 'Job-search and the Effectiveness of Job-Finding Methods', *Industrial and Labour Relations Review,* 25, 1971-72.

Reubens, Beatrice, 'Unemployment in War-Time Britain,' *Quarterly Journal of Economics,* LIX, 1945.

Richardson, J.H., *Industrial Employment and Unemployment in West Yorkshire,* London 1936.

Rose, A.G., *The Older Unemployed Man in Hull,* Hull 1953.

Rowntree, S., and Lasker, B., *Unemployment. A Social Study,* London 1911.

Saunders, C.T., 'The Importance of Seasonal Variations in Employment in the United Kingdom', *Economic Journal,* XLV, 1935.

Saunders, C.T., *Seasonal Variations in Employment,* London 1936.

Sawyer, M.C., 'The Effects of Unemployment Compensation on the Rate of Unemployment in Great Britain: A Comment', *Oxford Economic Papers,* 31, March 1979.

Schloss, D.F., 'The Reorganisation of our Labour Department', *Journal of the Royal Statistical Society,* LVI, 1893.

Scott, M., and Laslett, R., *Can We Get Back to Full Employment?,* London 1978.

'Seasonal Fluctuations in Employment', *International Labour Review,* XVII, March 1928.

'Seasonal Unemployment in the Clothing Industries', *International Labour Review,* XVIII, July 1928.

Showler, B., 'Incentives, Social Security Payments and Unemployment', *Social and Economic Administration,* 9, Summer 1975.

Sinfield, A., *The Long-Term Unemployed,* Paris 1968.

Sinfield, A., 'Poor and Out of Work in Shields', in P. Townsend, op. cit.

Sinfield, A., 'Unemployment and the Social Structure', in Worswick, op. cit.

Singer, H.W., 'The Process of Unemployment in the Depressed Areas (1935-1938)', *Review of Economic Studies,* VI, 1938-39.

Singer, H.W., 'Regional Labour Markets and the Process of Unemployment', *Review of Economic Studies*, VII, 1939–40.

Sirman, C.F., 'City Size and Unemployment: some new estimates', *Urban Studies*, 14, 1977.

Sleeper, R.D., 'Manpower Redeployment and the Selective Employment Tax', *Bulletin of the Oxford Institute of Economics and Statistics*, 32, 1970.

Smee, J., and Stern, J., *The Unemployed in a Period of High Unemployment: Some Notes on Characteristics and Benefit Status*, November 1978.

Smith, D.J., *The Facts of Racial Disadvantage*, Political and Economic Planning 1976.

Smith, P., 'Seasonal Fluctuations in the Motor Vehicle Industry: A Comment', *Journal of Industrial Economics*, 2, April 1973.

Smyth, D.J., and Lowe, P.D., 'The Vestibule to the Occupational Ladder and Unemployment: Some Econometric Evidence on United Kingdom Structural Unemployment', *Industrial Labour Relations Review*, 23, July 1970.

Smyth, R.L., 'Male Unemployment Problems in Large Ports and Urban Areas, with Special Reference to Kingston-upon-Hull', *Yorkshire Bulletin of Economic and Social Research*, 26, August 1953.

Spindler, Z.A., and Maki, D., 'More on the Effects of Unemployment Compensation on the Rate of Unemployment in Great Britain', *Oxford Economic Papers*, 31, March 1979.

Standing, G., 'A Million Unemployed Already', *New Society*, 14 October 1971.

Standing, G., *Labour Force Participation and Development*, Geneva 1979.

Stilwell, F.J.B., 'The Regional Distribution of Concealed Unemployment', *Urban Studies*, July 1970.

Surrey, M.S.C., 'The Seasonal Adjustment of Unemployment Statistics— A Note', *Bulletin of the Oxford University Institute of Economics and Statistics*, 34, 1972.

Tawney, J., 'Women and Unemployment', *Economic Journal*, XXI, 1911.

Taylor, J., 'High Unemployment and Coloured School-Leavers: the Tyneside pattern', *New Community*, 2, 1972/3.

Taylor, J., 'Hidden Female Labour Reserves', *Regional Studies*, 2, 1968.

Taylor, J., 'Hidden Unemployment, Hoarded Labour and the Phillips Curve', *Southern Economic Journal*, XXXVII, 1970.

Taylor, J., 'A Regional Analysis of Hidden Unemployment in Great Britain, 1951-66', *Applied Economics*, 3, 1971.

Taylor, J., 'The Behaviour of Unemployment and Unfilled Vacancies: Great Britain, 1958-71. An Alternative View', *Economic Journal*, 83, December 1972.

Taylor, J., 'Incomes Policy, the Structure of Unemployment and the Phillips Curve: the United Kingdom Experience 1953-70', in Parkin and Sumner, op. cit.

Taylor, J., *Unemployment and Wage Inflation*, London 1974.

Taylor, J., 'The Unemployment Gap in Britain's Production Sector, 1953-73' in Worswick (ed.)., op. cit.

Taylor, J., and McKendrick, S., 'How Should We Measure the Pressure of Demand?', *Lloyds Bank Review*, 115, January 1975.

'The Impact of War on Long-Term Unemployment in Great Britain', *International Labour Review*, XLV, 1942.

'The Use of the Employment Exchange Service in Great Britain as a Labour Clearing House', *International Labour Review*, 24, 1931.

Thirlwall, A.P., 'Regional Unemployment as a Cyclical Phenomenon', *Scottish Journal of Political Economy*, 13, June 1966.

Thirlwall, A.P., 'Types of Unemployment with Special Reference to "Non Demand-Deficient" Unemployment in the U.K.,' *Scottish Journal of Political Economy*, February 1969.

Thirlwall, A.P., 'Types of Unemployment in the Regions of Great Britain', *Manchester School*, 4, 1974.

Townsend, P., *The Concept of Poverty*, London 1970.

Turner, H., and Smith, R., 'The Slump in the Cotton Industry, 1952', *Bulletin of the Oxford University Institute of Statistics*, 15, 1953.

Turner, H.A., 'Unemployment in Textiles: A Note and some Conclusions', *Bulletin of the Oxford University Institute of Statistics*, 15, August 1953.

Turner, H.A., 'Measuring Unemployment', *Journal of the Royal Statistical Society*, 118, 1955.

Turner, H.A., 'Employment Fluctuations, Labour Supply and Bargaining Power', *Manchester School*, XXVII, 1959.

Universities–National Bureau Committee for Economic Research, *The Measurement and Behavior of Unemployment*, Princeton 1957.

Urwick, E.J., 'The St. Pancras Labour Bureau', *Economic Review*, 111, 1893.

Vipond, J., 'City Size and Unemployment', *Urban Studies*, 11, 1974.

Wabe, J.S., 'Labour Force Participation in the London Metropolitan Region', *Journal of the Royal Statistical Society,* 132, 1969.

Wabe, J.S. (ed.)., *Problems in Manpower Forecasting,* Saxon House, 1974.

Warren, R.S., 'The behaviour of unemployment and unfilled vacancies in Great Britain: a search–turnover view', *Applied Economics,* 9, 1977.

Webb, A., 'Statistics of Unemployment, with special reference to Seasonal Unemployment', in *National Conference on the Prevention of Destitution,* London 1911.

Webb, S., and Freeman, A., (eds.)., *Seasonal Trades by various Writers,* London 1912.

Weeden, R., 'Duration of Unemployment and Labour Turnover', University of Reading, Mimeo, May 1974.

Wilcock, R.C., 'The Secondary Labor Force and the Measurement of Unemployment', in Universities–National Bureau Committee, *The Measurement and Behavior of Unemployment.*

Wilson, Rt. Hon. J.H., 'Statistics and Decision-Making in Government– Bradshaw Revisited', *Journal of the Royal Statistical Society,* 136, 1973.

Wood, G.H., 'Some Statistics relating to Working Class Progress since 1860', *Journal of the Royal Statistical Society,* LXII, 1899.

Wood, G.H., 'Trade Union Expenditure on Unemployment Benefit since 1860', *Journal of the Royal Statistical Society,* LXIII, 1900.

Wood, J.B., *How Much Unemployment?,* Institute of Economic Affairs, 1971.

Wood, J.B., *How Little Unemployment?,* Institute of Economic Affairs, October 1975.

Woodfield, A., 'Job Search Costs and the Measurement of Structural Unemployment', *Scottish Journal of Political Economy,* XXII, 1975.

Worswick, G.D.N. (ed.)., *The Concept and Measurement of Involuntary Unemployment,* London 1976.

Woytinsky, W., *Three Sources of Unemployment,* Geneva 1935.

(b) Unpublished Sources

Davidson, R., 'Sir Hubert Llewellyn Smith and Labour Policy 1886-1916', Ph.D. thesis, Cambridge 1971.

Gayer, A.D., 'Unemployment in British Industries 1815-1850', D.Phil. thesis, Oxford 1930.

Shinton, D.A., 'Post-War Regional Unemployment and Development', M.A. thesis, University of Exeter 1965.

Showler, B., 'An Analysis of Adult Unemployment in the Sub-Region of Humberside since 1951', M.Sc.(Econ.) thesis, University of Hull 1969.

Index